Lab Manual for MCSE Guide to

Managing a Microsoft® Windows® Server 2003 Environment

Jennifer Guttormson

Dan DiNicolo

Kelly Reid

THOMSON

COURSE TECHNOLOGY

Australia • Canada • Mexico • Singapore • Spain • United Kingdom • United States

THOMSON
COURSE TECHNOLOGY

Lab Manual for MCSE Guide to Managing a Microsoft® Windows® Server 2003 Environment

by Jennifer Guttormson, Dan DiNicolo, and Kelly Reid

Managing Editor:
Will Pitkin III

Product Manager:
Nick Lombardi

Production Editor:
Jennifer Goguen

Technical Edit/Quality Assurance:
Marianne Snow
Chris Scriver
Shawn Day

Associate Product Manager:
Mirella Misiaszek
David Rivera

Editorial Assistant:
Amanda Piantedosi

Senior Manufacturing Coordinator:
Trevor Kallop

Senior Marketing Manager:
Jason Sakos

Text Designer:
GEX Publishing Services

Compositor:
GEX Publishing Services

Cover Design:
Steve Deschene

TABLE OF
Contents

CHAPTER 5

CHAPTER 6

Managing Disk and Data Storage   **155**

CHAPTER 7

Advanced File System Management   179

CHAPTER 8

Implementing and Managing Printers   225

CHAPTER 9

CHAPTER 10

CHAPTER 11

CHAPTER 12

CHAPTER 13

CHAPTER 14

Introduction

The objective of this lab manual is to assist you in preparing for the Microsoft Certification Exam 70-290: Managing and Maintaining a Microsoft Windows Server 2003 objectives to relevant lab activities. This Environment by applying the Windows Server 2003 objectives to relevant lab activities. This text is designed to be used in conjunction with *MCSE Guide to Managing a Microsoft Windows Server 2003 Environment* (0-619-12035-5), and it should be noted that many of the labs rely upon activities from the *MCSE Guide* being completed first. Without completing those activities first, students may get different results from the labs. Although this manual is written to be used in a classroom lab environment, it also may be used for self-study on a home network.

Features

In order to ensure a successful experience for instructors and students alike, this book includes the following features:

- **Lab Objectives** – The goal of each lab is clearly stated at the beginning.
- **Materials Required** – Every lab includes information on hardware, software, and other materials that you will need to complete the lab.
- **Estimated Completion Time** – Every lab has an estimated completion time, so that you can plan your activities more accurately.
- **Activity Background** – Activity Background information provides important details and prepares students for the activity that follows.
- **Activity Sections** – Labs are presented in manageable sections and include figures to reinforce learning.
- **Step-by-Step Instructions** – Steps provide practice, which enhances technical proficiency.
- **Microsoft Windows Server 2003 MCSE Certification Objectives** – For each chapter, the relevant objectives from MCSE Exam # 70-290 are listed.
- **Review Questions** – Review reinforces concepts presented in the lab.

Hardware Requirements

All hardware in the computer should be listed on the Hardware Compatibility List available at www.microsoft.com.

Operating System	Microsoft Windows Server 2003
CPU	Pentium 133MHz or higher (Pentium III 550MHz is recommended)
Memory	128 MB RAM (256 MB RAM recommended)
Disk Space	Minimum of two 4-GB partitions (C and D), with at least 1 GB of free space left on the drive for student exercises
Drives	CD-ROM Floppy Disk
Networking	All lab computers should be networked. Students will work in pairs for some lab exercises. A connection to the Internet via some sort of NAT or Proxy server is assumed.

Software Requirements

The following software is needed for proper setup of the labs:

- Microsoft Windows Server 2003, Enterprise Edition or Standard Edition

Setup Procedure

1. Install Windows Server 2003 onto drive C: of the instructor and student servers. The following specific parameters should be configured on individual servers during the installation process:

Parameter	Setting
Disk Partitioning	Create two 4-GB NTFS partitions during the installation process, C and D. Ensure that at least 1 GB of free space is left on the hard disk for student exercises.
Computer Names	Instructor (first server), ServerXX (subsequent student servers)
Administrator Password	Password01
Components	Default Settings
Network Adapter	IP Address: 192.168.1.X. The instructor computer should be allocated a unique IP address on the same subnet as client computers. The suggested IP address for the Instructor machine is 192.168.1.100.
	Subnet Mask: 255.255.255.0
	DNS: The IP address of the Instructor computer
	Default Gateway: The IP address for the classroom default gateway.
	If the Instructor computer will be used to provide Internet access via ICS or NAT, it will require a second network adapter card or modem.
Workgroup Name	Workgroup

In the table above, "X" or "XX" should represent a unique number to be assigned to each student. For example, student "1" would be assigned a computer name of Server01 and an IP address of 192.168.1.1.

2. Once the installation process is complete, use Device Manager to ensure that all devices are functioning correctly. In some cases, it may be necessary to download and install additional drivers for devices listed with a yellow question mark icon.

3. Create a new folder named Source on drive D: of all classroom servers. Copy the entire contents of the Windows Server 2003 CD to this folder on all servers.

4. Create a new folder named Shared on drive D: of the Instructor computer only. Share this folder using the shared folder name Shared, and ensure that the Everyone group is granted the Full Control shared folder permission. This folder will be used to store any supplemental files that may need to be made available to students during the course.

5. Download both the client and server components of Microsoft Update Services (SUS) to the Shared folder on the Instructor computer. Links to both downloads can be found at:
http://www.microsoft.com/windowsserversystem/sus/default.mspx.

6. Run dcpromo.exe on the Instructor computer to install Active Directory and DNS. Name the new domain (the first in a new forest) Dovercorp.net, ensure that both non-secure and secure dynamic updates are allowed, and accept all other default options.

7. On the Instructor server, open Active Directory Users and Computers. Right-click the Dovercorp.net domain and click Raise Domain Functional Level. Change the domain functional level of the Instructor server only to Windows Server 2003.

8. After the previous steps are completed and the Dovercorp.net domain is completely installed on the Instructor server, run dcpromo.exe on each student server to install Active Directory, making each a child domain of Dovercorp.net. Name the student domains DomainXX.Dovercorp.net, where *XX* is the student number assigned to each student. Once the process is completed on all classroom servers, all DNS zones should be configured to allow nonsecure and secure dynamic updates. The Active Directory structure in the classroom once this is complete is illustrated in the figure below.

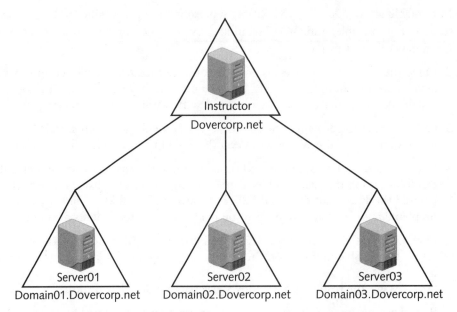

The Active Directory structure

9. In each child domain, use Active Directory Users and Computers to create a user account named AdminXX in the Users container, where XX corresponds to the student number assigned to each student. The password associated with this account should be Password01. This account should be added to the Domain Admins group in the same domain.

10. On each server, edit the Default Domain Controllers Group Policy object to grant the Domain Users group the right to log on locally. This is accomplished by opening Active Directory Users and Computers, right-clicking the Domain Controllers OU, and clicking Properties. Click the Group Policy tab, click the Default Domain Controllers Policy, and then click Edit. In the Group Policy Object Editor window, browse to the Computer Configuration\Windows Settings\Security Settings\Local Policies\User Rights Assignment node. Double-click the Allow log on locally right, and then add the Domain Users group to the list.

NOTE

Many of the labs rely upon activities from the *MCSE Guide to Managing a Microsoft Windows Server 2003 Environment* (0-619-12035-5), being completed first. Without completing those activities first, students may get different results from the labs.

ACKNOWLEDGMENTS

The authors would like to thank all the people from Course Technology who were involved in making this project run smoothly. Special thanks go to the following reviewers, whose attention to detail ensured that the information was accurate and conveyed in an easy to read fashion:

Patty Gillilan
Associate Professor
CIS Dept.
Sinclair Community College

C.J. Gray
Pittsburgh Technical Institute

Ronald Mashburn
Instructor in Computer Science at
West Texas A & M University

Robert Sherman
Sinclair Community College

1

INTRODUCTION TO WINDOWS SERVER 2003

Labs included in this chapter:

♦ Lab 1.1 An Introduction to Active Directory Users and Computers

♦ Lab 1.2 The Computer Management Console

♦ Lab 1.3 An Introduction to Securing Network Resources

♦ Lab 1.4 A Closer Look at Software Update Services

♦ Lab 1.5 An Introduction to the Active Directory Schema

Microsoft MCSE Exam #70-290 Objectives	
Objective	**Lab**
Identify and modify the scope of a group.	1.1
Create and modify user accounts by using the Active Directory Users and Computers MMC snap-in.	1.1
Monitor and analyze events. Tools might include Event Viewer and System Monitor.	1.2
Manage servers remotely.	1.2
Manage a server by using available support tools.	1.2
Configure access to shared folders.	1.3
Manage shared folder permissions.	1.3
■ Configure file system permissions.	1.3
■ Manage software update infrastructure.	1.4
■ Manage a server by using available support tools.	1.4, 1.5

Lab 1.1 An Introduction to Active Directory Users and Computers

Objectives

In this lab activity, you will investigate the default structure of Active Directory on the first domain controller in our organization: the Instructor computer in the Dovercorp.net domain.

Materials Required

This lab will require the following:

- Windows Server 2003 installed and configured according to the instructions at the beginning of this lab manual

Estimated completion time: **15 minutes**

Activity Background

The Active Directory Users and Computers console provides a graphical user interface through which you can administer your Windows Server 2003 domain. Active Directory contains information regarding objects in the domain, such as users, groups, computers, and domain resources (for example, published folders and printers). Through this interface, all objects within a domain can be managed. With the exception of Web Edition, all versions of Windows Server 2003 can be installed as domain controllers. The first domain in a forest is commonly referred to as the forest root domain. In this course, each student computer will be a domain controller in a child domain of Dovercorp.net.

ACTIVITY

Activity

1. Press **Ctrl+Alt+Delete** to access the Log On to Windows dialog box. Click **Options**.

2. In the Log On to Windows dialog box, type the following information and then click **OK**.

User Name	Administrator
Password:	Password01
Log on to:	DomainX.Dovercorp.net (where X is your assigned student number)

3. Click **Start**, and click **Manage Your Server**.

4. Under Managing Your Server Roles in the section titled Domain Controller (Active Directory), click the **green arrow** next to **Manage users and computers in Active Directory**. The Active Directory Users and Computers console will open.

5. Right-click **Active Directory Users and Computers** and click **Connect to Domain**. In the Connect to Domain dialog box, click **Browse**. In the Browse for Domain dialog box, click **Dovercorp.net** (as shown in Figure 1-1) and click **OK**.

Figure 1-1   The Browse for Domain dialog box

6. In the Connect to Domain dialog box, verify that the Domain field shows Dovercorp.net and click **OK** (as shown in Figure 1-2).

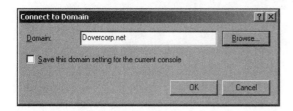

Figure 1-2   Connecting to the Dovercorp.net domain

7. In the Active Directory Users and Computers window, expand Dovercorp.net. Examine the default structure of Active Directory. Take note of the various icons that are used to represent objects in Active Directory. Click **Builtin**. This is a container object. Containers in Active Directory are represented by a folder icon. The Builtin container holds Domain Local security groups that have built-in rights on the system (as shown in Figure 1-3).

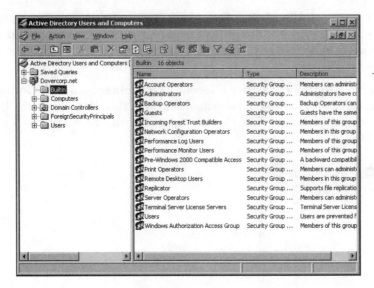

Figure 1-3   The Builtin container

8. Click **Computers**. This is also a container, as it is represented by a folder icon. For the purposes of this course, all student computers will be domain controllers and, therefore, this container will be empty.

9. Click **Domain Controllers**. This is an organizational unit. Organizational units are represented by folders with book icons on them. The Instructor computer is the only domain controller in the Dovercorp.net domain (as shown in Figure 1-4).

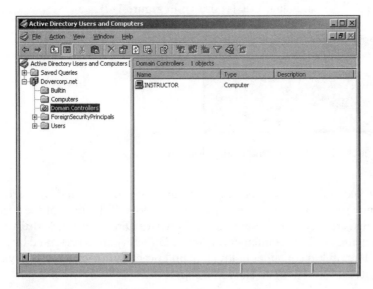

Figure 1-4   The Domain Controllers organizational unit

10. Click the **Users** container. The contents will appear on the right panel of your screen. Take note of the icons used to represent objects in this container. Icons with one head represent user accounts, whereas icons with two heads represent group accounts. These are the default user accounts and groups in Active Directory. There are three different types of security groups represented here: Domain Local, Global, and Universal (as shown in Figure 1-5).

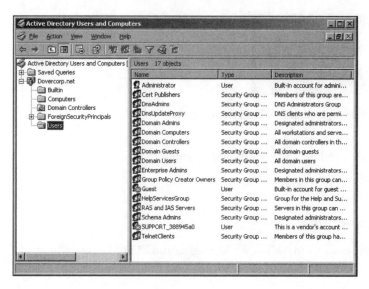

Figure 1-5   The Users container

11. There are two Universal security groups: the Enterprise Admins and the Schema Admins. These groups are only found in the very first domain in a forest. In your forest, Dovercorp.net is the forest root domain and, as such, contains these universal groups. There are two accounts that have a red X on them. This indicates that these objects are disabled. Right-click the **Guest** account. Click **Enable Account**.

> You will receive a message telling you that the object Guest has been enabled. For security reasons, it is not advised that you enable this account on your network.
>
> **NOTE**

12. Click **OK**.

13. Right-click the **Guest** account and click **Disable Account**. Click **OK** to accept the message telling you that the object Guest has been disabled.

14. Right-click the **Guest** account and click **Delete**. When asked if you are sure you want to delete this object, click **Yes**. A message will appear telling you that you cannot delete the Guest account, as it is a built-in account (as shown in Figure 1-6). The Administrator account is another built-in account and, therefore, cannot be deleted either. In a later chapter, you will examine Active Directory objects in more detail.

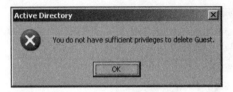

Figure 1-6   Attempting to delete a built-in account

15. Close Active Directory Users and Computers.

16. Log off.

Certification Objectives

Objectives for Microsoft Exam #70-290: Managing and Maintaining a Microsoft Windows Server 2003 Environment:

- Identify and modify the scope of a group.

- Create and modify user accounts by using the Active Directory Users and Computers MMC snap-in.

Review Questions

1. Which of the following are actions that can be taken with the Guest account? (Choose all that apply.)

   a. Rename

   b. Disable

   c. Reset password

   d. Delete

2. Which group(s) can only be found in the forest root domain? (Choose all that apply.)

   a. Administrators

   b. Domain Admins

   c. Enterprise Admins

   d. Schema Admins

3. Which account is disabled by default?

   a. Administrator

   b. Admin

   c. Guest

   d. No account is disabled by default

4. Which of the following objects in Active Directory are organizational units?

   a. Builtin

   b. Computers

   c. Domain controllers

   d. Users

5. What type of group is the Administrators group?

   a. Global

   b. Domain Local

   c. Universal

   d. All of the above

LAB 1.2 THE COMPUTER MANAGEMENT CONSOLE

Objectives

In this lab activity, you will identify the tools available in the Computer Management console.

Materials Required

This lab will require the following:

- Windows Server 2003 installed and configured according to the instructions at the beginning of this lab manual.

Estimated completion time: **15 minutes**

Activity Background

The Computer Management console is a built-in utility from which several administrative tools can be accessed within one console tree. In the Computer Management window, there are two panes. On the left is the console tree, which contains three items: System Tools, Storage, and Services and Applications. Once an item in the console tree has been selected, its subcomponents will be displayed in the right pane, commonly referred to as the details pane. The Computer Management console can be used for managing either local or remote systems.

ACTIVITY

Activity

1. If necessary, log on as **AdminX** to the **DomainX** domain (where *X* is your assigned student number) with a password of **Password01**.

2. Click **Start**, point to **Administrative Tools**, right-click **Computer Management**, and click **Run As**. In the Run As dialog box, click **The following user** and type **Dovercorp\Administrator**. Tab to the Password field and type **Password01** (as shown in Figure 1-7). Click **OK**. The Computer Management console window appears. The administrative tools available in this window have been separated into three different categories: System Tools, Storage, and Services and Applications.

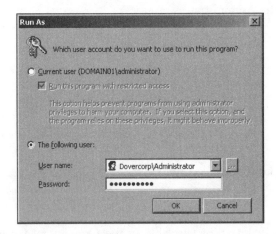

Figure 1-7   The Run As dialog box

3. Expand **System Tools**, if necessary. Click **Event Viewer**. There are several log files available in Event Viewer. The default logs available on any Windows 2003 Server are the Application, Security, and System logs. Your server also has two other logs: a Directory Service log and a File Replication Service log. These logs are present because your system is a domain controller (as shown in Figure 1-8).

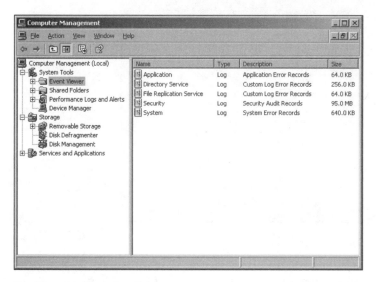

Figure 1-8   Event Viewer

4. Double-click **System** under Event Viewer. There are three types of events generated: Information, Warning, and Error (as shown in Figure 1-9).

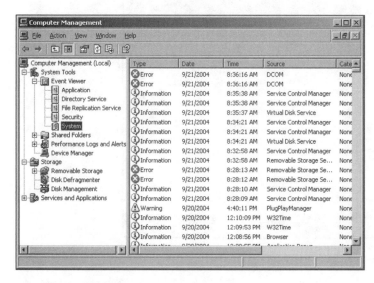

Figure 1-9   The System Log in Event Viewer

5. Double-click **Security** under Event Viewer. Note that Security auditing has been turned on by default, as Success Audit events have been generated in this field (as shown in Figure 1-10).

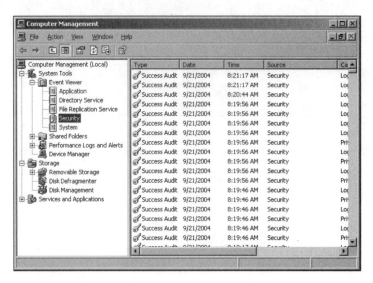

Figure 1-10   The Security log

6. Expand **Shared Folders**. Under Shared Folders, click **Shares**. In the details pane, the default shares will be displayed (as shown in Figure 1-11). Shares will be discussed in greater detail in the next lab activity.

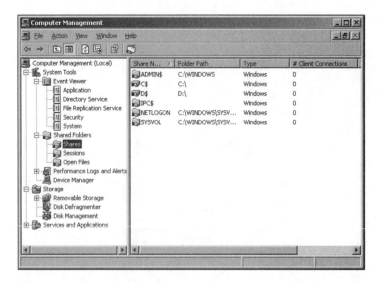

Figure 1-11   Shares

7. Click **Performance Logs and Alerts**. There are two types of logs that can be created: Counter Logs and Trace Logs. Alerts can also be generated with this utility as well (as shown in Figure 1-12).

Figure 1-12   Performance Logs and Alerts

8. Click **Device Manager**. This utility can also be accessed through the System applet in Control Panel (as shown in Figure 1-13).

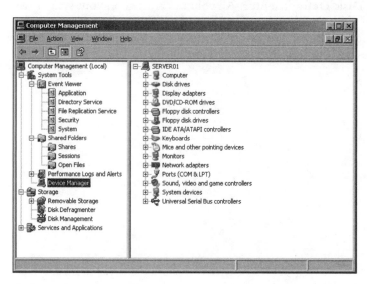

Figure 1-13   Device Manager

9. Expand **Storag**e under Computer Management (Local), if necessary. The three utilities available are: Removable Storage, Disk Defragmenter, and Disk Management. Click **Removable Storage**. Removable Storage can be used to manage removable media, such as tapes and optical discs (as shown in Figure 1-14).

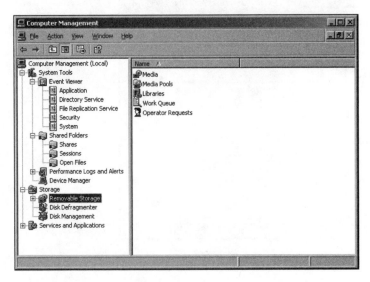

Figure 1-14   Removable Storage

10. Click **Disk Defragmenter**. All volumes created on your system will be displayed. Disk Defragmenter can be used to analyze the folders and files on these volumes and to consolidate them so that they are written to contiguous sectors on the hard drive (as shown in Figure 1-15).

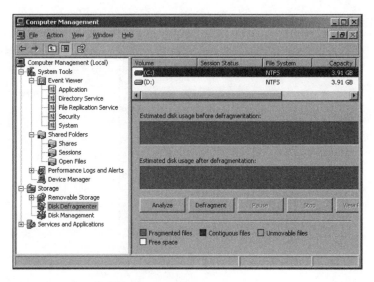

Figure 1-15   Disk Defragmenter

11. Click **Computer Management (Local)** and click **Connect to another computer**. In the Select Computer dialog box, click **Browse**. Click **Locations**. Click **Dovercorp.net** and click **OK**. Click **Advanced**. Click **Find Now**. In the Search Results field, click **Instructor** and click **OK**. Instructor should appear under the Enter the object name to select section. Click **OK**. The Select Computer dialog box indicates that this snap-in will now manage another computer called instructor.Dovercorp.net. Click **OK**. In the Computer Management console, double-click **Storage** and click **Disk Defragmenter**. Disk Defragmenter does not support the defragmentation of remote volumes (as shown in Figure 1-16).

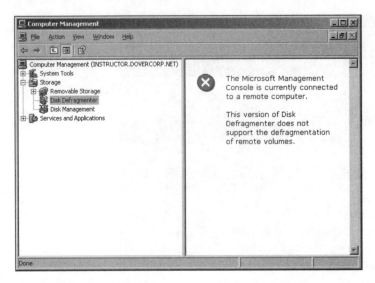

Figure 1-16 Disk Defragmenter and Remote Management

12. In the Computer Management (local) window, double-click **Storage** and click **Disk Management**. This is the utility used to manage partitions, volumes, and hard drives on Windows Server 2003 systems. This utility now replaces Disk Administrator that was available on Windows NT 4.0 systems.

13. Double-click **Services and Applications**. By default, services and applications on your system can be managed using the tools available from this menu. Available items include: Telephony, Services, WMI Control, and the Indexing Service (as shown in Figure 1-17).

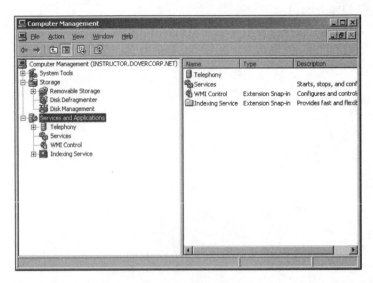

Figure 1-17 Services and Applications

14. Close the Computer Management console window.

Certification Objectives

Objectives for Microsoft Exam #70-290: Managing and Maintaining a Microsoft Windows Server 2003 Environment:

- Monitor and analyze events. Tools might include Event Viewer and System Monitor.

- Manage servers remotely.

- Manage a server by using available support tools.

REVIEW QUESTIONS

1. Which of the following tools would you use to create, manage, and delete partitions and volumes?

   a. Shared Folders

   b. Device Manager

   c. Removable Storage

   d. Disk Management

2. Which of the administrative tools in the Computer Management console would you use to update drivers for installed hardware?

   a. Removable Storage

   b. Device Manager

   c. Disk Defragmenter

   d. Disk Management

3. Which of the tools found in the Computer Management console are not available on domain controllers?

   a. Event Viewer

   b. Shared Folders

   c. Local users and groups

   d. Device Manager

4. Which of the following utilities does not support remote management functionality?

a. Event Viewer

b. Shared Folders

c. Local users and groups

d. Disk Defragmenter

5. When connected to another computer remotely in the Computer Management Console, which administrative tool only allows you to view the configuration information of the system to which you have connected, rather than to be able to modify it?

a. Shared Folders

b. Local users and groups

c. Device Manager

d. Disk Management

Lab 1.3 An Introduction to Securing Network Resources

Objectives

Windows Server 2003 provides two methods by which you can manage access to files and folders on your network: Windows Explorer and Shared Folders in the Computer Management console. In this lab activity, you will share folders using both methods.

Materials Required

This lab will require the following:

- Windows Server 2003 installed and configured according to the instructions at the beginning of this lab manual

Estimated completion time: **15 minutes**

Activity Background

One of the tasks you will need to perform as an Administrator will be to provide and secure access to network resources.

After completing this lab, you will be able to:

- Share folders using Windows Explorer

- Share folders using Shared Folders in Computer Management

■ Identify when Shared Folder permissions apply

■ Identify when NTFS permissions apply

■ Identify the default hidden shares

Activity

1. Log on as **AdminX** to the **DomainX** domain (where *X* is your assigned student number) with a password of **Password01**.

2. Right-click the **Start** button and click **Explore**.

3. Click **Local Disk (C:)**. Click **File** on the menu, point to **New**, and click **Folder**. Type **Example** and press **Enter**.

4. Right-click the **Example** folder and click **Sharing and Security**. In the Example Properties dialog box, notice that the default setting is **Do not share this folder**.

5. Click the **Share this folder** option. Notice how it defaults to the Share name Example, and that the User limit is set to Maximum allowed (as shown in Figure 1-18).

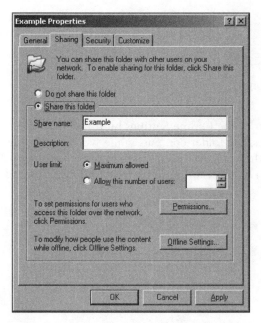

Figure 1-18   Sharing the Example folder

6. Read the description next to the Permissions button. These options control the type of permissions users have when they access this resource from across the network. Users who access the resource locally will not be affected by shared folder permissions. Click **Permissions**. The default permission is to grant the Everyone group Read permission (as shown in Figure 1-19). Click **Cancel** to exit the Permissions for Example dialog box.

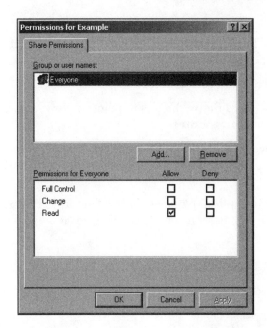

Figure 1-19 Default share permissions

7. Read the description next to the Offline Settings button. This option is used to modify how users access the folder contents while working off-line. Click **Offline Settings**. View the available options in the Offline Settings dialog box (as shown in Figure 1-20). Click **Cancel** to exit the Offline Settings dialog box.

1

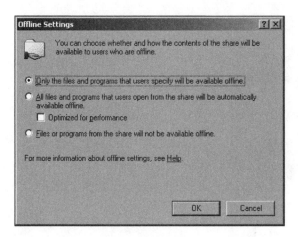

Figure 1-20   Offline Settings

8. Click **OK** to close the Example Properties dialog box. A hand now appears underneath the Example folder.

9. Right-click the **Example** folder and click **Properties**. In the Example Properties dialog box, click the **Security** tab.

10. The default permission assigned to the Administrators group of your domain is Full Control (as shown in Figure 1-21). Under Group or user names, click **Users (DOMAINX\USERS)** where *X* is your domain name. Notice the permissions assigned to the Users group (as shown in Figure 1-22). These are the default NTFS permissions assigned to this resource. This dialog box is the access control list for the Example folder. NTFS permissions control both local and network access to a resource and will apply to you regardless of whether you are connecting across the network or sitting physically at that computer and accessing files on the local drive.

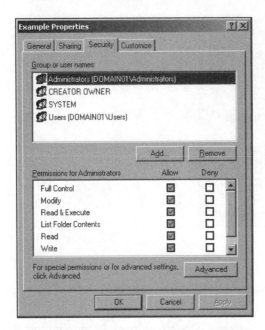

Figure 1-21   Administrators default NTFS permissions

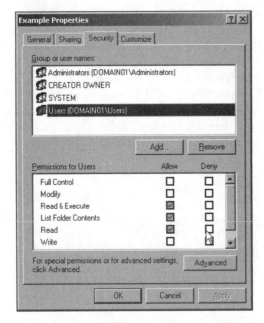

Figure 1-22   Users default NTFS permissions

11. Click **OK** to close the Example Properties dialog box.

12. Click **Start**, right-click **My Computer**, and click **Manage**.

13. In the Computer Management window, under System Tools, click **Shared Folders**.

14. Double-click **Shares**. Note that there are other shares in addition to the one you have just created (as shown in Figure 1-23).

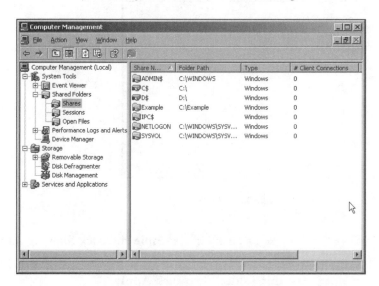

Figure 1-23   Shared Folders in Computer Management

15. Click **Start**, click **Run**, type **\\ServerX** (where *X* is your assigned student number), and click **OK**. Those shares that had a $ (dollar sign) appended to their share name in the Computer Management window will not appear (as shown in Figure 1-24). Shares with a $ appended to the share name will be hidden.

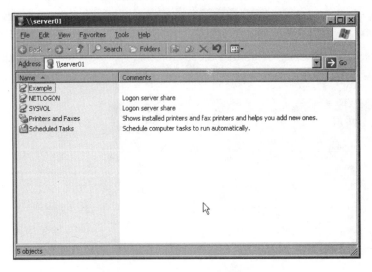

Figure 1-24   Using Run to view available shares

16. In Windows Explorer, right-click **C:\Example** and click **Sharing and Security**.

17. Click **Do not share this folder**, then click **Apply**.

18. Click the **Share this folder** option. Place your cursor in the Share name field at the end of Example and type **$**. Click **OK**. You have just created a hidden share.

19. In the Computer Management window, press **F5** to refresh the changes you have just made. The share now has a dollar sign appended to the share name.

20. Click **Start**, click **Run**, type **\\ServerX**, and click **OK**. The Example$ share is not visible. If the display doesn't update, click **F5** to refresh the view.

21. Click **Start**, click **Run**, type **\\ServerX\Example$** (as shown in Figure 1-25), and click **OK**. Even though the share is hidden, if you provide the full path to the share name you can access the Example folder.

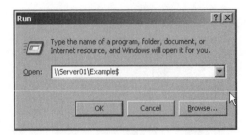

Figure 1-25   Using Run to connect to hidden shares

1

22. In Windows Explorer, right-click the **C:\Example** folder and click **Delete**. When asked if you are sure you want to remove the Example folder and all its contents to the Recycle Bin, click **Yes**. A message appears indicating that you are sharing the folder and that others may be using files in this folder, it will no longer be shared. Are you sure you want to delete it? Click **Yes**.

23. Close all windows.

Certification Objectives

Objectives for Microsoft Exam #70-290: Managing and Maintaining a Microsoft Windows Server 2003 Environment:

- Configure access to shared folders.

- Manage shared folder permissions.

- Configure file system permissions.

REVIEW QUESTIONS

1. What is the default share permission granted to the Everyone group?

   a. Read

   b. Change

   c. Modify

   d. Full control

2. When creating a hidden share, what character is appended to the end of the share name?

   a. !

   b. $

   c. %

   d. *

3. Which of the following is the default for Offline Settings on a shared folder?

   a. All files and programs that users open from the share will be automatically available offline.

   b. Only the files and programs that users specify will be available offline.

   c. Files or programs from the share will not be available offline.

   d. None of the above.

4. Which command-line utility is used to view the maximum number of users who can access a shared resource and the maximum open files per session? (Use Help and Support, if necessary.)

   a. Net File

   b. Net Config

   c. Net Share

   d. Net View

5. Which command-line utility can be used to create, delete, manage, and display shared resources? (Use Help and Support, if necessary.)

   a. Net File

   b. Net Config

   c. Net Share

   d. Net View

LAB 1.4 A CLOSER LOOK AT SOFTWARE UPDATE SERVICES

Objectives

This lab activity will introduce Software Update Services and will identify system requirements and recommendations for installing this service.

Materials Required

This lab will require the following:

- Windows Server 2003 installed and configured according to the instructions at the beginning of this lab manual

- Internet connectivity

Estimated completion time: **15 minutes**

Activity Background

Software Update Services (SUS) is a utility that administrators can use to manage and distribute critical operating system patches to clients running Windows 2000, Windows XP, and Windows Server 2003 operating systems. By using SUS, administrators have the capability of downloading and testing critical updates before deploying them to systems on your network.

Activity

ACTIVITY

1. If necessary, log on as **AdminX** to the **DomainX** domain (where *X* is your assigned student number) with a password of **Password01**.

2. Click **Start**, and click **Help and Support**.

3. In the Help and Support Center window, type **Software Update Services** in the search field and click the **green arrow**.

4. In the Search Results field, click **Microsoft Knowledge Base (50 results)**. Under Technical Articles, click the article titled **Server Requirements and Recommendations for Installing Microsoft Software Update Services** (Article Q322365). Read the documentation on Software Update Services. The Review Questions will refer back to information found in this article. When you have completed the Review Questions, close the Help and Support Center window.

Certification Objectives

Objectives for Microsoft Exam #70-290: Managing and Maintaining a Microsoft Windows Server 2003 Environment:

- Manage software update infrastructure.

- Manage a server by using available support tools.

REVIEW QUESTIONS

1. On which of the following systems would you be able to install Microsoft SUS? (Choose all that apply.)

    a. Microsoft Windows 2000 Server, Microsoft Windows 2000 Advanced Server, or Microsoft Windows 2000 Datacenter Server with Service Pack 2 (SP2) or later

    b. Windows 2000 Domain Controller

    c. Small business server

    d. None of the above

2. Which of the following are recommendations for installing Microsoft SUS on an existing server? (Choose all that apply.)

   a. Ensure that the computer is free of viruses and that the latest service pack, security rollups, or patches have been applied.

   b. Apply all security patches to IIS and run the IIS lockdown tool.

   c. Create an emergency repair disk.

   d. Turn off antivirus software.

3. You are trying to install Microsoft SUS but are experiencing technical difficulty. Which of the following could be possible reasons for the installation to fail?

   a. IIS is not detected on the computer.

   b. The drive is not formatted to NTFS.

   c. You are not logged on as an Administrator.

   d. All of the above.

4. When you are trying to install Microsoft SUS, it continues to fail. After checking and verifying that you have met all system requirements, which of the following recommendations should you follow? (Choose all that apply.)

   a. Enable antivirus software.

   b. Stop all services that are not required.

   c. Check Event Viewer.

   d. Try upgrading to Microsoft Windows Installer Version 2.0.

5. Which of the following are recommendations if you want to run Microsoft SUS? (Choose all that apply.)

   a. Host only SUS.

   b. Be sure the system is secure and free of viruses.

   c. Install the Microsoft Security Tool Kit.

   d. All of the above.

LAB 1.5 AN INTRODUCTION TO THE ACTIVE DIRECTORY SCHEMA

Objectives

In this lab activity, you will add the Active Directory Schema snap-in to a Microsoft Management console in order to view the schema.

Materials Required

This lab will require the following:

- Windows Server 2003 installed and configured according to the instructions at the beginning of this lab manual

Estimated completion time: **10 minutes**

Activity Background

The Active Directory Schema defines objects that can be found in Active Directory. Should the existing schema not meet the requirements of your organization, it can be extended by adding classes and attributes. By default, this snap-in is not available from either the Administrative Tools menu or the list of available snap-ins in the Microsoft Management console. As modifications to the schema will affect all domains in the forest, only members of the Schema Admins group have permission to modify or extend the schema.

ACTIVITY

Activity

1. If necessary, log on as **AdminX** to the **DomainX** domain (where *X* is your assigned student number) with a password of **Password01**.

2. Click **Start**, and click **Administrative Tools**. The Active Directory Schema console is not available from the Administrative Tools menu.

3. Click **Start**, click **Run**, type **mmc**, and click **OK**.

4. In the Console1 [Console Root] window, click **File** on the menu and click **Add/Remove Snap-in**.

5. In the Add/Remove Snap-in dialog box, click **Add**. In the Add Standalone Snap-in dialog box, note that the Active Directory Schema snap-in is not available from the list of options that can be added to the Microsoft Management Console window at this time. In order to make the Active Directory Schema console available, you must register the .dll. Close the mmc console window.

6. Click **Start**, click **Run**, type **regsvr32 schmmgmt.dll** (as shown in Figure 1-26), and click **OK**. A message will appear telling you that the DllRegister Server in schmmgmt.dll succeeded. Click **OK**.

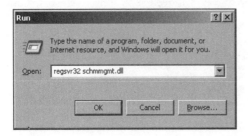

Figure 1-26   Registering the Schema Management .dll

7. Click **Start**, and then click **Administrative Tools**. The Active Directory Schema console is not available from the programs menu.

8. Click **Start**, click **Run**, type **mmc**, and click **OK**.

9. In the Console1 [Console Root] window, click **File** on the menu and click **Add/Remove Snap-in**.

10. In the Add/Remove Snap-in dialog box, click **Add**.

11. Active Directory Schema now appears in the list of available snap-ins. Click **Active Directory Schema** (as shown in Figure 1-27) and click **Add**.

Figure 1-27   The Active Directory Schema snap-in

12. Click **Close** to exit the Add Standalone Snap-in dialog box.

13. Click **OK** to close the Add/Remove Snap-in dialog box.

14. In the Console1 [Console Root] window, expand **Active Directory Schema**. There are two types of objects found in the Active Directory Schema: Classes and Attributes.

15. Click **Classes**. In the right pane of the screen, note the different classes that are available (as shown in Figure 1-28).

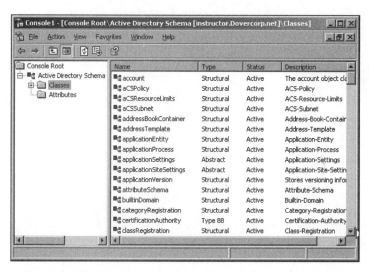

Figure 1-28 Classes

16. Click **Attributes**. Note the different attributes that objects in the schema can have (as shown in Figure 1-29).

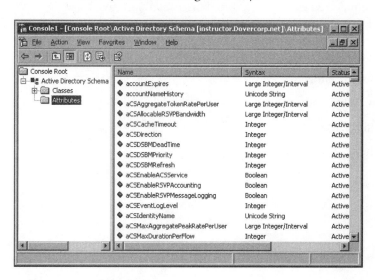

Figure 1-29 Attributes

17. In the Console1 window, click **Help** on the shortcut menu.

18. Under **Active Directory Schema**, click **Best practices** and read the recommendations on this page.

19. Click **Troubleshooting**. Notice the various types of problems that you may encounter or need to troubleshoot with the schema. Close the Microsoft Management Console window.

20. Close the Console1 window. If asked whether you want to save the console settings to Console1, click **No**.

Certification Objectives

Objectives for Microsoft Exam #70-290: Managing and Maintaining a Microsoft Windows Server 2003 Environment:

- Manage a server by using available support tools.

Review Questions

1. Which of the following will enable you to view the Active Directory Schema?

   a. Click **Active Directory Schema** from the Administrative Tools menu.

   b. Click **Active Directory Users and Computers**, right-click **Your Domain Name**, and click the **Schema** tab.

   c. Run regsvr32 schmmgmt.dll and then click **Active Directory Schema** from the Administrative Tools menu.

   d. Run regsvr32 schmmgmt.dll and then add the Active Directory Schema Snap-in from an MMC console.

2. To what group must you belong if you want to modify the schema?

   a. Administrators

   b. Domain Admins

   c. Enterprise Admins

   d. Schema Admins

3. Which of the following are recommendations to be followed with regards to the Active Directory Schema? (Choose all that apply.)

a. Develop and test schema modifications in an isolated test forest before moving them to production.

b. Remove all users from the Schema Admins group and only add users to this group when schema modifications need to be made. Once changes have been made, remove the users from the group.

c. Disable the use of signed or encrypted LDAP traffic for Active Directory administrative tools.

d. Do not casually modify the schema.

4. In order to identify the Schema Master, which of the following actions would you perform? (Choose all that apply.)

a. From Active Directory users and computers, right-click the **Domain** and click **Properties**. The Schema Master is listed on the Schema tab.

b. Open **Active Directory Schema**, right-click **Active** Directory Schema and click **Operations Master**. Look in the current Schema Master field.

c. Open a **Command** prompt and type **DSQuery Server – HASFSMO Schema**.

d. All of the above.

5. Which of the following are not true about Active Directory Schema? (Select all that apply.)

a. Each domain in a forest has one Schema Master.

b. You do not need administrative credentials to view the identity of the Schema Master.

c. Active Directory Schema is not found on the Administrative Tools menu by default.

d. To enable schema changes on a Schema Master, open **Registry Editor** and add the **Schema Update Allowed** key with a value of 1.

2

MANAGING HARDWARE DEVICES

Labs included in this chapter:

♦ Lab 2.1 Determining Compatible Hardware Using the Windows Server Catalog

♦ Lab 2.2 Installing Non-Plug and Play Hardware

♦ Lab 2.3 Viewing Memory and Performance Settings

♦ Lab 2.4 Configuring Hardware Profiles

♦ Lab 2.5 Investigating Power Options: The Hibernate Feature

Microsoft MCSE Exam #70-290 Objectives	
Objective	**Lab**
Monitor server hardware. Tools might include Device Manager, the Hardware Troubleshooting Wizard, and appropriate Control Panel items.	2.1, 2.4, 2.5
Install and configure server hardware devices.	2.2
Configure resource settings for a device.	2.5
Configure device properties and settings.	2.4
Monitor and optimize a server environment for application performance.	2.3

Lab 2.1 Determining Compatible Hardware Using the Windows Server Catalog

Objectives

The goal of this lab is to use Device Manager to determine which hardware components are installed on your system and then use the Windows Server 2003 Catalog to verify whether the devices are supported.

Materials Required

This lab will require the following:

- Windows Server 2003 installed and configured according to the instructions at the beginning of this lab manual

- Internet access

Estimated completion time: **30 minutes**

Activity Background

Before purchasing new hardware for systems that will be running the Windows Server 2003 operating system, it is important that you verify whether the hardware will be compatible. Microsoft has implemented the Windows Server 2003 Catalog to facilitate this process. The Windows Server 2003 Catalog is an online reference that can be consulted before making any new hardware purchase for a Windows Server 2003 system.

ACTIVITY

Activity

1. Log on as **AdminX** to the **DomainX** domain (where *X* is your assigned student number) with a password of **Password01**.

2. Click **Start**, right-click **My Computer**, and click **Properties**.

3. In the System Properties dialog box, click the **Hardware** tab.

4. On the Hardware tab, click the **Device Manager** button in the Device Manager section.

5. Determine and record the manufacturer and model of the following devices:

(Hint: Click the **+** (plus symbol) next to the type of device, and then double-click the item to display the Properties window.)

Display adapter _____

Network adapter _____

DVD/CD-ROM drives _____

Disk drives _____

6. Close the **Device Manager** window.

7. Click **OK** to close the **System Properties** dialog box.

8. Click **Start** and click **Help and Support**.

9. In the Help and Support Center window under Support Tasks, click **Compatible Hardware and Software**.

10. A message appears indicating that Microsoft Internet Explorer's Enhanced Security Configuration is currently enabled on your server. This enhanced level of security reduces the risk of attack from Web-based content that is not secure, but it may also prevent Web sites from displaying correctly and restrict access to network resources. Click to select the **In the future, do not show this message** check box, and click **OK**. The Windows Server Catalog Web page appears in your browser window. (Note: If you receive a content blocked warning message, uncheck the **Continue to prompt when Web site content is blocked** check box, then click **Close**.) There appear to be two tabs on the Windows Server Catalog page: Home Page and Hardware.

11. Click the link for the **Hardware** tab.

12. Under Browse hardware, click **Networking and Modems**. On the Networking and Modems page, click **LAN Cards**. Use the sort features available on this page to find your network adapter card faster.

13. Use the Browse hardware options to look up compatibility for your Display, DVD/CD-ROM drives, and Disk drives.

14. When you have finished looking up whether your hardware is on this list, click the link for **Home Page**.

15. Under More Windows Server Catalog Links, click **More Information about the Windows Server Catalog**. On the section of the Web page titled More Resources, there is a link for manufacturers to register their products with the Windows Server Catalog.

16. Click the **Back** shortcut on the menu bar to take you to the previous page.

17. Under More Windows Server Catalog Links, click **Hardware Compatibility List**. A new browser window opens. Notice the Search feature available on this page.

18. Close all instances of Internet Explorer and then close the Help and Support Center window.

Certification Objectives

Objectives for Microsoft Exam #70-290: Managing and Maintaining a Microsoft Windows Server 2003 Environment:

- Monitor server hardware. Tools might include Device Manager, the Hardware Troubleshooting Wizard, and appropriate Control Panel items.

REVIEW QUESTIONS

1. Which Windows utility would you use to see a list of locally installed hardware?

   a. Device manager

   b. Event Viewer

   c. System Monitor

   d. Disk Management

2. You have decided to upgrade a device driver currently installed on your machine. Which utility would you choose to accomplish this?

   a. Event Viewer

   b. Device Manager

   c. Disk Defragmenter

   d. System Information

3. Which of the following are aspects of the "Designed for Windows" logo program? (Choose all that apply.)

   a. It helps customers identify products that are compatible with the Microsoft Windows operating systems.

   b. Products display the "Designed for Windows" logo on product and packaging.

   c. Drivers contain a digital signature indicating that they have passed Windows compatibility testing.

   d. Customers can download signed drivers from the Windows update site, and qualified products are listed in the Windows Catalog.

2

4. Which of the following is/are true about the Microsoft Application Compatibility Analyzer?

   a. Available for download from Microsoft

   b. Available through the Application Compatibility Toolkit

   c. Gathers an inventory of applications on your network and determines the compatibility results for those applications

   d. All of the above

5. Which of the following methods can you use to verify whether your hardware is compatible with Windows Server 2003?

   a. Begin upgrade or new installation. Setup will check both software and hardware compatibility and report problems to you.

   b. From the CD-ROM, run \I386\winnt32.exe with the /checkupgradeonly switch.

   c. Check the Microsoft Web site to verify hardware and software.

   d. All of the above.

LAB 2.2 INSTALLING NON-PLUG AND PLAY HARDWARE

Objectives

The goal of this lab is to manually install non–plug and play devices using the Add Hardware Wizard in Control Panel.

Materials Required

This lab will require the following:

- Windows Server 2003 installed and configured according to the instructions at the beginning of this lab manual

Estimated completion time: **10 minutes**

Activity Background

Installing devices onto your Windows Server 2003 system is a relatively easy operation. For the most part, newer devices will be plug and play. Plug and play devices are easy to configure. Simply attach them to your system, and the operating system will detect and configure the device for you. Non–plug and play devices need to be manually installed using the Add Hardware Wizard in Control Panel. When configuring these devices, it is recommended that you follow the instructions provided by the device manufacturer. In this lab activity, you will install a device using the Add Hardware Wizard.

ACTIVITY

Activity

1. Log on as **AdminX** to the **DomainX** domain (where *X* is your assigned student number) with a password of **Password01**.

2. Click **Start**, point to **Control Panel**, and click **Add Hardware**.

3. On the Welcome to the Add Hardware Wizard page, click **Next**. Wait while the wizard searches for hardware that has been connected to your computer recently, but not installed.

4. When asked if the hardware is connected to your computer, click **Yes, I have already connected the hardware** and click **Next**.

5. On the page titled "The following hardware is already installed on your computer", scroll to the bottom of the list of devices and click **Add a new hardware device** (as shown in Figure 2-1). (Note that your system may contain different hardware devices than the ones shown here.) Click **Next**.

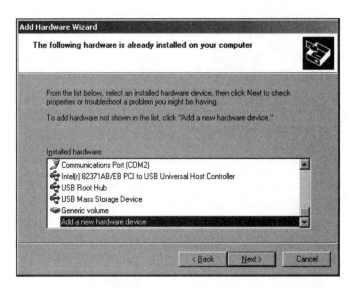

Figure 2-1   Adding a new hardware device

6. When asked what you want the wizard to do, click the **Install the hardware that I manually select from a list (Advanced)** option and click **Next**.

7. Under Common Hardware types, click **Modems** and click **Next**.

8. On the Install New Modem page, click to select the **Don't detect my modem; I will select it from a list** check box and click **Next**.

9. Under the Models listed for Standard Modem Types, scroll through the list until you see the Standard 56000 bps Modem (as shown in Figure 2-2), click the **Standard 56000 bps Modem**, and click **Next**.

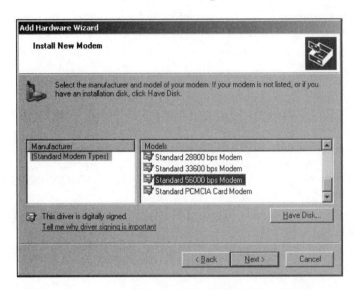

Figure 2-2   Selecting the Standard 56000 bps Modem

10. On the page asking On which ports do you want to install it?, click **COM1** under Selected ports and then click **Next**.

11. Click **Finish** to close the Add Hardware Wizard.

12. Click **Start**, point to **Control Panel**, and click **System**. Click the **Hardware** tab, and then click the **Device Manager** button in the Device Manager section. Expand **Modems**. The Standard 56000 bps Modem has now been installed.

13. Close Device Manager.

14. Click **OK** to close the System Properties dialog box.

Certification Objectives

Objectives for Microsoft Exam #70-290: Managing and Maintaining a Microsoft Windows Server 2003 Environment:

■ Install and configure server hardware devices.

REVIEW QUESTIONS

1. Under what conditions would you need to be logged on as a member of the Administrators group in order to install or configure a device? (Choose all that apply.)

    a. The device driver is already installed on the computer.

    b. The device driver has not been digitally signed.

    c. The device needs to be configured in Device Manager.

    d. Policy settings on the network prevent hardware installations.

2. Which of the following are methods by which you can install non–plug and play devices? (Choose all that apply.)

    a. Physically connect the device to your computer, and Windows Server 2003 will take care of the rest.

    b. Use the Add Hardware Wizard from the Hardware tab on the system applet in Control Panel.

    c. Use the Add Hardware applet from Control Panel.

    d. All of the above.

3. Which of the following is/are true regarding disabling devices in Device Manager?

    a. When a device is disabled, the device remains connected but the device driver is not loaded.

    b. Resources that were allocated to disabled devices can be assigned to other devices.

    c. Some devices such as disk drives and processors cannot be disabled.

    d. All of the above.

4. Which of the following is/are true regarding troubleshooting remote systems using Device Manager?

    a. Computer management does not support remote access to computers running Windows 95.

    b. The remote registry service must be started on the remote computer.

    c. Device Manager works in read-only mode when connected to remote systems.

    d. All of the above.

5. You have updated a device driver and now your system is unstable. You are logged onto your system. Which of the following is your best course of action?

   a. Use the Add Hardware Wizard to reinstall the device.

   b. Use Device Manager to uninstall the device.

   c. Use the Device Driver roll back feature to undo the driver update.

   d. None of the above.

LAB 2.3 VIEWING MEMORY AND PERFORMANCE SETTINGS

Objectives

The goal of this lab is to use the Advanced tab in the System Properties dialog box to adjust settings manually for visual effects, processor time, and virtual memory allocation.

Materials Required

This lab will require the following:

- Windows Server 2003 installed and configured according to the instructions at the beginning of this lab manual

Estimated completion time: **10 minutes**

Activity Background

Although Windows allocates memory and processor time according to the resources available on your system, you have the ability to adjust these settings manually as well.

By default, Windows Server 2003 is configured to "Let Windows choose what's best for my computer." However, visual effects settings can be adjusted for best appearance, best performance, or a custom configuration, if desired. Windows Server 2003 can be configured to allocate more processor time to programs or background services. Memory settings can also be configured to allocate more memory to programs or the system's cache.

Additionally, Windows uses a file on the local hard drive to simulate system RAM. The paging file (pagefile.sys) is commonly referred to as virtual memory and can be enlarged or moved to improve system performance.

ACTIVITY

Activity

1. Log on as **AdminX** to the **DomainX** domain (where X is your assigned student number) with a password of **Password01**.

2. Click **Start**, point to **Control Panel**, and click **System**.

3. In the System Properties dialog box, click the **Advanced** tab.

4. Under Performance, click **Settings**.

5. Notice the Visual Effects tab (as shown in Figure 2-3). The system defaults to Let Windows choose what's best for my computer. Scroll through the settings to see which features have been turned on or off.

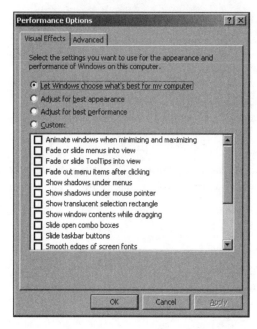

Figure 2-3   The Visual Effects tab

6. Click the **Adjust for best appearance** option. View the features that have been selected.

7. Click the **Adjust for best performance** option. Again view the features that have been selected.

8. Click the **Let Windows choose what's best for my computer** option.

9. Click the **Advanced** tab (as shown in Figure 2-4). By default, Processor scheduling is configured to allocate more processor resources to background services. With this option selected, all programs receive equal amounts of processor resources. You would select the Programs option if more processor resources needed to be given to a particular application than were currently being allocated. The default setting for Memory usage is to allocate more system memory to the system cache. This option is optimal if you are using the system as a server or if programs that you are running call for a larger system cache. You would select the Programs option if you were using the system as a workstation and wanted your applications to run faster.

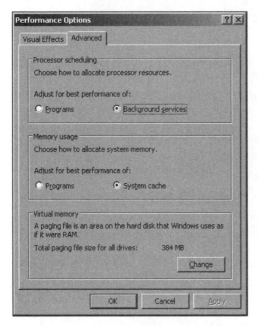

Figure 2-4 The Advanced tab

10. Look at the Virtual memory section on the Advanced tab. Note that your Total paging file size for all drives has been configured to be approximately 1.5 times the amount of RAM installed on your system. Click the **Change** button.

11. The paging file resides on drive C: (as shown in Figure 2-5; please note that, depending on the amount of memory installed on your system, the memory values shown in this figure may be different from the values your system displays). The three options available for your paging file settings are Custom size, System managed size, and No paging file. Note that after changing your paging file settings, if you have selected the Custom size option (which is the default), you can use the Set button to apply the initial and maximum size settings for the paging file on the selected drive.

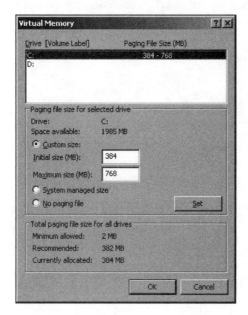

Figure 2-5   Virtual Memory settings

12. Click **Cancel** to exit the Virtual Memory dialog box.

13. Click **Cancel** to close the Performance Options dialog box.

14. Click **OK** to close the System Properties dialog box.

Certification Objectives

Objectives for Microsoft Exam #70-290: Managing and Maintaining a Microsoft Windows Server 2003 Environment:

■ Monitor and optimize a server environment for application performance.

REVIEW QUESTIONS

2

1. Which of the following is/are true about virtual memory? (Choose all that apply.)

   a. It is often called the paging file.

   b. The paging file is similar to the UNIX swap file.

   c. During installation, the size of the page file is equal to 1.5 times the amount of RAM on your computer.

   d. The page file is called pagefile.sys.

2. Which of the following is/are ways to optimize virtual memory?

   a. Move the page file off slower hard drives.

   b. Move the page file off heavily accessed drives.

   c. If possible, move the page file onto a different drive from the system files.

   d. All of the above.

3. Which of the following is/are true regarding the paging file and virtual memory management?

   a. The computer management snap-in can be used to change the size of the page file remotely using system properties.

   b. To delete a page file, set both the initial size and maximum size to zero.

   c. Use the pagefileconfig.vbs command-line utility to view and configure the page file settings.

   d. All of the above.

4. Which of the following is not a recommended option for virtual memory management?

   a. Custom size

   b. System managed size

   c. No paging file

   d. All of the above are recommended options

5. Which of the following is/are true regarding the pagefileconfig.vbs command-line utility? (Choose all that apply.)

a. Can only be used to configure local page file settings

b. Can be used to add or create an additional paging file to a system

c. Can be used to delete a paging file from a system

d. Can be used to query a system's paging file virtual memory settings

LAB 2.4 CONFIGURING HARDWARE PROFILES

Objectives

The goal of this lab is to demonstrate the steps necessary to create, configure, and delete a hardware profile.

Materials Required

This lab will require the following:

- Windows Server 2003 installed and configured according to the instructions at the beginning of this lab manual

Estimated completion time: **40 minutes**

Activity Background

Hardware profiles specify which devices to start and which device drivers to load when the computer is booted into Windows Server 2003. By default, all devices attached when the operating system is installed will be enabled. Hardware profiles can be used to configure laptops for use in different environments. Using Device Manager, devices can be enabled or disabled in each hardware profile.

Occasionally, you may find the need to set up different hardware configuration settings for your Windows Server 2003 system. Hardware profiles are a way of accomplishing just that. By enabling or disabling certain hardware devices, you can test applications and system configuration settings in your environment.

ACTIVITY

Activity

1. Log on as **AdminX** to the **DomainX** domain (where *X* is your assigned student number) with a password of **Password01**.

2. Click **Start**, point to **Control Panel**, and click **System**. (Alternatively, you can also open the System applet using the keyboard shortcut **Windows key + Pause Break**.)

3. In the System Properties dialog box, click the **Hardware** tab.

4. Under the section titled Hardware Profiles, click **Hardware Profiles**.

5. In the Hardware Profiles dialog box (as shown in Figure 2-6), if necessary, click **Profile 1 (Current)** and click **Copy**. In the Copy Profile dialog box, type **Home** and click **OK**.

2

Figure 2-6   The Hardware Profiles dialog box

6. In the Hardware Profiles dialog box, there are now two hardware profiles available: Profile 1 (Current) and Home. You have the ability to rename a profile to help identify hardware configuration settings when booting up your computer. The word Current appears next to the profile with which you have started your computer. At this moment, you are using Profile 1. You are only able to modify the device settings for your current hardware profile. If you wish to modify device settings for the Home profile you have just created, you will need to restart your computer and boot up with the Home profile before going into Device Manager to modify these settings. First, you will modify the startup settings for Hardware Profiles. In the Hardware Profiles dialog box, you have two options as to how your computer will behave with regards to hardware profiles: Wait until I select a hardware profile and Select the first profile listed if I don't select a profile in 30 seconds. You can change the number of seconds that the profile list will be displayed before starting up. Type **0** in the seconds field. The option should now read Select the first profile listed if I don't select a profile in 0 seconds. When restarting your computer with this configuration (0 seconds), the list of hardware profiles will not appear, and the first profile in the list will be used to start your computer.

7. Under Available hardware profiles, if necessary, click **Home** and click the **Up arrow**. The Hardware Profiles dialog box should now appear (as shown in Figure 2-7).

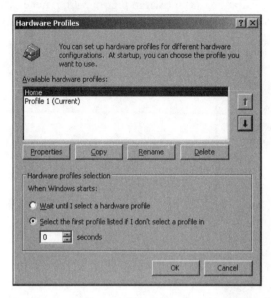

Figure 2-7 The modified Hardware Profiles dialog box

8. Click **OK** to close the Hardware Profiles dialog box.

9. Click **OK** to close the System Properties dialog box.

10. Shut down and restart your computer. The hardware profiles list does not appear because you have set the amount of time the list will display to 0 seconds.

11. Log on as **AdminX** to the **DomainX** domain (where *X* is your assigned student number) with a password of **Password01**.

12. Click **Start**, point to **Control Panel**, and click **System**.

13. Click the **Hardware** tab and click **Hardware Profiles**. Home is the current hardware profile. Click **Cancel** to exit the Hardware Profiles dialog box.

14. On the Hardware tab, click **Device Manager**.

15. In the Device Manager window, expand **Network adapters**.

16. Right-click your **network adapter card** and click **Properties**. On the General tab under Device usage, click the **drop-down arrow** and click **Do not use this device in the current hardware profile (disable)**, as shown in Figure 2-8. Click **OK** to close the Properties dialog box for your network card. Your network adapter card now has a red X on the icon.

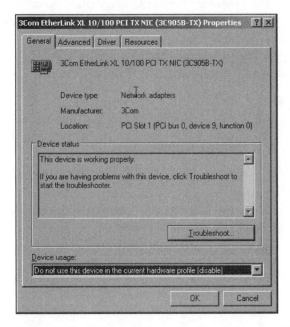

Figure 2-8   Disabling the network adapter card in the Home profile

17. Close Device Manager and close the System Properties window.

18. Click **Start**, click **Run**, type **cmd**, and click **OK**.

19. In the Command Prompt window, type **ping 192.168.1.x** (where *x* is the unique host IP address of another computer in your classroom) and press **Enter**. The ping was unsuccessful. You will receive the message Destination Host Unreachable. This is because the network adapter card is disabled in this hardware profile.

20. Close the Command Prompt window. You are now going to delete the hardware profile.

21. Click **Start**, click **Control Panel**, and click **System**.

22. In the System Properties dialog box, click the **Hardware** tab and click **Hardware Profiles**.

23. If necessary, click **Home (Current)**. The Delete option is not available.

24. Click **Profile 1**. You have the ability to delete a hardware profile if it is not the profile currently in use by the operating system.

25. In the Hardware profiles selection dialog box under Hardware Profiles, click **Wait until I select a hardware profile**. Click **OK** to close the Hardware Profiles dialog box.

26. Click **OK** to close the System Properties dialog box.

27. Restart your computer. The Hardware Profile/Configuration Recovery Menu appears. Using the down arrow on your keyboard, select **Profile 1** and press **Enter**.

28. Log on as **AdminX** to the **DomainX** domain (where *X* is your assigned student number) using a password of **Password01**.

29. Click **Start**, click **Control Panel**, and click **System**.

30. In the System Properties dialog box, click the **Hardware** tab.

31. On the Hardware tab, click **Hardware Profiles**.

32. In the Hardware Profiles dialog box under Available hardware profiles, click **Home** and click **Delete**.

33. In the Confirm Profile Delete dialog box, click **Yes** to indicate that you are sure you want to delete the hardware profile "Home."

34. Click **OK** to close the Hardware Profiles dialog box.

35. Click **OK** to close the System Properties dialog box.

Certification Objectives

Objectives for Microsoft Exam #70-290: Managing and Maintaining a Microsoft Windows Server 2003 Environment:

- Monitor server hardware. Tools might include Device Manager, the Hardware Troubleshooting Wizard, and appropriate Control Panel items.

- Configure device properties and settings.

Review Questions

1. To create a hardware profile, which Control Panel applet do you use?

   a. Add hardware

   b. Add or remove programs

   c. Display

   d. System

2. Which of the following is/are true regarding hardware profiles?

   a. All devices installed when Windows is installed will be enabled in the Profile 1 hardware profile.

   b. You cannot delete a hardware profile if currently in use.

   c. If a service is disabled in a hardware profile, the startup type setting for that service will override the hardware profile settings.

   d. All of the above.

3. Which of the following is/are true about hardware profiles?

   a. When a device is disabled in a hardware profile, the device drivers are uninstalled from the system.

   b. When a device is disabled in a hardware profile, the device drivers are not loaded when the computer is started.

   c. You must be a member of the Administrators local group to create hardware profiles.

   d. All of the above.

4. Which of the following is/are true about hardware profiles?

   a. Hardware profiles instruct Windows as to which devices or services to start when starting the computer or which settings to use for each device.

   b. The default profile will be the hardware profile at the top of the list if more than one profile resides on that computer.

   c. If you want to select a different hardware profile, press **spacebar** during startup to choose a profile from the list.

   d. All of the above.

5. Which of the following procedures is/are the right ways to configure a hardware profile?

   a. Using the system applet in control panel, click the **Hardware** tab, click **Device Manager**, select the device you wish to configure, and on the Device Properties dialog box click the **Disable** option next to the name of the profile you wish to modify.

   b. Using the system applet in Control Panel, click the **Hardware** tab, then click **Hardware Profiles**. Copy the hardware profile and switch to Device Manager to enable or disable device drivers.

   c. Using the system applet in Control Panel, click the Hardware tab. Click Hardware Profiles, and copy the hardware profile. Restart your computer using the new hardware profile. Using Device Manager, enable or disable appropriate device drivers for that profile.

   d. All of the above.

Lab 2.5 Investigating Power Options: The Hibernate Feature

Objectives

The goal of this lab is to configure power options to reduce the amount of power that your Windows Server 2003 system uses.

Materials Required

This lab will require the following:

- Windows Server 2003 installed and configured according to the instructions at the beginning of this lab manual

Estimated completion time: **15 minutes**

Activity Background

One of the available power options is the ability to put your computer into hibernation. When a system is hibernated, the contents of RAM are saved to the local hard drive and the computer is shut down. Once the system is restarted, all applications and processes are restored. This feature can be used if you will be away from your system for an extended period of time.

Activity

1. Log on as **AdminX** to the **DomainX** domain (where X is your assigned student number) with a password of **Password01**.

2. Click **Start**, point to **Control Panel**, and click **Power Options**.

3. In the Power Options Properties dialog box, click the **Hibernate** tab.

4. Under Hibernate, click **Enable hibernation**. Under Disk space for hibernation, note that it shows two values: Free disk space and Disk space required to hibernate. The value under Disk space required to hibernate matches the amount of RAM installed on your system (as shown in Figure 2-9).

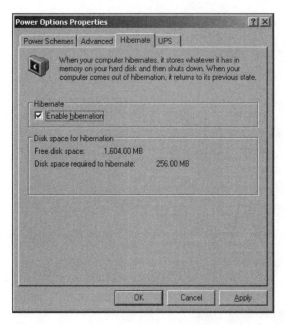

Figure 2-9   Enabling Hibernation

5. Click the **Advanced** tab and note that the available options now include Always show icon on the taskbar. Click the **Hibernate** tab and click **Apply**. Click the **Advanced** tab. The option Prompt for password when computer resumes from standby now appears under options.

6. Click **OK** to close the Power Options Properties dialog box.

7. Click **Start**, point to **All Programs**, point to **Accessories**, and click **Notepad**. In Notepad, type **This message will appear after you hibernate this system**.

8. Click **Start**, point to **Control Panel**, and double-click **Network Connections**. After hibernating your system, you are going to see if the windows that you have just opened are still there once you have restarted your system.

9. Click **Start** and click **Shut Down**.

10. In the Shut Down Windows dialog box under What do you want the computer to do?, click the **drop-down arrow** and click **Hibernate**. Once you have selected this option, a description of "Hibernate" is provided (as shown in Figure 2-10).

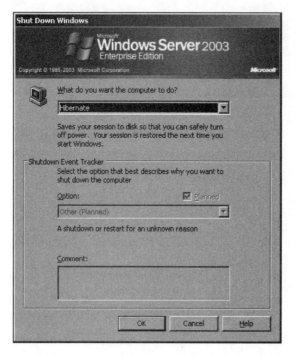

Figure 2-10   Selecting the Hibernate option in the Shut Down Windows dialog box

11. Click **OK** to hibernate your computer.

12. Restart your computer. The Computer Locked dialog box appears. The message "This computer is in use and has been locked" appears.

13. Log on as **AdminX** to the **DomainX** domain (where *X* is your assigned student number) with a password of **Password01**. All applications that were open when you hibernated your computer are still running.

14. Close all open applications.

15. Click **Start**, point to **Control Panel**, and click **Power Options**.

16. In the Power Options Properties dialog box, click the **Hibernate** tab.

17. Under Hibernate, click to clear the **Enable hibernation** option.

18. Click **OK** to close the **Power Options Properties** dialog box.

Certification Objectives

Objectives for Microsoft Exam #70-290: Managing and Maintaining a Microsoft Windows Server 2003 Environment:

2

- Monitor server hardware. Tools might include Device Manager, the Hardware Troubleshooting Wizard, and appropriate Control Panel items.

- Configure resource settings for a device.

REVIEW QUESTIONS

1. Which of the following statements is/are true about the hibernate feature?

   a. It saves everything in memory to disk, turns off the monitor and hard drive, and shuts down the computer.

   b. It requires an amount of free disk space equal to the amount of memory installed on the computer.

   c. It is a method to reduce power consumption of devices on the system.

   d. All of the above.

2. Which of the following are true about the POWERCFG command-line utility? (Choose all that apply.)

   a. Creates and deletes specified power schemes.

   b. Changes settings for a specified power scheme.

   c. Turns hibernate feature on or off.

   d. Configures time-out settings for turning the computer off after a specified period of time for both AC and battery power.

3. Which of the following statements is/are true of both the standby and hibernate features?

   a. Both are methods of reducing power consumption of the system.

   b. Both save the contents of the desktop to the local hard drive.

   c. Both offer methods by which you can recover unsaved information in the event of a power failure.

   d. All of the above.

4. Which of the following statements is/are true? (Choose all that apply.)

   a. Both hibernate and standby are useful methods of conserving battery power on portable systems.

   b. It is advised that you choose standby rather than hibernate if you will be away from your computer for an extended period of time or overnight.

   c. When rebooting after hibernation, the desktop is locked by the user account that hibernated the computer.

   d. When rebooting after hibernation, the desktop will be restored to the state it was in when it was hibernated.

5. Which of the following must be in place in order to enable your system to hibernate automatically?

   a. You must click the **APM** tab and click **Enabled Advanced Power Management Support**.

   b. Your computer must support this option.

   c. You must have free disk space equal to the amount of RAM installed on your system.

   d. All of the above.

3

CREATING AND MANAGING USERS

Labs included in this chapter:

◆ Lab 3.1 Using CSVDE to Create Accounts in Active Directory

◆ Lab 3.2 Creating and Modifying Accounts Using Command-Line Utilities

◆ Lab 3.3 Moving and Deleting Accounts Using Command-Line Utilities

◆ Lab 3.4 Troubleshooting User Authentication Issues

◆ Lab 3.5 Modifying the Default Profile

Microsoft MCSE Exam #70-290 Objectives	
Objective	Lab
Manage local, roaming, and mandatory user profiles.	3.5
Create and manage user accounts.	3.1, 3.2, 3.3
Create and modify user accounts by using automation.	3.2, 3.3
Import user accounts.	3.1
Diagnose and resolve account lockouts.	3.4
Diagnose and resolve issues related to user account properties.	3.4
Troubleshoot user authentication issues.	3.4

LAB 3.1 USING CSVDE TO CREATE ACCOUNTS IN ACTIVE DIRECTORY

Objectives

In this lab activity, you will use the CSVDE command-line utility to create user accounts in Active Directory Users and Computers and create a text file to be used with the CSVDE command-line utility.

Materials Required

This lab will require the following:

- Windows Server 2003 installed and configured according to the instructions at the beginning of this lab manual

Estimated completion time: **15 minutes**

Activity Background

One of the most common tasks to be performed by a domain administrator will be to create and modify user accounts in Active Directory. One command-line utility that can be used to create user accounts in Active Directory is CSVDE.

Activity

1. Log on as **AdminX** to the **DomainX** domain (where *X* is your assigned student number) with a password of **Password01**.

2. Click **Start**, point to **All Programs**, point to **Accessories**, and click **Notepad**.

3. In Notepad, type the following: givenName,sn,displayName, sAMAccount-Name,userPrincipalName,department, userAccountControl,DN,objectClass and then press Enter twice.

4. Type **John,Doe, John Doe,Johnd,Johnd@domainX. dovercorp.net,IT,514," cn=John Doe,cn=users,dc=domainX, dc=dovercorp,dc=net",user** (where *X* is your assigned student number) and press **Enter**.

5. Type **Joy,Smith, Joy Smith,Joys,Joys@domainX. dovercorp.net,IT,514,"cn=Joy Smith,cn=users,dc=domainX, dc=dovercorp,dc=net",user** (where *X* is your assigned student number) and press **Enter**.

6. Type **Jack,Wilson, Jack Wilson,Jackw,Jackw@domainX. dovercorp.net,IT,514,"cn=Jack Wilson,cn=users,dc=domainX, dc=dovercorp,dc=net",user** (where *X* is your assigned student number) and press **Enter**.

7. Click **File** and click **Save As**. Click the **drop-down arrow** in the Save in field and click **Local Disk (C:)**.

8. In the File name field, type **NewUsers** and click **Save**.

9. Click **Start**, click **Run**, type **cmd**, and click **OK**.

10. In the command prompt window, type **csvde –i –f c:\newusers.txt** and press **Enter**. The command prompt window should appear (as in Figure 3-1).

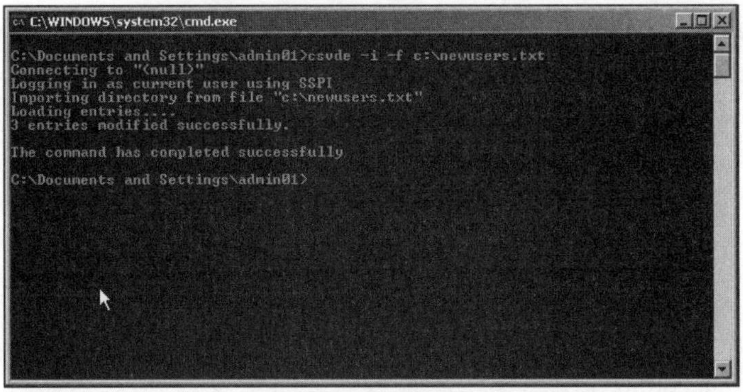

Figure 3-1   Using the CSVDE command-line utility

11. Close the command prompt window.

12. Click **Start**, click **Administrative Tools**, and click **Active Directory Users and Computers**. The three user accounts that you have just created appear as disabled. This is because you entered 514 as the userAccountControl value. The value 512 is used to enable accounts, and the value 514 is used to disable accounts. Close Active Directory Users and Computers.

Certification Objectives

Objectives for Microsoft Exam #70-290: Managing and Maintaining a Microsoft Windows Server 2003 Environment:

- Create and manage user accounts.

- Import user accounts.

REVIEW QUESTIONS

1. Which of the following are true with regards to Password reset disks? (Choose all that apply.)

   a. They can only be used for local computer accounts.

   b. They can only be used for domain accounts.

   c. If you try to change your password and create a password reset disk at the same time, the new password information will not be saved.

   d. You do not have to create a new password reset disk if you change your password or if the password is reset manually.

2. Which of the following are true? (Choose all that apply.)

   a. When the Administrator account is disabled, it can still be used to gain access to a domain controller using Safe Mode.

   b. It is recommended that you rename or disable the built-in Administrator and Guest accounts.

   c. A renamed user account retains its security ID (SID).

   d. The password must meet complexity requirements; security setting is disabled on stand-alone servers by default.

3. Which of the following are considered to be weak passwords? (Choose all that apply.)

   a. Leaving the password blank

   b. Contains your user name or your given name

   c. Contains a complete dictionary word

   d. Contains uppercase and lowercase letters, numerals, and other keyboard symbols

4. Which of the following are advisable security practices to follow with regards to password protection? (Choose all that apply.)

   a. Use a different password for each of your different user accounts.

   b. If your password has been compromised, change it immediately.

   c. Keep your password to yourself.

   d. If it must be written down, store your password in a secure location and destroy when it is no longer required.

5. Which of the following are true regarding the system key utility? (Choose all that apply.)

   a. If the disk that contains the system key is lost or if the password is forgotten, you cannot start the computer without restoring the registry to the state it was in before the system key was used.

   b. To run the system key, click **Run** and type **syskey**.

   c. According to the Securing the Windows Account Database dialog box that appears when you run the syskey utility, once enabled, encryption cannot be disabled.

   d. The most secure syskey option is to store the key on a floppy disk rather than encrypted on the local computer.

LAB 3.2 CREATING AND MODIFYING ACCOUNTS

Objectives

In this lab activity, you will be using the DSMOD command-line utility to create and modify user accounts in Active Directory.

Materials Required

This lab will require the following:

- Windows Server 2003 installed and configured according to the instructions at the beginning of this lab manual

Estimated completion time: **20 minutes**

Activity Background

There are several ways that user accounts can be created on Windows Server 2003. In addition to the CSVDE and LDIFDE command-line utilities, user accounts can also be created using either the Active Directory Users and Computers console or through command-line utilities. DSADD is a command-line utility that can be used to create objects in Active Directory, such as computers, contacts, groups, organizational units, or users. In this lab activity, you will use DSADD to create user accounts. Once objects such as computers, contacts, groups, organizational units, servers, or users have been created in Active Directory, they can be modified using the DSMOD command-line utility. The DSMOD command-line utility can be used to modify the attributes of one or more user accounts in Active Directory.

Activity

1. Log on as **AdminX** to the **DomainX** domain (where *X* is your assigned student number) with a password of **Password01**.

2. First, you will create an OU where the user accounts will be placed in Active Directory. Click **Start**, then click **Help and Support**. In the Help and Support Center window, type **dsadd** in the Search field and click the **green arrow**.

3. In the Search Results under Help Topics, click **Dsadd: Command-line reference**.

4. Expand **dsadd ou** in the details pane and view the syntax for dsadd ou. You are going to use this command to create the organizational unit where the users in this activity will be created.

5. Click **Start**, click **Run**, type **cmd**, and click **OK**.

6. In the command prompt window, type **dsadd ou "ou=Chapter3, dc=domainX, dc=dovercorp, dc=net"** (where *X* is your assigned student number) and press **Enter**.

7. Click **Start**, point to **Administrative Tools**, and Click **Active Directory Users and Computers**. Double-click to expand the **DomainX.Dovercorp.net** domain (where *X* is your assigned student number), if necessary. The Chapter3 organizational unit you created appears.

8. Switch to the command prompt window.

9. In the command prompt window, type **dsadd user "cn=Bob White,ou=Chapter3,dc=domainX,dc=dovercorp,dc=net" –samid bwhite –upn bwhite@domainX.dovercorp.net** (where *X* is your assigned student number) and press **Enter**. When you receive the dsadd succeeded message, switch to the Active Directory Users and Computers console.

10. In the Active Directory Users and Computers console, click the **Chapter3** organizational unit. The Bob White account appears. By default, the account has been disabled. Right-click the **Bob White** account and click **Properties**. Click the **Account** tab. The User logon name field has been filled in with the user principal name (UPN) that you entered in the dsadd utility, and the pre-Windows 2000 User logon name is bwhite (as shown in Figure 3-2). Click **Cancel** to exit the Bob White Properties dialog box.

3

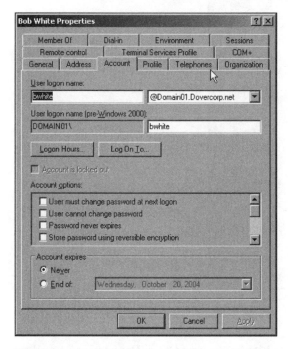

Figure 3-2   An account created using DSADD user

11. Now you are going to create another account using different parameters in the dsadd user utility. In the command prompt window, type **dsadd user "cn=Alice Green,ou=Chapter3,dc=domainX, dc=dovercorp,dc=net" –samid Aliceg –pwd * –mustchpwd yes –acctexpires 365 –disabled no** (where *X* is your assigned student number) and press **Enter**.

12. When asked to Enter User Password, type **Password01** and press **Enter**.

13. When asked to Confirm User Password, type **Password01** and press **Enter**.

14. When the dsadd succeeded message appears, switch to Active Directory Users and Computers. In the Active Directory Users and Computers console window, click the **Chapter3** organizational unit, click **Action** on the menu, and click **Refresh**. The Alice Green user account appears and is not disabled. Next, you will review some of the other options that you entered when creating this account.

15. Right-click the **Alice Green** account and click **Properties**. Click the **Account** tab. The User must change password at next logon option has been checked. The account is also set to expire one year from this day (as shown in Figure 3-3). Click **OK** to close the Alice Green Properties dialog box.

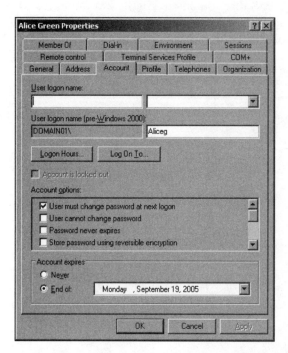

Figure 3-3   The Alice Green user account properties

16. Right-click the **Bob White** account and click **Properties**. Recall that we did not specify information for the First name and Last name fields. As a result, these fields are blank. Click the **Account** tab. Note that the account options have not been configured for this user account and that the Account expires options have defaulted to Never. Click **OK** to close the Bob White Properties dialog box.

17. In the Help and Support Center window, type **dsmod** in the Search field and click the **green arrow**. In the Search Results under Help Topics, click **Dsmod: Command-line reference**. Review the syntax for the dsmod user command.

18. In the command prompt window, type **dsmod user "cn=Bob White, ou=Chapter3, dc=domainX, dc=dovercorp, dc=net" –fn Bob –ln White –pwd Password01 –pwdneverexpires yes –disabled no** (where *X* is your assigned student number) and press **Enter**.

19. When the dsmod succeeded message appears, switch to the Active Directory Users and Computers window. In the Active Directory Users and Computers console window, click the **Chapter3** organizational unit, click **Action** on the menu, and click **Refresh**. Note that the Bob White user account is no longer disabled. Right-click the **Bob White** user account and click **Properties**. Note that the First name and Last name fields have now been filled in. Click the **Account** tab. Note that the Account options have been modified to Password never expires. Click **Cancel** to exit the Bob White Properties dialog box.

20. You can also use the dsmod user command-line utility to modify the attributes of more than one account at the same time. Switch to the command prompt window.

21. In the command prompt window, type **dsmod user "cn=Bob White, ou=Chapter3,dc=domainX,dc=dovercorp,dc=net" "cn=Alice Green,ou=Chapter3,dc=domainX,dc=dovercorp,dc=net" –pwd P@ssw0rd! –mustchpwd yes** (where *X* is your assigned student number) and press **Enter** (as shown in Figure 3-4).

Figure 3-4   Modifying properties for more than one account with DSMOD user

22. When the dsmod succeeded message appears, close the command prompt window. You have just reset the passwords for the Bob White and Alice Green user accounts to P@ssw0rd!, and both accounts are set to force the user to change their password at the next logon.

23. Close Active Directory Users and Computers and close the Help and Support Center window.

Certification Objectives

Objectives for Microsoft Exam #70-290: Managing and Maintaining a Microsoft Windows Server 2003 Environment:

■ Create and manage user accounts.

■ Create and modify user accounts by using automation.

REVIEW QUESTIONS

1. Which of the following are false regarding creating user accounts?

   a. A new user account that has the same name as a deleted account will not have the same permissions and group memberships as the deleted account.

   b. A new user account will have a unique SID.

   c. A user account that is created by copying an existing user account will belong to the same groups it was copied from.

   d. All of the above.

2. To use the Dsadd user command-line utility to create new accounts in Active Directory, to which of the following groups must your user account belong? (Choose all that apply.)

   a. Account Operators

   b. Domain Admins

   c. Enterprise Admins

   d. Server Operators

3. Which of the following can be accomplished by using the dsmod user command-line utility? (Choose all that apply.)

   a. Create a new user account.

   b. Delete a user account.

   c. Disable or re-enable a user account.

   d. Rename a user account.

4. Which of the following must be specified when using the dsmod user command-line utility?

   a. User distinguished name

   b. User principal name

   c. User name

   d. All of the above

5. When using the dsadd user command-line utility and you specify –pwd *, what will the resulting password be?

a. Blank

b. *

c. You will be prompted to enter a password.

d. None of the above

LAB 3.3 MOVING AND DELETING ACCOUNTS USING COMMAND-LINE UTILITIES

Objectives

In this lab activity, you will be using command-line utilities to manipulate objects in Active Directory. After completing this lab activity, you will be able to move and rename objects in Active Directory using the DSMOVE command-line utility and delete objects in Active Directory using the DSRM command-line utility.

Materials Required

This lab will require the following:

- Windows Server 2003 installed and configured according to the instructions at the beginning of this lab manual

Estimated completion time: **20 minutes**

Activity Background

Administrators will often have to move or delete objects in Active Directory. To accomplish this task, the Active Directory Users and Computers console can be used, as well as the command-line utilities. The DSMOVE command-line utility can be used to move and/or rename objects in Active Directory. The DSRM command-line utility can be used to delete objects in Active Directory.

ACTIVITY

Activity

1. Log on as **AdminX** to the **DomainX** domain (where *X* is your assigned student number) with a password of **Password01**.

2. Click **Start**, then click **Help and Support**. In the Help and Support Center window, type **dsmove** in the Search field and click the **green arrow**. In the Search Results under Help Topics, click **Dsmove: Command-line reference**. Review the syntax for the dsmove command.

3. Click **Start**, click **Run**, type **cmd**, and click **OK**.

4. In the command prompt window, type **dsmove "cn=Bob White, ou=Chapter3, dc=domainX, dc=dovercorp, dc=net" –newname "Kaitlyn Gutterstorm"** (where *X* is your assigned student number) and press **Enter**. Note that you are putting quotes around Kaitlyn Gutterstorm, as there is a space and the command will otherwise fail—it will recognize Gutterstorm as an unknown parameter. (Note: Under normal circumstances, we would use the dsmod utility to modify other user parameters, such as the logon name, for example.)

5. Click **Start**, point to Administrative Tools, and click **Active Directory Users and Computers**. In the Active Directory Users and Computers console click the **Chapter3** organizational unit. The Bob White account in the Chapter3 organizational unit has now been replaced with the Kaitlyn Gutterstorm object. Right-click the **Kaitlyn Gutterstorm** user account and click **Properties**. Note that the First name and Last name field would need to be modified, as well as the User logon names on the Account tab. Click **Cancel** to close the Kaitlyn Gutterstorm Properties dialog box.

6. In the command prompt window, type **dsmod user "cn=Kaitlyn Gutterstorm,ou=Chapter3,dc=domainX,dc=dovercorp, dc=net" –fn Kaitlyn –ln Gutterstorm –upn Kaitlyng@domainX.dovercorp.net** (where *X* is your assigned student number) and press **Enter**.

7. Switch to the Active Directory Users and Computers console window. In the Active Directory Users and Computers console, right-click **Chapter3** and click **Refresh**.

8. Right-click the **Kaitlyn Gutterstorm** account and click **Properties**. On the General tab, note that both the First name and Last name fields have now been changed. Click the **Account** tab. Note that the User logon name has now been modified (as shown in Figure 3-5). Tab down to the **User logon name** (pre-Windows 2000) field and type **Kaitlyng**. Click **OK** to close the Kaitlyn Gutterstorm Properties dialog box.

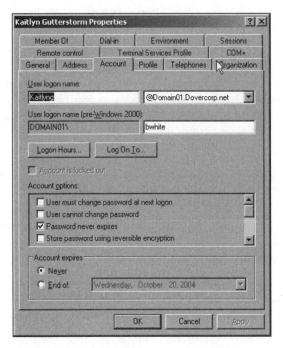

Figure 3-5   Modifying the renamed account properties

9. Switch back to the command prompt window. We are now going to create an organizational unit in which to move the Alice Green account. In the command prompt window, type **dsadd ou "ou=dsmove, ou=Chapter3,dc=domainX,dc=dovercorp,dc=net"** (where *X* is your assigned student number) and press **Enter**.

10. When you see the dsadd succeeded message, switch to the Active Directory Users and Computers console window. In the Active Directory Users and Computers console window, right-click the **Chapter3** organizational unit and click **Refresh**. If the dsmove organizational unit does not appear, wait a few seconds and click **Refresh** again.

11. Switch back to the command prompt window. In the command prompt window, type **dsmove "cn=Alice Green,ou=Chapter3, dc=domainX,dc=dovercorp,dc=net" –newname "Mackenzie Benoit" –newparent "ou=dsmove,ou=Chapter3, dc=domainX,dc=dovercorp,dc=net"** (where *X* is your assigned student number) and press **Enter**. When the dsmove succeeded message appears, switch to the Active Directory Users and Computers console window.

12. In the Active Directory Users and Computers console window, right-click the **Chapter3** organizational unit and click **Refresh**. The Alice Green user account is no longer there. Expand the Chapter3 organizational unit, if necessary, and then click the **dsmove** organizational unit. It now contains a user account by the name of Mackenzie Benoit.

13. You are going to delete the objects you created in this lab using the dsrm command-line utility. In the Help and Support Center window, type **dsrm** in the Search field and click the **green arrow**. In the Search Results under Help topics, click **Dsrm: Command-line reference**. Review the syntax for this command-line utility.

14. In the command prompt window, type **dsrm –subtree –exclude –noprompt "ou=dsmove,ou=Chapter3,dc=domainX, dc=dovercorp,dc=net"** (where *X* is your assigned student number) and press **Enter**. When the message dsrm succeeded appears, switch to the Active Directory Users and Computers console window.

15. In the Active Directory Users and Computers console window, click **Action** and click **Refresh**. The contents of the dsmove organizational unit have been deleted.

16. In the command prompt window, type **dsrm –subtree "ou=Chapter3, dc=domainX, dc=dovercorp, dc=net"** (where *X* is your assigned student number) and press **Enter**.

17. When asked "Are you sure you wish to delete ou=Chapter3, dc=domainX,dc=dovercorp,dc=net (Y/N)?", type **Y** and press **Enter**. When the message dsrm succeeded appears, close the command prompt window.

18. Switch to the Active Directory Users and Computers console window, click **DomainX.Dovercorp.net**, and then click **Action** on the menu, and click **Refresh**. The Chapter3 organizational unit and its contents have now been deleted.

19. Click the **Users** container. Click the **Jack Wilson** account, hold down the **Ctrl** key on your keyboard, and click the **Joy Smith** account. All three user accounts that you created during this lab activity will be selected. Press **Delete** on your keyboard. When asked if you are sure you want to delete these three objects, click **Yes**.

20. Close Active Directory Users and Computers and close the Help and Support Center window.

Certification Objectives

Objectives for Microsoft Exam #70-290: Managing and Maintaining a Microsoft Windows Server 2003 Environment:

- Create and manage user accounts.

- Create and modify user accounts by using automation.

REVIEW QUESTIONS

1. Which of the following are true regarding moving user accounts in Active Directory?

   a. Right-click the user account you want to move, click **Move**, and then select the location where you want to move the account.

   b. To move user accounts between domains, you must use the Movetree support tool.

   c. Click the object you want to move, and drag and drop it onto the new organizational unit or container.

   d. All of the above.

2. Membership in which of the following groups will allow you to move accounts in Active Directory?

   a. Account Operators

   b. Domain Admins

   c. Enterprise Admins

   d. All of the above

3. Which of the following is true when deleting user accounts? (Choose all that apply.)

   a. Once an account is deleted, all permissions and group memberships associated with it are deleted as well.

   b. A new user account created with identical properties to a deleted user account will still have its own unique SID.

   c. User accounts cannot be restored from backup.

   d. All of the above.

4. Which of the following are methods by which a user account can be deleted?

   a. Right-click the user account and click **Delete**.

   b. Click the user account in Active Directory and press the **Delete** key on your keyboard.

   c. Use the dsrm command-line utility.

   d. All of the above.

5. Which of the following options will work to restore a deleted account and all of its memberships and permissions?

   a. Create another account using the same user logon name.

   b. In Active Directory Users and Computers, use the Action Undo Delete option.

   c. Restore the account from backup.

   d. All of the above.

LAB 3.4 TROUBLESHOOTING USER AUTHENTICATION ISSUES

Objectives

In this lab activity, you will configure user account properties and then log on to observe the messages users receive when they attempt to log on. After completing this lab activity, you will also be able to troubleshoot user logon issues.

Materials Required

This lab will require the following:

- Windows Server 2003 installed and configured according to the instructions at the beginning of this lab manual

> Estimated completion time: **10 minutes**

Activity Background

Some user account properties may restrict when users are allowed to log onto the domain, which workstations they are allowed to log onto, and when their accounts will expire. As a result, there will be times when you need to troubleshoot these circumstances.

ACTIVITY

Activity

1. Log on as **AdminX** to the **DomainX** domain (where *X* is your assigned student number) with a password of **Password01**.

2. Click **Start**, point to **Administrative Tools**, and click **Active Directory Users and Computers**.

3. Right-click the **DomainX.Dovercorp.net** domain, point to **New**, and click **Organizational Unit**. In the New Object—Organizational Unit dialog box, type **Troubleshooting Lab** and click **OK**.

4. Right-click the **Troubleshooting Lab** organizational unit, point to **New**, and click **User**.

5. In the New Object—User dialog box, tab down to the **Full name** field and type **Troubleshooting Logon Hours**. Tab down to the **User logon name** field and type **Hours**, and then click **Next**. Type **Password01** in the Password and Confirm password fields, then click to clear the **User must change password at next logon** check box, and click **Next**. Click **Finish**.

6. Create two other user accounts in the Troubleshooting Lab organizational unit using **Password01** as your password and using the same account settings as the Hours account in the previous step. Use the following parameters:

Full name	Troubleshooting Workstation Logon
User Logon name	Workstation
Full name	Troubleshooting Expired Accounts
User Logon name	Expired

7. Right-click the **Troubleshooting Logon Hours** account and click **Properties**. Click the **Account** tab. Click **Logon Hours**. Click the day of the week that you are performing this lab activity and click **Logon Denied** (as shown in Figure 3-6). Click **OK**, and then click **OK** again to close the Troubleshooting Logon Hours Properties dialog box.

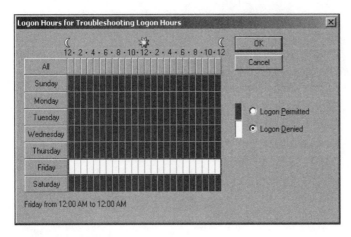

Figure 3-6 Configuring Logon Hours

8. Right-click the **Troubleshooting Workstation Logon** account and click **Properties**. Click the **Account** tab. Click the **Log On To** button. In the Logon Workstations dialog box, click **The following computers**. In the Computer name field, type **ComputerX** (where *X* is your assigned student number). (See Figure 3-7.) Note that you are intentionally typing the name of a computer that does not exist in your lab environment. Click **Add** and click **OK**. Click **OK** to close the Troubleshooting Workstation Logon Properties dialog box.

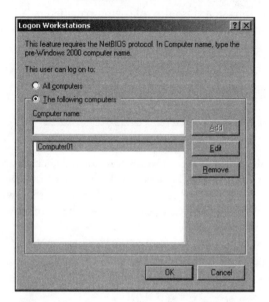

Figure 3-7   Configuring Logon Workstations

9. Right-click **Troubleshooting Expired Accounts** and click **Properties**. Click the **Account** tab. Under Account expires, click to select the **End of** option. Then click the **drop down arrow** and select the day before the day shown on your system clock date and time settings (as shown in Figure 3-8). Click **OK**.

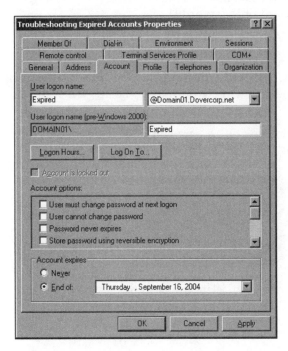

Figure 3-8   Configuring Account Expires

10. Close Active Directory Users and Computers.

11. Log off.

12. Log on as **Hours** to the **DomainX** domain (where *X* is your assigned student number) with a password of **Password01**. You will receive a message telling you that your account has time restrictions that prevent you from logging on at this time, and inviting you to please try again later. Click **OK**.

13. Log on as **Workstation** to the **DomainX** domain (where *X* is your assigned student number) with a password of **Password01**. You should receive a message telling you that your account is configured to prevent you from using this computer, and inviting you to please try another computer. Click **OK**.

14. Log on as **Expired** to the **DomainX** domain (where *X* is your assigned student number) with a password of **Password01**. You will receive a message telling you that your account has expired, and to please see your system administrator. Click **OK**.

15. Next, try to log on as **Guest** to the **DomainX** (where *X* is your assigned student number). You will receive a message telling you that your account has been disabled, and to please see your system administrator. This account is disabled by default. Click **OK**.

16. Log on as **AdminX** to the **DomainX** domain (where *X* is your assigned student number) with a password of **Password01**.

17. Click **Start**, point to **Administrative Tools**, and click **Active Directory Users and Computers**.

18. In Active Directory Users and Computers, click the **Troubleshooting Lab** organizational unit and press **Delete** on your keyboard. When asked if you are sure you want to delete this object, click **Yes**.

19. A message appears asking if you are sure you want to delete the container and the objects it contains (as shown in Figure 3-9). Click **Yes**.

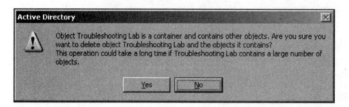

Figure 3-9   Message when attempting to delete container holding other objects

Certification Objectives

Objectives for Microsoft Exam #70-290: Managing and Maintaining a Microsoft Windows Server 2003 Environment:

- Diagnose and resolve issues related to user account properties.

- Troubleshoot user authentication issues.

3

REVIEW QUESTIONS

1. Which of the following are true regarding deleting a user account? (Choose all that apply.)

   a. Security IDs are mapped to user names, and therefore, a new user account and a previously deleted user account with the same name will both have the same SID.

   b. If you wish to disallow logging onto a domain for a user account temporarily for security reasons, it is recommended that you disable the account rather than delete it.

   c. The DSRM command-line utility can be used to delete user accounts.

   d. All of the above.

2. You have accidentally deleted a user account. You need to allow that user access to the same resources as they previously had. Which of the following could work to accomplish this? (Choose all that apply.)

   a. Perform an authoritative restore using your most recent backup tape before the deletion.

   b. Recreate the user account in Active Directory Users and Computers with the same account settings and group memberships as the deleted account.

   c. Recreate the user account in Active Directory Users and Computers with the same account settings and group memberships that had been assigned to the deleted account. If permissions had been assigned directly to the old user account, reset the permissions to allow access to the newly created account.

   d. All of the above.

3. To modify user account properties, you must be a member of which of the following groups? (Choose all that apply.)

   a. Account Operators

   b. Domain Admins

   c. Enterprise Admins

   d. None of the above

4. Which of the following are true? (Choose all that apply.)

 a. To modify properties for multiple users at the same time, hold down **CTRL** and then click each user account. Right-click the accounts you selected and click **Properties**. Modify the property that you wish to change.

 b. To prevent a particular user from logging on for security reasons, you can disable accounts rather than delete them.

 c. The DSMOD user command-line utility can be used to reset passwords.

 d. All of the above

5. Which of the following statements are not true about the Guest account? (Choose all that apply.)

 a. It is disabled by default.

 b. It requires a password.

 c. It can be assigned rights and permissions like any other user account.

 d. It can be used by people who do not have an actual account in the domain.

LAB 3.5 MODIFYING THE DEFAULT PROFILE

Objectives

The goal of this activity is to create and configure a new default profile for users who have logged onto a workstation for the first time.

Materials Required

This lab will require the following:

■ Windows Server 2003 installed and configured according to the instructions at the beginning of this lab manual

Estimated completion time: **15 minutes**

Activity Background

Should you wish to create a domain-wide default profile, see the article titled "To create a preconfigured user profile" in Help and Support. This exercise will walk you through the basic steps in creating a default profile. Should you wish to create a more detailed default profile, you would further customize the user desktop and install all applications that you wanted to be a part of your new default user template.

ACTIVITY

Activity

1. Log on as **AdminX** to the **DomainX** domain (where *X* is your assigned student number) with a password of **Password01**.

2. Click **Start**, point to **Administrative Tools**, and click **Active Directory Users and Computers**.

3. Right-click the **Users** container, click **New**, and click **User**.

4. In the New Object—User dialog box, tab down to the **Full name** field and type **Default01 Profile**. Tab down to the **User logon name** field and type **Default01**. Click **Next**. Type **Password01** in both the Password and Confirm password fields. Click to clear the **User must change password at next logon** check box and click **Next**. Then click **Finish**.

5. Close Active Directory Users and Computers.

6. Log off as **AdminX**.

7. Log on as **Default01** to the **DomainX** domain (where *X* is your assigned student number) with a password of **Password01**. Note the default desktop for this new user account.

8. Right-click the **desktop** and click **Properties**. In the Display Properties dialog box, click the **Desktop** tab and scroll down to the **Windows Server 2003** background. Click **Windows Server 2003** and click **OK**. Note that your wallpaper has just changed.

9. Log off as **Default01**.

10. Log on as **AdminX** to the **DomainX** domain (where *X* is your assigned student number) with a password of **Password01**.

11. Right-click **Start** and click **Explore**. Click **Tools** on the menu and click **Folder Options**.

12. In the Folder Options dialog box, click the **View** tab. Click to select the **Show Hidden files and folders** option and click **OK**.

13. Press the **Windows** key on your keyboard and the **Pause Break** key at the same time. (Note that the Windows key is between the Ctrl and Alt keys on your keyboard, if you are unfamiliar with its functions.) If you do not have a Windows key, click **Start**, click **Control Panel**, and click **System**.

14. In the System Properties dialog box, click the **Advanced** tab. Under User Profiles, click the **Settings** button.

15. In the User Profiles dialog box, click the **DomainX\Default01** profile (where *X* is your assigned student number) (as shown in Figure 3-10) and click **Copy To**.

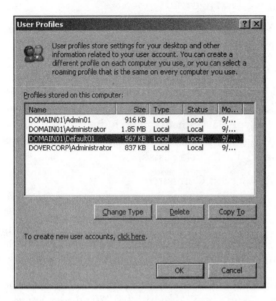

Figure 3-10   Copying the Default01 profile

16. In the Copy To dialog box, click **Browse** and select **C:\Documents and Settings\Default User** (as shown in Figure 3-11) and click **OK**.

Figure 3-11   Selecting Default User

17. In the Copy To dialog box, under Permitted to use, click **Change**. In the **Select User or Group** dialog box, click **Locations**. Double-click **Dovercorp.net**, click **DomainX.Dovercorp.net** (where *X* is your assigned student number), and click **OK**. Click **Advanced**. In the Name field next to Starts with, type **E** and click **Find Now**.

18. In the Search results field, click the **Everyone** account and click **OK**.

19. Click **OK** to close the Select User or Group dialog box.

20. The Copy To dialog box should now appear as shown in Figure 3-12. Click **OK** to close the Copy To dialog box.

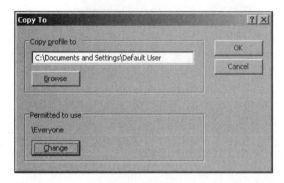

Figure 3-12   How the Copy To dialog box should now appear

21. When the Confirm Copy message appears indicating that C:\Documents and Settings\Default User already exists and that the current contents of this directory or file will be deleted during this operation, click **Yes** to show that you are sure you want to continue.

22. Click **OK** to close the User Profiles dialog box.

23. Click **OK** to close the System Properties dialog box. Next, you are going to create a new user account to test the new default profile settings.

24. Click **Start**, point to **Administrative Tools**, and click **Active Directory Users and Computers**.

25. Right-click the **Users** container, click **New**, and click **User**.

26. In the New Object—User dialog box, tab down to the **Full name** field and type **DefaultTest**. Tab down to the **User logon name** field and type **DefaultTest**, and click **Next**. In the Password and Confirm password fields, type **Password01**. Click to clear the **User must change password at next logon** check box and click **Next**. Click **Finish** to close the New Object—User dialog box.

27. Close Active Directory Users and Computers.

28. Log off as **AdminX**.

29. Log on as **DefaultTest** to the **DomainX** domain (where *X* is your assigned student number) with a password of **Password01**. The desktop shows the Windows Server 2003 wallpaper.

30. Log off as **DefaultTest**.

31. Log on as **AdminX** to the **DomainX** domain (where *X* is your assigned student number) with a password of **Password01**.

32. Click **Start**, point to **Administrative Tools**, and click **Active Directory Users and Computers**.

33. In the Active Directory Users and Computers console, click the **Users** container. Click the **Default01 Profile** account and then, holding down the **Shift** key, click the **Default01 Test** account. Press **Delete** on your keyboard. When asked if you are sure you want to delete these two objects, click **Yes**.

34. Close Active Directory Users and Computers and log off.

Certification Objectives

Objectives for Microsoft Exam #70-290: Managing and Maintaining a Microsoft Windows Server 2003 Environment:

- Manage local, roaming, and mandatory user profiles.

REVIEW QUESTIONS

1. To create a domain-wide default profile, you would use the System applet in Control Panel to copy the profile settings to which of the following locations?

   a. SYSTEMROOT\DOCUMENTS and SETTINGS\DEFAULT user folder on the local machine

   b. SYSTEMROOT\DOCUMENTS and SETTINGS\DEFAULT user folder on the Domain Controller

   c. NETLOGON\DEFAULT user on the local machine

   d. NETLOGON\DEFAULT user on the Domain Controller

2. To create a new local default user profile, you would use the System applet in Control Panel to copy the profile settings to which of the following locations?

   a. SYSTEMROOT\DOCUMENTS and SETTINGS\DEFAULT user folder on the local machine

   b. SYSTEMROOT\DOCUMENTS and SETTINGS\DEFAULT user folder on the Domain Controller

   c. NETLOGON\DEFAULT user on the local machine

   d. NETLOGON\DEFAULT user on the Domain Controller

3. Which of the following are not true about user profiles?

   a. You cannot copy or delete a user profile that belongs to the currently logged on user or to any user whose profile is in use.

   b. EFS is not compatible with roaming profiles.

   c. Roaming user profiles used with Terminal Services clients replicate to the server when the interactive user logs off and the interactive session is closed.

   d. A mandatory user profile is created for each user when they log on to the computer for the first time.

4. Which of the following are not true regarding profiles?

   a. If you are logged on to more than one computer at the same time and are using a roaming user profile, the registry settings from the computer you log off from last will be saved.

   b. In order to delete a roaming user profile, you need to take ownership of the profile's folder first.

   c. Roaming profiles must be stored on domain controllers.

   d. Every user profile begins as a copy of Default User.

5. Which of the following are recommendations to keep in mind when creating user profiles? (Choose all that apply.)

   a. Turn off Offline Folder caching on the shared directory where roaming user profiles are stored to avoid synchronization problems.

   b. Allow for different hardware because different video cards and display monitors may affect how well the profile works.

   c. Try to create the user profile on a computer that has the same type of video hardware as the users who will have the profile.

   d. Create a single mandatory profile for a group of users only if all computers have the same video hardware.

IMPLEMENTING AND MANAGING GROUPS

Labs included in this chapter:

♦ Lab 4.1 Introducing ADSI Edit

♦ Lab 4.2 The DSADD Command-line Utility

♦ Lab 4.3 The DSMOD Command-line Utility

♦ Lab 4.4 The DSQUERY and DSGET Command-line Utilities

♦ Lab 4.5 The DSMOVE and DSRM Command-line Utilities

Microsoft MCSE Exam #70-290 Objectives	
Objective	Lab
Create and manage groups.	4.2, 4.3, 4.4, 4.5
Manage group membership.	4.2, 4.3, 4.4, 4.5
Create and modify groups by using automation.	4.2, 4.3, 4.4, 4.5
Reset computer accounts.	4.3
Manage a server by using available support tools.	4.1

Lab 4.1 Introducing ADSI Edit

Objectives

The goal of this lab activity is to use Active Directory Service Interfaces (ADSI) Edit to view Active Directory information and to manipulate objects in Active Directory.

Materials Required

This lab will require the following:

- Windows Server 2003 installed and configured according to the instructions at the beginning of this lab manual

Estimated completion time: **25 minutes**

Activity Background

ADSI Edit is a snap-in available in the Microsoft Management Console (MMC). ADSI Edit can be used to add, delete, and move objects in Active Directory. Additionally, it can be used to view, change, or delete the attributes of an object. In order to run this utility, you either need to have installed the Windows Support Tools on your system or you need to register the file adsiedit.dll using the regsvr32 command. In this lab activity, we are running ADSI Edit from our domain controllers. This utility can actually be run from any client computer or server. Client computers do not have to be members of the domain. In order to connect to a domain, you must provide the domain name and credentials. Exercise caution when using this utility.

ACTIVITY

Activity

1. If necessary, log on as **AdminX** to the **DomainX** domain (where X is your assigned student number) with a password of **Password01**.

2. In order to demonstrate ADSI Edit, you need first to install the Windows Support Tools. If you have already installed these tools, proceed to step 8.

3. Navigate to the **D:\Source\SUPPORT\TOOLS** directory and double-click the **SUPTOOLS.MSI** file. The Welcome to the Windows Support Tools Setup Wizard page appears. Click **Next**.

4. On the End User License Agreement page, click **I Agree** and click **Next**. On the User Information page, type **Student** in the Name field and type **Dover Corp** in the Organization field. Click **Next**.

5. Accept the default settings for the destination directory and click **Install Now**.

6. On the Completing the Windows Support Tools Setup Wizard page, click **Finish**.

7. Close the D:\Source\SUPPORT\TOOLS window.

8. Click **Start**, click **Run**, type **cmd**, and click **OK**.

9. In order to create, modify, move, delete or query objects in Active Directory using the command-line utilities, you must be able to provide the Distinguished Names of these objects. You are now going to create a new user called AdsiEdit Test in the Users container. As you proceed through the labs in this chapter, keep in mind that when creating or renaming objects in Active Directory, if you want the object to appear in Active Directory with capitalization, you must ensure that capitalization is part of the command-line syntax used. When modifying these objects later, capitalization will not be required. In the command prompt window, type **dsadd user "cn=AdsiEdit Test,cn=users, dc=domainX,dc=dovercorp,dc=net"** (where *x* is your assigned student number) and press **Enter**. The dsadd succeeded message appears (as shown in Figure 4-1).

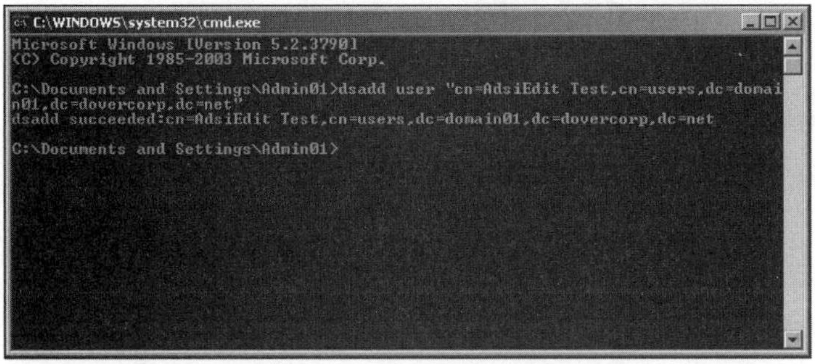

Figure 4-1   Creating the ADSIEDIT Test account

10. Click **Start**, point to **Administrative Tools**, and click **Active Directory Users and Computers**.

11. In the Active Directory Users and Computers console, double-click **DomainX.Dovercorp.net** to expand the node, if necessary.

12. Click the **Users** container. The AdsiEdit Test account will appear in the details pane of the window. As you did not specify –disable no as part of the dsadd user command, the account is disabled by default. Close Active Directory Users and Computers.

13. Click **Start**, click **Run**, type **mmc**, and then click **OK**.

14. In the Console1 window, click **File** and click **Add/Remove Snap-in**.

15. In the Add/Remove Snap-in dialog box, click **Add**.

16. In the Add Standalone Snap-in dialog box, click **ADSI Edit** (as shown in Figure 4-2) and click **Add**.

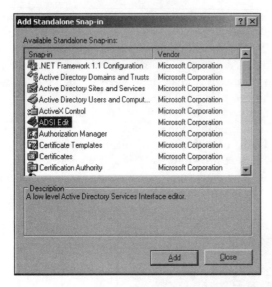

Figure 4-2   Adding the ADSI Edit snap-in to the MMC Console

17. Click **Close** to exit the Add Standalone Snap-in dialog box.

18. Click **OK** to close the Add/Remove Snap-in dialog box.

19. Maximize the **Console Root** window so that it occupies the entire Console1 window. In the Console Root window, double-click **ADSI Edit**. Notice that there are no items shown in this view.

20. Right-click **ADSI Edit** and click **Connect to...**.

21. In the Connection Settings dialog box, ADSI Edit is configured to connect to the domain or server that you logged on to (as shown in Figure 4-3). Click **OK**.

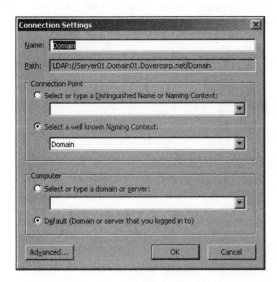

Figure 4-3   Connection Settings dialog box

22. Right-click **DomainX [ServerX.DomainX.Dovercorp.net]** (where *X* is your assigned student number) and click **Remove**. When a message appears asking if you are sure you want to remove Domain [ServerX.DomainX.Dovercorp.net], click **Yes**. This will only remove the connection point that links you to Active Directory through this utility.

 The Delete command in the ADSI Edit utility will remove objects from Active Directory. ADSI Edit is a very powerful utility, and you should exercise caution when using it.

23. Right-click **ADSI Edit** and click **Connect to...**.

24. In the Connection Settings dialog box, type **DomainX** (where *X* is your assigned student number) in the Name field. As shown in Figure 4-4, under the Computer section of the dialog box, click the **Select or type a domain or server** option and type **DomainX.Dovercorp.net**.

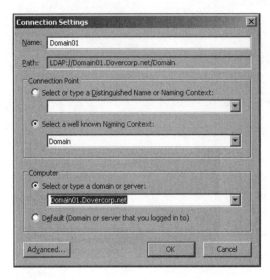

Figure 4-4   Connecting to the DomainX.Dovercorp.net domain

25. Click the **Advanced** button. If you are logged on with another user account, you can specify the credentials that you wish to use to connect to the Active Directory database (as shown in Figure 4-5). Click **OK** in the Advanced dialog box, then click **OK** in the Connection Settings dialog box.

Figure 4-5   The Specify Credentials check box

26. Click **DomainX [ServerX.DomainX.Dovercorp.net]** (where *X* is your assigned student number). The Distinguished Name for the domain object appears in the details pane.

27. Double-click **DC=DomainX,DC=Dovercorp,DC=net** (where *X* is your assigned student number). The Distinguished Name field displays the Distinguished Name for each container and organizational unit in your domain (as shown in Figure 4-6).

4

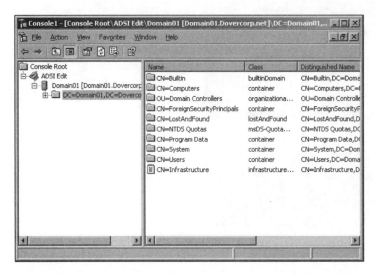

Figure 4-6 Viewing the Distinguished Names of objects in Active Directory

28. Double-click **OU=Domain Controllers**. The Distinguished Name for your domain controller object appears in the details pane.

29. Click **CN=Users**. The Distinguished Names of objects in the Users container appear in the details pane of the window.

You can use the ADSI Edit utility to help you determine the Distinguished Names of objects when using the Directory Services command-line utilities.

NOTE

30. Click the **CN=AdsiEdit Test** object in the details pane of the window. Scroll to the right of the screen and view the Distinguished Name of the object you created earlier in this exercise.

31. Right-click the **CN=AdsiEdit Test** user object in the details pane and click **Properties**.

32. In the CN=AdsiEdit Test Properties dialog box, scroll through the list of Attributes and click **description** (as shown in Figure 4-7), and click **Edit**.

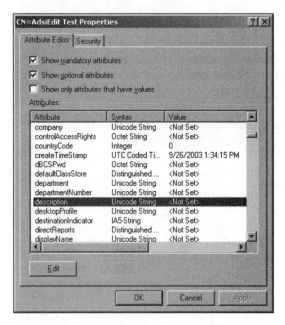

Figure 4-7   Viewing object properties using ADSI Edit

33. In the Multi-valued String Editor dialog box, type **Demonstration Account for ADSI Edit Lab** in the Value to add field, and then click **Add**. Click **OK** to close the Multi-valued String Editor dialog box. The description field has now been updated. Click **OK** to close the CN=AdsiEdit Test Properties dialog box.

34. Switch to the command prompt window, type **dsadd ou "ou=Chapter4,dc=domainX,dc=dovercorp,dc=net"**, and press **Enter**. When the dsadd succeeded message appears, close the command prompt window.

35. In the Console1 window, right-click **DC=DomainX, DC=Dovercorp,DC=net** and click **Refresh**. OU=Chapter4 appears in the Console1 window.

36. Click **CN=Users**. Right-click **CN=AdsiEdit Test** and click **Move**.

37. In the Move dialog box, click the **Chapter4** organizational unit and click **OK**.

38. Click **OU=Chapter4**. The CN=AdsiEdit Test object now appears.

39. Double-click **OU=Chapter4**. Right-click **CN=AdsiEdit Test** and click **Delete**. When asked if you are sure you want to delete this object, click **Yes**. The object is deleted.

40. Close the Console1 window. When asked if you want to save the console settings to Console1, click **No**.

41. Click **Start**, point to **Administrative Tools**, and click **Active Directory Users and Computers**. The Chapter4 organizational unit appears. Click the **Chapter4** organizational unit. The AdsiEdit account has been deleted. Close Active Directory Users and Computers.

42. Click **Start** and click **Help and Support**. In the Help and Support Center window, type **ADSI Edit** in the Search field and click the **green arrow**.

43. Under Search Results under Help Topics, click **Adsiedit.msc: ADSI Edit: Windows Support Tools**. Review the Help and Support documentation provided on ADSI Edit. Close the Help and Support Center window and log off.

Certification Objectives

Objectives for Microsoft Exam #70-290: Managing and Maintaining a Microsoft Windows Server 2003 Environment:

- Manage a server by using available support tools.

REVIEW QUESTIONS

1. Which of the following are actions that can be taken from within ADSI Edit?

   a. Add objects

   b. Delete objects

   c. Move objects

   d. All of the above

2. Which of the following are true about the ADSI Edit utility? (Choose all that apply.)

   a. You can connect to a domain controller from a computer that does not belong to the domain by providing credentials and specifying the domain information.

   b. The computer running ADSI Edit must be a member of the domain.

   c. The user running ADSI Edit must have rights to view the domain they are connecting to.

   d. ADSI Edit automatically tries to load the domain that the user is logged onto.

3. When creating a connection point to an object in Active Directory, what are the default credentials that will be used if none are specified in the Connection Settings dialog box?

   a. Administrator for the domain you are logged onto

   b. Administrator of the forest root domain

   c. Currently logged on user

   d. None of the above

4. Which of the following ADSI Edit options will remove the current objects in a container and repopulate the container with updated information from Active Directory?

   a. Update Schema Now

   b. Refresh

   c. Remove

   d. Delete

5. Which of the following are true about ADSI Edit? (Choose all that apply.)

   a. It is a GUI interface for viewing and making changes in Active Directory.

   b. It requires Adsiedit.dll and Adsiedit.msc.

   c. ADSI Edit will not run unless the adsiedit.dll is registered.

   d. The Delete command does not appear on the menu unless you have permissions to delete an object from Active Directory.

Lab 4.2 The DSADD Command-line Utility

Objectives

In this lab activity, you will be creating and adding computer accounts and groups using the DSADD computer command-line utility.

Materials Required

This lab will require the following:

- Windows Server 2003 installed and configured according to the instructions at the beginning of this lab manual

Estimated completion time: **15 minutes**

Activity Background

One of the more common tasks you will need to perform as a domain administrator will be to create objects in Active Directory. These tasks can be accomplished either by using the Active Directory Users and Computers console or through command-line utilities. This lab activity uses DSADD, a command-line utility used for adding objects to Active Directory. DSADD can be used for adding computers, contacts, groups, organizational units, users, and quotas.

Activity

1. Log on as **AdminX** to the **DomainX** domain (where *X* is your assigned student number) with a password of **Password01**.

2. Before using this utility, you will need to familiarize yourself with the syntax to be used with the dsadd command-line utility. Click **Start** and click **Help and Support**.

3. In the Help and Support Center window, type **dsadd** in the Search field and click the **green arrow**.

4. In the Search Results field under Help Topics, click the topic **Directory service command-line tools: Command-line reference**. Notice that there are other Active Directory command-line utilities in addition to the dsadd utility that you will be using in this exercise.

5. In the Search Results field under Help Topics, click the topic **Dsadd: Command-line reference**. The dsadd utility includes functionality for adding contacts, groups, organizational units, users, quotas, and computers. If necessary, you can refer to the Help and Support Center documentation for the syntax of these command-line utilities.

6. Click **Start**, click **Run**, type **cmd**, and click **OK**.

7. In the command prompt window, type **dsadd /?** and press **Enter**. Review the syntax for the dsadd computer command-line utility. First, you are going to add a computer account.

8. In the command prompt window, type **dsadd computer "cn=System1,cn=computers,dc=domainX,dc=dovercorp, dc=net"** (where *x* is your assigned student number) and press **Enter**. The dsadd succeeded message appears.

9. Click **Start**, point to **Administrative Tools**, and click **Active Directory Users and Computers**. Double-click **DomainX.Dovercorp.net** (where *X* is your assigned student number) if necessary.

10. Click the **Computers** container. The System1 computer account appears in the details pane.

11. Click the **Users** container. Right-click the **Domain Computers** group, and click **Properties**. Click the **Members** tab. Notice that the System1 computer account is a member of this group by default. Click **Cancel** to close the Domain Computers Properties dialog box.

12. In the command prompt window, type **dsadd computer "cn=System2, cn=computers,dc=domainX,dc=dovercorp, dc=net" –memberof "cn=ras and ias servers,cn=users, dc=domainX,dc=dovercorp,dc=net"** (where *x* is your assigned student number), and press **Enter**. When the dsadd succeeded message appears (as shown in Figure 4-8), switch back to the Active Directory Users and Computers console.

Figure 4-8   Using the DSADD computer command-line utility

13. Right-click the **Computers** container and click **Refresh**. The System2 computer account now appears in the details pane.

14. Click the **Users** container. Right-click the **RAS and IAS Servers** group, and click **Properties**. Click the **Members** tab. The System2 computer object appears as a member of this group. Click **Cancel** to exit the RAS and IAS Servers Properties dialog box.

15. In the Help and Support Center window, scroll down through the details pane and then click **dsadd group**. Review the syntax for this command-line utility.

16. In the command prompt window, type **dsadd group "cn=Chapter4 Computers,cn=users,dc=domainX,dc=dovercorp,dc=net" –secgrp yes –scope g –members "cn=System1,cn=computers, dc=domainX,dc=dovercorp,dc=net" "cn=System2, cn=computers,dc=domainX,dc=dovercorp,dc=net"** (where *X* is your assigned student number), and press **Enter**. When the dsadd succeeded message appears (as shown in Figure 4-9), switch back to the Active Directory Users and Computers console window.

4

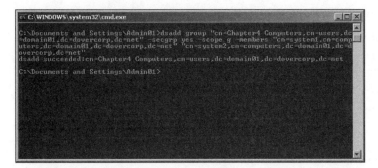

Figure 4-9   Using DSADD to create a group and add members to it in a single step

17. Right-click the **Users** container and click **Refresh**. The Chapter4 Computers group appears in the details pane. Right-click the **Chapter4 Computers** group and click **Properties**.

18. Click the **Members** tab. System1 and System2 both appear. Click **Cancel** to close the Chapter4 Computers Properties dialog box. Close Active Directory Users and Computers.

19. Close the command prompt window and the Help and Support Center window, and then log off.

Certification Objectives

Objectives for Microsoft Exam #70-290: Managing and Maintaining a Microsoft Windows Server 2003 Environment:

- Create and manage groups.

- Manage group membership.

- Create and modify groups by using automation.

REVIEW QUESTIONS

1. Which of the following are required parameters when running the DSADD computer command-line utility?

   a. ComputerDN

   b. –samid SAMName

   c. –memberof GroupDN

   d. All of the above

2. When using DSADD group to add a group to Active Directory, if you do not specify –samid SAMName, where is the SAM account name generated from?

   a. The Distinguished Name of the group

   b. The relative Distinguished Name of the group

   c. The description of the group

   d. None of the above

3. Which of the following formats would be unacceptable when specifying the –u UserName parameter with the DSADD utility?

   a. User name

   b. Domain\User name

   c. User principal name (UPN)

   d. All of the above are acceptable formats

4. If you were to type DSADD user –acctexpires 0, when would the user account expire?

   a. Today

   b. One year from today

   c. Never

   d. None of the above

5. Which of the following objects cannot be added using the DSADD command-line utility? (Choose all that apply.)

   a. Computer

   b. Contact

   c. Domain

   d. Quota

Lab 4.3 The DSMOD Command-line Utility

Objectives

The goal of this lab activity will be to use the DSMOD utility to modify the properties of computer accounts and groups, and to reset computer accounts.

Materials Required

This lab will require the following:

- Windows Server 2003 installed and configured according to the instructions at the beginning of this lab manual

Estimated completion time: **20 minutes**

Activity Background

Once objects have been created in Active Directory, you will often need to modify their properties. Again, this can be accomplished either by using the Active Directory Users and Computers console or through command-line utilities. This lab activity uses DSMOD, a command-line utility used for modifying the properties of objects in Active Directory. Using DSMOD, the attributes of objects such as computers, contacts, groups, organizational units, domain controllers, users, quotas, and partitions can be modified.

ACTIVITY

Activity

1. Log on as **AdminX** to the **DomainX** domain (where *X* is your assigned student number) with a password of **Password01**.

2. Click **Start** and click **Help and Support**. In the Help and Support Center window, type **dsmod** in the Search field and click the **green arrow**.

3. In the Search Results field under Help Topics, click **Dsmod: Command-line reference**. The dsmod utility can be used to modify existing objects in Active Directory, such as computers, contacts, groups, organizational units, domain controller properties, users, quotas, and partitions.

4. Click **dsmod computer**. This is the syntax that you will be following in this lab activity.

5. Click **Start**, click **Run**, type **cmd**, and click **OK**.

6. Now you will use the dsmod computer utility to reset a computer account. In the command prompt window, type **dsmod computer "cn=System1,cn=computers,dc=domainX,dc=dovercorp, dc=net" −reset** (where *X* is your assigned student number), and press **Enter**.

7. In the command prompt window, type **dsmod computer "cn=System2,cn=computers,dc=domainX,dc=dovercorp, dc=net" –disabled yes** (where *X* is your assigned student number), and press **Enter**. The command executes, and the dsmod succeeded message appears in the command prompt window (as shown in Figure 4-10).

Figure 4-10   Using a DSMOD computer to reset or disable computer accounts

8. Click **Start**, point to **Administrative Tools**, and click **Active Directory Users and Computers**.

9. If necessary, double-click to expand **DomainX.Dovercorp.net**. Click the **Computers** container. The System2 computer account is now disabled, and the icon is displayed with a Red X.

10. In the Help and Support Center window, scroll down in the details pane and then click **dsmod group**. Review the syntax and then switch to the command prompt window.

11. First, you are going to create a new computer account that will not belong to the Chapter4 Computers security group that you created in the previous lab activity. In the command prompt window, type **dsadd computer "cn=System3,cn=users,dc=domainX, dc=dovercorp,dc=net"** (where *X* is your assigned student number), and press **Enter**.

12. Now you are going to modify the membership of the RAS and IAS Servers group. Previously, you had added System2 to this group. In this next step, you will modify the group membership so as to include only the System3 computer account. In the command prompt window, type **dsmod group "cn=ras and ias servers, cn=users,dc=domainX,dc=dovercorp,dc=net" –chmbr "cn=System3,cn=users,dc=domainX,dc=dovercorp,dc=net"** (where *X* is your assigned student number), and press **Enter**. When the dsmod succeeded message appears (as shown in Figure 4–11), switch back to the Active Directory Users and Computers console window.

4

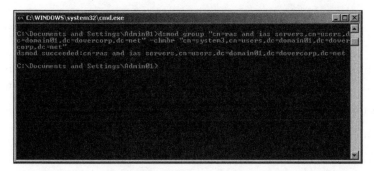

Figure 4-11   Using dsmod group to remove members from a group

13. Click the **Users** container. Right-click the **RAS and IAS Servers** group and click **Properties**. Click the **Members** tab. The System2 account has been removed, and the System3 account now appears. Click **Cancel** to close the RAS and IAS Servers Properties dialog box.

14. Close Active Directory Users and Computers and then close the Help and Support Center window.

15. Close the command prompt window and log off.

Certification Objectives

Objectives for Microsoft Exam #70-290: Managing and Maintaining a Microsoft Windows Server 2003 Environment:

- Create and manage groups.

- Manage group membership.

- Create and modify groups by using automation.

- Reset computer accounts.

REVIEW QUESTIONS

1. Which parameter do you need to specify when using the DSMOD command-line utility to report errors, but avoids having the command exit on the first error?

   a. –P

   b. –U

   c. –C

   d. –Q

2. Which of the following are correct syntax for disabling the Mike Williams user account in the Sales OU in the Dovercorp.net domain? (Choose all that apply.)

   a. Dsmod user "cn=Mike Williams,cn=Sales,dc=dovercorp,dc=net" –disable

   b. Dsmod user "cn=Mike Williams,ou=Sales,dc=dovercorp,dc=net" –disable

   c. Dsmod user cn=Mike Williams,cn=Sales,dc=dovercorp,dc=net –disable

   d. Dsmod user cn=Mike Williams,ou=Sales,dc=dovercorp,dc=net –disable

3. Which of the following would reset the System1 computer account in the Computers container in the Dovercorp.net domain? (Choose all that apply.)

   a. Dsmod computer "cn=System1,cn=computers,dc=dovercorp,dc=net" -reset

   b. Dsmod computer "cn=System1,ou=computers,dc=dovercorp,dc=net" –reset

   c. Dsmod computer cn=System1,cn=computers,dc=dovercorp,dc=net –reset

   d. Dsmod computer cn=System1,ou=computers,dc=dovercorp,dc=net –reset

4. Which is the correct syntax to configure the properties of the John Doe user account in the Users container in the Dovercorp.net domain to expire five days from now?

   a. Dsmod user "cn=John Doe,cn=Users,dc=Dovercorp,dc=net" –acctexpires –5

   b. Dsmod user "cn=John Doe,cn=Users,dc=Dovercorp,dc=net" –acctexpires 5

   c. Dsmod user "cn=John Doe,ou=Users,dc=Dovercorp,dc=net" –acctexpires –5

   d. Dsmod user "cn=John Doe,ou=Users,dc=Dovercorp,dc=net" –acctexpires 5

5. Which of the following are valid commands with the DSMOD command-line utility? (Choose all that apply.)

   a. Server

   b. User

   c. Quota

   d. Partition

4

LAB 4.4 THE DSQUERY AND DSGET COMMAND-LINE UTILITIES

Objectives

The goals of this lab activity are to find objects in Active Directory using the DSQUERY command-line utility, modify objects in Active Directory using DSQUERY along with DSMOD, and to view properties of objects in Active Directory using DSGET.

Materials Required

This lab will require the following:

- Windows Server 2003 installed and configured according to the instructions at the beginning of this lab manual

Estimated completion time: **15 minutes**

Activity Background

In order to save time, you may need to use queries to help you find objects that need to be modified in Active Directory. Windows Server 2003 offers the Saved Queries option through the Active Directory Users and Computers console. Additionally, queries can be performed on Active Directory objects using command-line utilities. This lab activity introduces the DSQUERY command-line utility, which is used to find specific objects in Active Directory, such as computers, contacts, groups, organizational units, sites, servers, users, quotas, and partitions. Adding to its functionality is the ability of this utility to be combined with other command-line utilities to modify, move, delete, or display properties of objects in Active Directory. This lab will also investigate the DSGET command-line utility, which can be used to display properties of objects in Active Directory.

Activity

1. Log on as **AdminX** to the **DomainX** domain (where *X* is your assigned student number) with a password of **Password01**.

2. Click **Start** and click **Help and Support**. In the Help and Support Center window, type **dsquery** in the Search field and then click the **green arrow**.

3. In the Search Results field, click **Dsquery: Command-line reference**. Click **dsquery computer** and review the syntax for this command.

4. Click **Start**, click **Run**, type **cmd**, and click **OK**.

5. In the command prompt window, type **dsquery computer –disabled** and press **Enter**. The command executes and returns the value "CN=System2,CN=Computers,DC=DomainX,DC=Dovercorp,DC=net" (where X is your assigned student number).

6. You will now modify this query to return the results in a different format. In the command prompt window, type **dsquery computer –o rdn –disabled** and press **Enter**. The command executes and "System2" displays in the command prompt window (as shown in Figure 4-12).

Figure 4-12   Using DSQUERY to find disabled computer accounts

7. Next, you are going to use the dsmod group command to add the System3 computer account to the Chapter4 Computers group that you created previously. In the command prompt window, type **dsquery group "cn=Chapter4 computers,cn=users,dc=domainX, dc=dovercorp,dc=net" | dsmod group –addmbr "cn=System3, cn=users,dc=domainX,dc=dovercorp,dc=net"** (where X is your assigned student number), and press **Enter**. The command executes, and the message dsmod succeeded appears.

8. Click **Start**, point to **Administrative Tools**, and click **Active Directory Users and Computers**.

9. Double-click to expand DomainX.Dovercorp.net (where X is your assigned student number), if necessary. Click the **Users** container. Right-click the **Chapter4 Computers** group and click **Properties**. Click the **Members** tab. System1, System2, and System3 all appear as members of this group. Click **Cancel** to close the Chapter4 Computers Properties dialog box.

10. In the command prompt window, type **dsquery computer –o rdn –name system*** and press **Enter**. The command executes, and the names System1, System2, and System3 are displayed.

11. You are now going to run a query that will find any computers whose names start with system in the Users container and move them to the Computers container. In the command prompt window, type **dsquery computer "cn=users,dc=domainX,dc=dovercorp,dc=net" –name system* |dsmove –newparent "cn=computers, dc=domainX,dc=dovercorp, dc=net"** (where *X* is your assigned student number), and press **Enter**. The command executes and the message dsmove succeeded appears (as shown in Figure 4-13).

Figure 4-13   Using DSQUERY to move specific computers in Active Directory

12. Switch to the Active Directory Users and Computers console window. Right-click the **Computers** container and click **Refresh**. The System3 computer account now appears.

13. In the command prompt window, type **dsadd ou "ou=Disabled Computers Query,dc=domainX,dc=dovercorp,dc=net"**, and press **Enter**.

14. You are now going to run a query that will move disabled computer accounts into the Disabled Computers Query organizational unit that you just created. In the command prompt window, type **dsquery computer –disabled |dsmove –newparent "ou=disabled computers query,dc=domainX,dc=dovercorp,dc=net"**, and press **Enter**. When the dsmove succeeded message appears, switch to the Active Directory Users and Computers console window.

15. Right-click **DomainX.Dovercorp.net** and click **Refresh**. The Disabled Computers Query organizational unit appears. Click the **Disabled Computers Query** organizational unit. The System2 computer account appears.

16. Close the Active Directory Users and Computers console and close the Help and Support Center window.

17. Close the command prompt window and log off.

Certification Objectives

Objectives for Microsoft Exam #70-290: Managing and Maintaining a Microsoft Windows Server 2003 Environment:

- Create and manage groups.

- Manage group membership.

- Create and modify groups by using automation.

REVIEW QUESTIONS

1. When using the DSQUERY computer command-line utility, what is the default node at which the search will start?

    a. Forestroot

    b. Domainroot

    c. Computers container

    d. None of the above

2. When using DSQUERY to perform a search, what is the default format of the output from this command?

    a. Distinguished Name

    b. Relative Distinguished Name

    c. SAM account name

    d. None of the above

3. When performing a new query using the Active Directory Users and Computers console, which of the following types of objects can be found?

    a. Users

    b. Groups

    c. Computers

    d. All of the above

4. When performing a query from within the Active Directory Users and Computers console, what is the Query root?

   a. The root of the domain

   b. The root of the forest

   c. The same container or organizational unit that your user account is located within

   d. None of the above

5. Which of the following attributes can be displayed using the DSGET group command-line utility?

   a. The Distinguished Names of the groups

   b. The group security IDs (SIDs)

   c. Scope type

   d. All of the above

4

LAB 4.5 THE DSMOVE AND DSRM COMMAND-LINE UTILITIES

Objectives

In this lab activity, you will move and rename objects in Active Directory using the DSMOVE command-line utility, and delete objects in Active Directory using the DSRM command-line utility.

Materials Required

This lab will require the following:

- Windows Server 2003 installed and configured according to the instructions at the beginning of this lab manual

Estimated completion time: **25 minutes**

Activity Background

As an administrator, you may often need to move and delete objects in Active Directory as part of your day-to-day administrative tasks. Like other actions that can be taken on objects in Active Directory, this can either be accomplished through the Active Directory Users and Computers console or through command-line utilities. This lab activity introduces the DSMOVE command-line utility, which is a multifunctional utility used for moving or renaming objects in Active Directory. Additionally, we will also be using the DSRM command-line utility, which can be used for deleting objects from Active Directory.

ACTIVITY

Activity

1. Log on as **AdminX** to the **DomainX** domain (where *X* is your assigned student number) with a password of **Password01**.

2. Click **Start** and click **Help and Support**.

3. In the Help and Support Center window, type **dsmove** in the Search field and click the **green arrow**.

4. Under Search Results in the section titled Help Topics, click **Dsmove: Command-line reference**. Read over the information regarding the dsmove command-line utility. Note that it can be used to move an object in the domain and can also be used to rename an object without moving it in Active Directory.

5. In order to move an object to a new location in Active Directory, first you'll create an organizational unit to demonstrate this properly.

6. Click **Start**, click **Administrative Tools**, and click **Active Directory Users and Computers**.

7. In the Active Directory Users and Computers console window, expand **DomainX.Dovercorp.net** (where *X* is your assigned student number). You could create the organizational unit using Active Directory Users and Computers, but as this lab is demonstrating a command-line utility, you will again use the dsadd utility to accomplish this. Leave Active Directory Users and Computers open, because you will be using it to verify that your changes have been made throughout the exercise.

8. Click **Start**, click **Run**, type **cmd**, and click **OK**.

9. In the command prompt window, type **dsmove "cn=system2, ou=disabled computers query,dc=domainX,dc=dovercorp, dc=net" –newname Disabled2** (where *X* is your assigned student number), and press **Enter**. When the message dsmove succeeded appears, switch to the Active Directory Users and Computers console.

10. In the Active Directory Users and Computers console, press **F5** to refresh the display. Prior to running the dsmove utility, the System2 computer account was in the Disabled Computers Query organizational unit. Click the **Disabled Computers Query** organizational unit. The System2 computer account has now been renamed Disabled2.

11. You are now going to move the Disabled2 computer account from the Disabled Computers Query organizational unit into the Chapter4 organizational unit. At the same time, you are going to rename the computer account back to System2. In the command prompt window, type **dsmove "cn=disabled2,ou=disabled computers query, dc=domainX, dc=dovercorp,dc=net" –newname System2 –newparent "ou=Chapter4,dc=domainX,dc=dovercorp,dc=net"** (where *X* is your assigned student number), and press **Enter**. When the message dsmove succeeded appears (as shown in Figure 4-14), switch to the Active Directory Users and Computers console.

Figure 4-14   Using DSMOVE to move and rename objects in a single step

12. In the Active Directory Users and Computers console, press **F5** on your keyboard to refresh the display. Click the **Disabled Computers Query** organizational unit. The Disabled2 computer account no longer appears. Click the **Chapter4** organizational unit. It now contains a computer account called System2.

13. You will now use the dsrm utility to delete the objects you have created in this lab activity. In the Help and Support Center window, type **dsrm** in the Search field and click the **green arrow**.

14. In the Search Results field under Help Topics, click **Dsrm: Command-line reference**. Note that the dsrm utility can be used to delete objects from Active Directory. Take note of the syntax for this utility. You may want to refer back to this page later on during this lab activity.

15. In the command prompt window, type **dsmove "cn=Chapter4 computers,cn=users,dc=domainX,dc=dovercorp,dc=net" –newparent "ou=Chapter4, dc=domainX, dc=dovercorp, dc=net"** (where *X* is your assigned student number), and press **Enter**.

16. When the dsmove succeeded message appears, type **dsquery ou –name disabled* | dsmove –newparent "ou=Chapter4,dc=domainX, dc=dovercorp,dc=net" –newname "Just Moved"** (where *X* is your assigned student number), and press **Enter**. When the dsmove succeeded message appears (as shown in Figure 4-15), switch back to the Active Directory Users and Computers console window.

Figure 4-15   Using DSQUERY to move and rename an organizational unit

17. Right-click **DomainX.Dovercorp.net** and click **Refresh**. Click the **Chapter4** organizational unit. Both the Chapter4 Computers group and the Just Moved organizational unit appear. The Chapter4 organizational unit now contains a computer account, a global group, and an organizational unit.

18. You are now going to delete the computer objects from this organizational unit. In the command prompt window, type **dsquery computer –name system* | dsrm –noprompt** and press **Enter**. The command executes, and the dsrm succeeded message appears once for each computer object that has been deleted (as shown in Figure 4-16). You were not prompted to confirm the deletion of these objects because you specified –noprompt as part of the command syntax.

Figure 4-16   Using DSQUERY to find and delete computer accounts in Active Directory

19. Switch to the Active Directory Users and Computers console window. Right-click **DomainX.Dovercorp.net** and click **Refresh**. Click the **Chapter4** organizational unit. The System2 computer account no longer appears. Click the **Computers** container. The System1 and System3 computer accounts have also been deleted.

20. In the command prompt window, type **dsrm –subtree –exclude –c "ou=Chapter4,dc=domainX,dc=dovercorp,dc=net"** (where *X* is your assigned student number), and press **Enter**.

21. When asked "Are you sure you wish to delete all children of ou=Chapter4,dc=domainX,dc=dovercorp,dc=net (Y/N)?", press **Y** and press **Enter**.

22. When the dsrm succeeded message appears, switch to the Active Directory Users and Computers console window. Right-click **DomainX.Dovercorp.net** and click **Refresh**. Click the **Chapter4** organizational unit. Its contents have now been deleted. By using the exclude option, you were able to delete the contents of the organizational unit but not the organizational unit itself.

23. Next, you will delete the Chapter4 organizational unit. In the command prompt window, type **dsrm "ou=Chapter4,dc=domainX, dc=dovercorp,dc=net" –noprompt** (where *X* is your assigned student number), and press **Enter**. After the command executes and the dsrm succeeded message appears, close the command prompt window.

24. In Active Directory Users and Computers, right-click **DomainX.Dovercorp.net** and click **Refresh**. The Chapter4 organizational unit no longer appears.

25. Close Active Directory Users and Computers and log off.

Certification Objectives

Objectives for Microsoft Exam #70-290: Managing and Maintaining a Microsoft Windows Server 2003 Environment:

- Create and manage groups.

- Manage group membership.

- Create and modify groups using automation.

REVIEW QUESTIONS

1. One of your users in the Sales organizational unit in the Dovercorp.net domain has recently divorced and decided to use her maiden name. Her married name was Erin Wild, and you need to change her account to Erin Chancellor. Which of the following is the correct syntax for this command?

   a. Dsmove "cn=Erin Wild,cn=Sales,dc=Dovercorp,dc=net" –newname "Erin Chancellor"

   b. Dsmove "cn=Erin Wild,ou=Sales,dc=Dovercorp,dc=net" –newname "Erin Chancellor"

   c. Dsmove cn=Erin Wild,cn=Sales,dc=Dovercorp,dc=net –newname Erin Chancellor

   d. Dsmove cn=Erin Wild,ou=Sales,dc=Dovercorp,dc=net –newname Erin Chancellor

2. Chris Pavlov of Accounting has been promoted to the Corporate Sales Department in the Dovercorp.net domain. Which of the following is the proper syntax for this move?

   a. Dsmove "cn=Chris Pavlov,cn=Accounting,dc=Dovercorp,dc=net" –newparent "Corporate Sales"

   b. Dsmove "cn=Chris Pavlov,ou=Accounting,dc=Dovercorp,dc=net" –newparent "Corporate Sales"

   c. Dsmove "cn=Chris Pavlov,cn=Accounting,dc=Dovercorp,dc=net" –newparent "cn=Corporate Sales,dc=Dovercorp,dc=net"

   d. Dsmove "cn=Chris Pavlov,ou=Accounting,dc=Dovercorp,dc=net" –newparent "ou=Corporate Sales,dc=Dovercorp,dc=net"

3. Kim Storm has just left your company, and the employee you've hired to replace her will be working out of the Calgary office instead. In order for the new employee to receive the appropriate group policy settings, you need to move the account to the appropriate organizational unit. To make things easier, you have decided to rename the old user account. Which of the following is the correct syntax for this command?

a. Dsmove "cn=Kim Storm,ou=Calgary,dc=Dovercorp,dc=net" –newparent "ou=Winnipeg,dc=Dovercorp,dc=net" –newname "Nicole Tache"

b. Dsmove "cn=Kim Storm,ou=Winnipeg,dc=Dovercorp,dc=net" –newparent "ou=Calgary,dc=Dovercorp,dc=net" –newname "Nicole Tache"

c. Dsmove "cn=Kim Storm,ou=Calgary,dc=Dovercorp,dc=net" –newparent Winnipeg –newname "Nicole Tache"

d. Dsmove "cn=Kim Storm,ou=Winnipeg,dc=Dovercorp,dc=net" –newparent Calgary –newname "Nicole Tache"

4. Which of the following are recommendations when using the DSMOVE command-line utility?

a. If a value that you supply contains spaces, use quotation marks around the text.

b. When entering multiple values for a parameter, use spaces in between to separate the values.

c. If moving an object to another domain, use the Movetree command-line tool.

d. All of the above

5. When renaming an object using the DSMOVE utility, what information follows the –newname parameter?

a. The Relative Distinguished Name

b. The Distinguished Name

c. The User Principal Name

d. None of the above

5

MANAGING ACCESS TO FILES

Labs included in this chapter:

- ♦ Lab 5.1 Demonstrating Special NTFS Permissions: Change Permissions
- ♦ Lab 5.2 Demonstrating Special NTFS Permissions: Take Ownership
- ♦ Lab 5.3 Demonstrating Effective Permissions
- ♦ Lab 5.4 Using NET SHARE to Create and Delete Shares
- ♦ Lab 5.5 Troubleshooting Access to Files and Shared Folders

Microsoft MCSE Exam #70-290 Objectives	
Objective	Lab
Configure access to shared folders.	5.4, 5.5
Manage shared folder permissions.	5.4, 5.5
Configure file system permissions.	5.1, 5.2, 5.3, 5.5
Verify effective permissions when granting permissions.	5.3
Change ownership of files and folders.	5.2
Troubleshoot access to files and shared folders.	5.5
Find domain groups in which a user is a member.	5.5
Manage group memberships.	5.5

Lab 5.1 Demonstrating Special NTFS Permissions: Change Permissions

Objective

The goal of this lab activity will be to investigate the special NTFS permission Change Permissions.

Materials Required

This lab will require the following:

- Windows Server 2003 installed and configured according to the instructions at the beginning of this lab manual

Estimated completion time: **30 minutes**

Activity Background

On drives formatted with the NTFS file system, you have the ability to configure NTFS permissions. NTFS permissions will apply to users regardless of whether they are connecting to a resource locally, or from across the network. NTFS permissions always apply. In order to change the NTFS permissions on a resource, you need either to be the owner of that resource or to have been granted permission by the owner of that resource. A user who has been granted the NTFS Change Permissions has the ability to configure the access control list for a resource on an NTFS partition or volume.

ACTIVITY

Activity

1. If necessary, log on as **AdminX** to the **DomainX** domain (where *X* is your assigned student number) with a password of **Password01**.

2. Click **Start**, point to **Administrative Tools**, and click **Active Directory Users and Computers**.

3. In the Active Directory Users and Computers console window, if necessary, double-click to expand the **DomainX.Dovercorp.net** domain (where *X* is your assigned student number).

4. Right-click **DomainX.Dovercorp.net**, point to **New**, and click **Organizational Unit**.

5. In the New Object—Organizational Unit dialog box, type **Chapter5** and click **OK**.

6. Right-click the **Chapter5** organizational unit, point to **New**, and click **User**.

7. In the New Object—User dialog box, tab down to the Full name field and type **Change Permissions Account**. Tab down to the User logon name field and type **cp**. Click **Next**.

8. Type **Password01** in both the Password and Confirm password fields. Click to clear the **User must change password at next logon** check box. Click to select the **User cannot change password** check box. Click **Next**. Click **Finish**.

9. Create three more user accounts in the Chapter5 organizational unit using the information given below, having the same password and password settings as the account you created in the previous step.

Full name	Change Permissions Test Account
User logon name	cptest
Full name	Take Ownership Account
User logon name	to
Full name	Take Ownership Test Account
User logon name	totest

10. You now have four accounts in the Chapter5 organizational unit that will be used in Lab 5.1 and Lab 5.2. Close Active Directory Users and Computers.

11. Right-click **Start** and click **Explore**.

12. Click **Local Disk (C:)**, and then click **File** on the menu bar, point to **New**, and click **Folder**. Type **Special NTFS Permissions Labs** and press **Enter**.

13. Right-click the **Special NTFS Permissions Labs** folder and click **Sharing and Security**.

14. In the Special NTFS Permissions Labs Properties dialog box, click the **Security** tab. Click **Advanced**.

15. In the Advanced Security Settings for Special NTFS Permissions Labs dialog box, click the **Owner** tab. Under the Current owner of this item field, the Administrators group of the DomainX domain (where *X* is your assigned student number) appears (as shown in Figure 5-1). The owner of a resource has the ability to assign permissions to a resource.

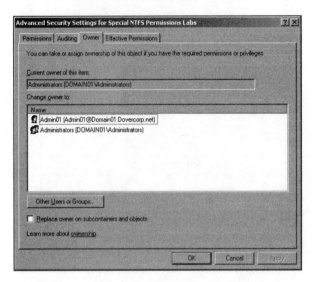

Figure 5-1   Current owner of this item: Administrators

16. Click **Cancel** to exit the Advanced Security Settings for Special NTFS Permissions Labs dialog box.

17. On the Security tab, click **Add**. In the Select Users, Computers, or Groups dialog box, click **Advanced**. Under Common Queries, click in the **Name** field and type **c**. Click **Find Now**. Under Search results, double-click on the line separating the Name (RDN) column and the E-Mail Address column. The Name (RDN) field will expand to show the complete names of the accounts found in the search. In the Search results field, click the **Change Permissions Account** (as shown in Figure 5-2) and click **OK**. Note that the Search results you receive may be somewhat different than those shown in the figure. Click **OK** to close the Select Users, Computers, or Groups dialog box.

Figure 5-2   Selecting Change Permissions Account

18. In the Special NTFS Permissions Labs Properties dialog box, click **Advanced**.

19. In the Advanced Security Settings for Special NTFS Permissions Labs dialog box, click the **Change Permissions Account** and click **Edit**.

20. In the Permission Entry for Special NTFS Permissions Labs dialog box, scroll through the list of Permissions until you see Change Permissions. Click to select the **Allow** check box for **Change Permissions** (as shown in Figure 5-3). Click **OK** to close the Permission Entry for Special NTFS Permissions Labs dialog box. Click **OK** to close the Advanced Security Settings for Special NTFS Permissions Labs dialog box.

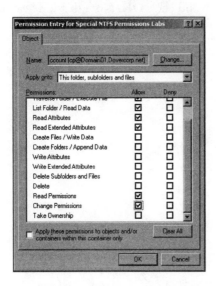

Figure 5-3   Assigning Change Permissions

21. In the Permissions for Change Permissions Account field of the Special NTFS Permissions Labs Properties dialog box, scroll to the bottom of the list of permissions. There will now be a check in the Allow check box next to Special Permissions. Click **OK** to close the Special NTFS Permissions Labs Properties dialog box. Close Windows Explorer.

22. Log off as **AdminX**.

23. Log on as **cptest** (Change Permissions Test Account) to the **DomainX** domain (where *X* is your assigned student number) with a password of **Password01**.

24. Right-click **Start** and click **Explore**.

25. Click **Local Disk (C:)**. Right-click the **Special NTFS Permissions Labs** folder and click **Properties**. Click the **Security** tab. The Add and Remove buttons are not available (as shown in Figure 5-4). The Change Permissions Test Account has not been assigned Change Permissions for this resource. Click **Cancel** to exit the Special NTFS Permissions Labs Properties dialog box.

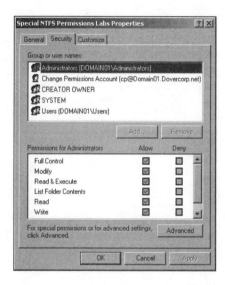

Figure 5-4   Add and Remove buttons are unavailable

26. Log off as **cptest**.

27. Log on as **cp** (Change Permissions Account) to the **DomainX** domain (where *X* is your assigned student number) with a password of **Password01**.

28. Right-click **Start** and click **Explore**.

29. Click **Local Disk (C:)**. Right-click the **Special NTFS Permissions Labs** folder and click **Properties**. Click the **Security** tab. The Add and Remove buttons are now available. The Change Permissions Account has been assigned Change Permissions for this resource.

30. Click **Add**. In the Select Users, Computers, or Groups dialog box, click **Advanced**. Under Common Queries, click in the **Name** field, type **t**, and click **Find Now**. Under Search results, double-click the line separating the Name (RDN) and the E-Mail Address columns. The Name (RDN) column will expand to show the complete names of the objects in that field. Click **Take Ownership Account** and click **OK**. Click **OK** to close the Select Users, Computers, or Groups dialog box.

31. In the Special NTFS Permissions Labs Properties dialog box, click **Advanced**.

32. In the Advanced Security Settings for Special NTFS Permissions Labs dialog box, click **Take Ownership Account** and click **Edit**.

33. In the Permission Entry for Special NTFS Permissions Labs dialog box, scroll to the bottom of the list of Permissions and click to select the **Allow** check box for the **Take Ownership** permission (as shown in Figure 5-5). Click **OK** to close the Permission Entry for Special NTFS Permissions Labs dialog box. Close Windows Explorer.

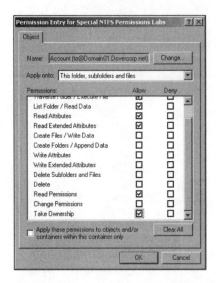

Figure 5-5   Assigning Take Ownership permission

34. Click **OK** to close the Advanced Security Settings for Special NTFS Permissions Labs dialog box.

35. Click **OK** to close the Special NTFS Permissions Labs Properties dialog box.

36. Log off as **cptest**.

Certification Objectives

Objectives for Microsoft Exam #70-290: Managing and Maintaining a Microsoft Windows Server 2003 Environment:

■ Configure file system permissions.

REVIEW QUESTIONS

1. Which of the following individual permissions are not granted with the Modify permission on a folder?

    a. Delete Subfolders and Files

    b. Change Permissions

    c. Take Ownership

    d. All of the above

2. By default, what permissions are granted to the Users group on a folder created on an NTFS partition or volume? (Choose all that apply.)

    a. Read & Execute

    b. List Folder Contents

    c. Read

    d. Write

3. Which of the following will allow you to change inherited permissions?

    a. Configure the opposite permission (allow or deny).

    b. Modify parent permissions that will be inherited by the child object.

    c. Click to clear the **Allow inheritable permissions from the parent to propagate to this object and all child objects** check box.

    d. All of the above.

4. Which of the following are true with regards to explicit permissions and inherited permissions?

    a. Explicit permissions override inherited permissions.

    b. Inherited permissions override explicit permissions.

    c. An inherited deny permission will override an explicit allow permission.

    d. All of the above.

5. Which of the following are recommendations for assigning NTFS permissions?

    a. Use security templates to assign permissions if possible.

    b. Never deny the Everyone group access to a file or folder.

    c. Privileges may override permissions.

    d. All of the above.

LAB 5.2 DEMONSTRATING SPECIAL NTFS PERMISSIONS: TAKE OWNERSHIP

Objective

The goal of this lab activity will be to investigate the special NTFS permission called Take Ownership.

Materials Required

This lab will require the following:

- Windows Server 2003 installed and configured according to the instructions at the beginning of this lab manual

Estimated completion time: **30 minutes**

Activity Background

When an object is created on an NTFS partition or volume it will have an owner. The owner of a resource has the ability to assign the permission to that resource. If you are assigned the Take ownership of files or other objects user right, or have been assigned the Take Ownership permission, or have been assigned the Restore files and directories user right, you will be able to take ownership of a resource. The Administrators group has been assigned the Take ownership of files or other objects user right by default and can therefore take ownership resources on an NTFS partition or volume.

A new feature on Windows Server 2003 is the ability to transfer ownership to another user. This option was not available on previous versions of Windows. If you have the Restore files and directories user right, you will be able to assign ownership to another user or group. If you do not have this right and are the owner of a resource, you can assign the Take Ownership permission to a user and let them take ownership from you.

Activity

1. Log on as **totest** (Take Ownership Test Account) to the **DomainX** domain (where X is your assigned student number) with a password of **Password01**. This user account was created in Lab 5.1. If you did not complete Lab 5.1 in this lab manual, you will need to do so before continuing with this next lab activity.

2. Right-click **Start** and click **Explore**.

3. Click **Local Disk (C:)**. Right-click the **Special NTFS Permissions Labs** folder and click **Properties**.

4. In the Special NTFS Permissions Labs Properties dialog box, click the **Security** tab. The Add and Remove buttons are not available at this time, as the Take Ownership Test Account has not been assigned Change Permissions. Click **Advanced**. The Add and Remove buttons are not available on the Permissions tab in the Advanced Security Settings for Special NTFS Permissions Labs dialog box.

5. Click the **Owner** tab. A message appears indicating that you only have permission to view the current owner on Special NTFS Permissions Labs. Click **OK** to close the message box.

6. On the Owner tab, the Current owner of this item field displays the Administrators group for the DomainX domain (where X is your assigned student number). This folder was created by the AdminX account (where X is your assigned student number), which is a member of this group (as shown in Figure 5-6). Click **OK** to exit the Advanced Security Settings for Special NTFS Permissions Labs dialog box.

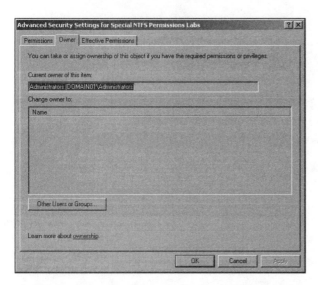

Figure 5-6   Viewing the Current owner of this item field

7. Click **OK** to close the Special NTFS Permissions Labs Properties dialog box. Close Windows Explorer.

8. Log off as **totest**.

9. Log on as **to** (Take Ownership Account) to the **DomainX** domain (where X is your assigned student number) with a password of **Password01**.

10. Right-click **Start** and click **Explore**.

11. Click **Local Disk (C:)**. Right-click the **Special NTFS Permissions Labs** folder and click **Properties**.

12. In the Special NTFS Permissions Labs Properties dialog box, click the **Security** tab. The Add and Remove buttons do not appear. Click **Advanced**.

13. In the Advanced Security Settings for Special NTFS Permissions Labs dialog box, click the **Owner** tab. The Change owner to field is now available (as shown in Figure 5-7), whereas before when Take Ownership Test Account was logged on, this field appeared grey.

Figure 5-7   Change owner to field

14. In the Change owner to field, click **Take Ownership Account** and click **Apply**. The Current owner of this item is now Take Ownership Account (as shown in Figure 5-8).

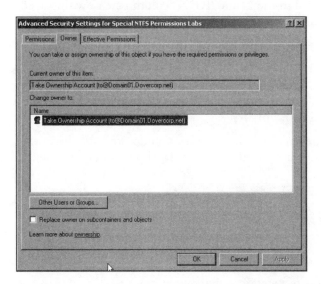

Figure 5-8   Take Ownership Account as the current owner of this item

15. Click **OK** to close the Advanced Security Settings for Special NTFS Permissions Labs dialog box.

16. Click **OK** to close the Special NTFS Permissions Labs Properties dialog box.

17. Right-click the **Special NTFS Permissions Labs** folder and click **Properties**.

18. Click the **Security** tab. The Add and Remove buttons now appear. The owner of a resource has the ability to change permissions for that resource. Click **Take Ownership Account**. This account has Read & Execute, List Folder Contents, Read, and the Take Ownership special permission assigned for this resource. If you scroll down through the list of permissions for this account, you will see that the Allow check box for Special Permissions has been selected. Click to select the **Allow** check box for the **Full Control** permission, and click **Apply**. As the current owner of this resource, you have the ability to assign permissions to this resource.

19. Click **OK** to close the Special NTFS Permissions Properties dialog box.

20. Right-click the **Special NTFS Permissions Labs** folder and click **Properties**.

21. Click the **Security** tab and then click **Advanced**. In the Advanced Security Settings for Special NTFS Permissions Labs dialog box, click the **Owner** tab. The only account that appears under the Change owner to field is Take Ownership Account.

22. Click **Other Users or Groups**. In the Select Users, Computers, or Groups dialog box, click **Advanced**.

23. Under Common Queries, click in the **Name** field and type **t**. Click **Find Now**. Under Search results, double-click the line between the Name (RDN) column and the E-Mail Address column. The column expands, and the complete names of the objects listed in the Name (RDN) column are now displayed. Click **Take Ownership Test Account** and click **OK**.

24. Click **OK** to close the Select Users, Computers, or Groups dialog box.

25. In the Advanced Security Settings for Special NTFS Permissions Labs dialog box, both Take Ownership Account and Take Ownership Test Account appear in the Change owner to field. Click **Take Ownership Test Account** (if necessary) and click **Apply**.

26. An error message appears indicating that you do not have the restore privilege required to set this user/group as owner (as shown in Figure 5-9). Click **OK**.

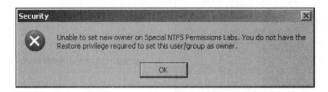

Figure 5-9   Restore privilege required to assign ownership

27. Click **Cancel** to exit the Advanced Security Settings for Special NTFS Permissions Labs dialog box.

28. Click **OK** to close the Special NTFS Permissions Labs Properties dialog box. Close Windows Explorer.

29. Log off as **to**.

30. Log on as **AdminX** to the **DomainX** domain (where *X* is your assigned student number) with a password of **Password01**.

31. Right-click **Start** and click **Explore**.

32. Click **Local Disk (C:)**. Right-click the **Special NTFS Permissions Labs** folder and click **Properties**.

33. In the Special NTFS Permissions Labs Properties dialog box, click the **Security** tab. Click **Advanced**.

34. In the Advanced Security Settings for Special NTFS Permissions Labs dialog box, click the **Owner** tab. The Current owner of this item field displays Take Ownership Account.

35. Click **Other Users or Groups**. In the Select User, Computer, or Group dialog box, click **Advanced**.

36. Under Common Queries, click in the **Name** field and type **t**. Click **Find Now**. In the Search results field, double-click on the line between the Name (RDN) column and the E-Mail Address column. The column expands, and the complete names of the objects in the Name (RDN) column are now displayed. Click **Take Ownership Test Account** and click **OK**. Click **OK** to close the Select User, Computer, or Group dialog box.

37. On the **Owner** tab, in the Change owner to field, click to select **Take Ownership Test Account** and click **Apply**. Take Ownership Test Account now appears as the current owner of this item (as shown in Figure 5-10).

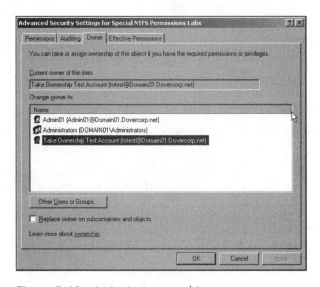

Figure 5-10   Assigning ownership

38. Click **OK** to close the Advanced Security Settings for Special NTFS Permissions Labs dialog box.

39. Click **OK** to close the Special NTFS Permissions Labs Properties dialog box.

40. Right-click the **Special NTFS Permissions Labs** folder and click **Delete**. When asked if you are sure you want to remove the Special NTFS Permissions Labs folder and move all its contents to the Recycle Bin, click **Yes**. Close Windows Explorer.

41. Log off as **AdminX**.

Certification Objectives

Objectives for Microsoft Exam #70-290: Managing and Maintaining a Microsoft Windows Server 2003 Environment:

- Configure file system permissions.

- Change ownership of files and folders.

REVIEW QUESTIONS

1. Which of the following are true with regards to the Take Ownership permission? (Choose all that apply.)

   a. Even when denied all access to a folder, the owner can change permissions.

   b. The Administrators group has the ability to take ownership.

   c. The owner of a resource can give ownership to another user.

   d. All of the above.

2. On Windows Server 2003, who is the default owner on resources created on an NTFS partition?

   a. Domain users

   b. Domain guests

   c. Administrators

   d. None of the above

3. Which of the following are not true about NTFS permissions?

   a. If the check boxes are shaded, the permissions have been inherited from the parent folder.

   b. To change permissions, you must be the owner or have been granted Change Permission by the owner.

   c. Groups or users having Full Control permission on a folder can delete files within the folder, regardless of individual file or subfolder permissions.

   d. All of the above.

4. Which group(s) has the ability to take ownership by default?

   a. Domain users

   b. Server operators

   c. Administrators

   d. All of the above

5. Which of the following would enable you to take ownership of a folder or file?

   a. Being a member of the Administrators group

   b. Being assigned Take Ownership permission for that object

   c. Having the Restore files and directories user right

   d. All of the above

5

LAB 5.3 DEMONSTRATING EFFECTIVE PERMISSIONS

Objective

The goal of this lab activity will be to demonstrate Effective Permissions, a new feature available with the NTFS file system on Windows Server 2003.

Materials Required

This lab will require the following:

- Windows Server 2003 installed and configured according to the instructions at the beginning of this lab manual

Estimated completion time: **20 minutes**

Activity Background

Effective Permissions allows an Administrator to determine exactly what permissions a user has on a folder or file on an NTFS partition. The tool takes into account both those permissions applied directly to the object as well as those permissions that may have been inherited by parent objects. All local groups, as well as domain groups, are taken into consideration (with the exception of the Special Identities groups).

When effective permissions are calculated, share permissions are not taken into consideration. Therefore, when troubleshooting permission problems, shared permissions will have to be analyzed separately.

Activity

1. Log on as **AdminX** to the **DomainX** domain (where *X* is your assigned student number) with a password of **Password01**. First, you are going to create a user account and place that user account into several groups, in order to illustrate this tool on a more complex level.

2. Click **Start**, point to **Administrative Tools**, and click **Active Directory Users and Computers**.

3. In the Active Directory Users and Computers console window, right-click the **Chapter5** organizational unit, point to **New** and click **User**.

4. In the New Object—User dialog box, tab down to the Full name field and type **Effective Permissions Account**. Tab down to the User logon name field and type **ep**. Click **Next**. Type **Password01** in both the Password and Confirm password fields. Click to clear the **User must change password at next logon** option. Click to select the **User cannot change password** option. Click **Next** and then click **Finish**.

5. Right-click the **Chapter5** organizational unit, point to **New**, and click **Group**.

6. In the New Object—Group dialog box, type **EP Demo Allowed** in the Group name field and click **OK**.

7. Right-click the **Chapter5** organizational unit, point to **New**, and click **Group**.

8. In the New Object—Group dialog box, type **EP Demo Denied** in the Group name field and click **OK**.

9. Click **Effective Permissions Account**. (You want to deselect the other security principles that you have just created, as they are highlighted as well). Right-click **Effective Permissions Account** and click **Properties**. (You are not going to use the Add to a group option, as you will be adding Effective Permissions Account to more than one group.)

10. In the Effective Permissions Account Properties dialog box, click the **Member Of** tab.

11. On the Member Of tab, click **Add**.

12. In the Select Groups dialog box, click **Advanced**. Under Common Queries, click in the **Name** field and type an **e**. Click **Find Now**. Both EP Demo Allowed and EP Demo Denied should appear in the Search results field. The EP Demo Allowed group should be highlighted. Press the **Ctrl** key on your keyboard, and at the same time, click the **EP Demo Denied** group. Both EP Demo Allowed and EP Demo Denied should now be selected. Release the **Ctrl** key and click **OK**.

13. In the Select Groups dialog box, **EP Demo Allowed** and **EP Demo Denied** should appear in the object names to select field. Click **OK** to close the Select Groups dialog box.

14. The Effective Permissions Account now belongs to the Domain Users group as well as EP Demo Allowed and EP Demo Denied (as shown in Figure 5-11). Click **OK** to close the Effective Permissions Properties dialog box.

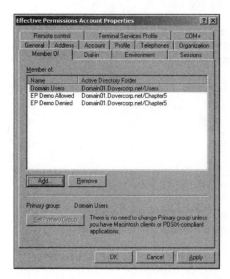

Figure 5-11   The Member Of tab for Effective Permissions Account

15. Close Active Directory Users and Computers.

16. Right-click **Start** and click **Explore**.

17. Click **Local Disk (C:)**.

18. Click **File** on the menu bar, point to **New**, and click **Folder**.

19. Type **Effective Permissions Lab** and press **Enter**.

20. Right-click the **Effective Permissions Lab** folder and click **Sharing and Security**.

21. In the Effective Permissions Lab Properties dialog box, click the **Security** tab.

22. On the Security tab, click **Add**.

23. In the Select Users, Computers, or Groups dialog box, click **Advanced**.

24. Under Common Queries, click in the **Name** field and type an **e**. Click **Find Now**. The Search results field shows several entries. Double-click the line between the Name (RDN) column and the E-Mail Address column. The column expands, and the complete names of the objects in the Name (RDN) column are displayed.

25. Click **EP Demo Allowed**, and then holding down the **Ctrl** key on your keyboard, click to select **EP Demo Denied**, and then click again to select **Effective Permissions Account**. Once all three have been selected, release the **Ctrl** key and click **OK**.

26. Click **OK** to close the Select Users, Computers, or Groups dialog box. On the Security tab, click **Effective Permissions Account**. The default permissions include Read & Execute, List Folder Contents, and Read. You will not be modifying the permissions for this account.

27. Click **EP Demo Allowed**. Under Permissions for EP Demo Allowed, click to select the **Allow** check box for the **Modify** permission. The Write permission has also been assigned when you clicked the Modify check box (as shown in Figure 5-12).

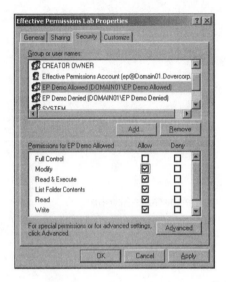

Figure 5-12 Assigning EP Demo Allowed the Allow Modify permission

28. You are not going to change the permissions assigned to the EP Demo Denied group at this time. Click **Apply**.

29. Click **Advanced**. In the Advanced Security Settings for Effective Permissions Lab dialog box, click the **Effective Permissions** tab. By default, no group or user name is currently selected.

30. Click **Select**. In the Select User, Computer, or Group dialog box, click **Advanced**.

31. Under Common Queries, click in the **Name** field and type an **e**. Click **Find Now**.

32. Double-click the line between the Name (RDN) column and the E-Mail Address column. The Name (RDN) column expands to show the complete names of objects in this field. Click **Effective Permissions Account** and click **OK**.

33. Click **OK** to close the Select User, Computer, or Group dialog box.

34. The Effective Permissions tab displays all permissions assigned to Effective Permissions Account for this folder (as shown in Figure 5-13). Click **OK** to close the Advanced Security Settings for Effective Permissions Labs dialog box.

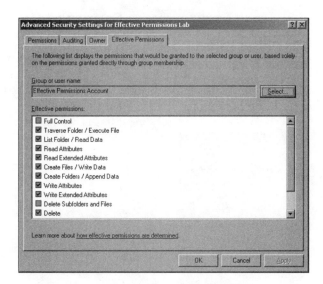

Figure 5-13 The Effective Permissions for Effective Permissions Account

35. On the Security tab, click the **EP Demo Denied** account. In the Permissions for EP Demo Denied, click to select the **Deny** check box for the **Write** permission. Click **Apply**. You will receive a message telling you that you are setting a deny permissions entry that will take precedence over allow entries. Click **Yes**. (See Figure 5-14.)

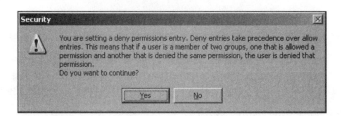

Figure 5-14 Warning message when applying the Deny permission

36. Click **Advanced**. In the Advanced Security Settings for Effective Permissions Lab dialog box, click the **Effective Permissions** tab.

37. Click **Select**. In the Select User, Computer, or Group dialog box, click **Advanced**.

38. Under Common Queries, click in the **Name** field and type an **e**. Click **Find Now**.

39. Double-click the line between the Name (RDN) field and the E-Mail Address field. The column expands, and the complete contents of the Name (RDN) field are displayed. Select **Effective Permissions Account** and click **OK**.

40. Click **OK** to close the Select User, Computer, or Group dialog box.

41. The permissions have now changed on the Effective Permissions tab (as shown in Figure 5-15). This user account belongs to two groups. One group has been assigned Modify, and the other group has been assigned Deny Write. Deny permissions override Allow permissions (with some exceptions). Click **OK** to close the Advanced Security Settings for Effective Permissions Lab dialog box.

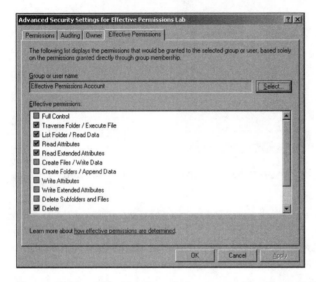

Figure 5-15   Effective Permissions once the Deny Write permission has been applied

42. Click **OK** to close the Effective Permissions Lab Properties dialog box.

43. In Windows Explorer, right-click the **Effective Permissions Lab** folder and click **Delete**. When asked if you are sure you want to remove the Effective Permissions Lab folder and move all its contents to the Recycle Bin, click **Yes**.

44. Close Windows Explorer and log off.

Certification Objectives

Objectives for Microsoft Exam #70-290: Managing and Maintaining a Microsoft Windows Server 2003 Environment:

- Configure file system permissions.

- Verify effective permissions when granting permissions.

REVIEW QUESTIONS

1. Which of the following are true with regards to the Effective Permissions tool?

   a. It looks up all domain and local groups in which the user or group is a member.

   b. Special Identities group membership (logon–specific information) cannot be determined by the Effective Permissions tool.

   c. Share permissions are not part of the Effective Permissions calculation.

   d. All of the above.

2. Which of the following are true about permissions? (Choose all that apply.)

   a. Explicit permissions take precedence over inherited permissions, even inherited Deny permissions.

   b. The Backup files and directories user right overrides File and directory permissions for the purposes of backing up the system.

   c. Explicit permissions are set by default when an object is created by a user.

   d. Inherited permissions are propagated to an object from a parent object.

3. Which of the following are true regarding Effective Permissions? (Choose all that apply.)

   a. Information on the Effective Permissions tab is read-only.

   b. Permissions can be modified on the Effective Permissions tab.

   c. Effective Permissions is a feature of NTFS formatted partitions or volumes.

   d. All of the above.

4. When do NTFS permissions apply?

   a. When connecting to a resource across the network

   b. When accessing a file on the local hard drive

   c. When accessing files on a terminal server

   d. All of the above

5. What is the rule when combining NTFS and Shared Folder permissions on a resource?

a. The effective permissions are the most restrictive permissions.

b. The effective permissions are the least restrictive permissions.

c. NTFS permissions always override share permissions.

d. None of the above.

LAB 5.4 USING **NET SHARE** TO CREATE AND DELETE SHARES

Objective

This goal of this lab activity will be to investigate the use of the NET SHARE command-line utility.

Materials Required

This lab will require the following:

- Windows Server 2003 installed and configured according to the instructions at the beginning of this lab manual

Estimated completion time: **25 minutes**

Activity Background

There are several methods by which shared folders can be created, such as Windows Explorer, Shared Folders in Computer Management, and NET SHARE. The NET SHARE command-line utility can be used to create, delete, display, and manage shared resources.

Activity

1. Log on as **AdminX** to the **DomainX** domain (where *X* is your assigned student number) with a password of **Password01**.

2. Click **Start**, point to **Administrative Tools**, and click **Active Directory Users and Computers**.

3. In the Active Directory Users and Computers console window, double-click to expand the **DomainX.Dovercorp.net** domain (if necessary). Right-click the **Chapter5** organizational unit, point to **New**, and click **User**.

4. In the New Object—User dialog box, tab down to the Full name field and type **Lab 4 User 1**. Tab down to the User logon name field and type **lab4user1**. Click **Next**. Type **Password01** in both the Password and Confirm password fields. Click to clear the **User must change password at next logon** check box. Click to select the **User cannot change password** check box. Click **Next** and click **Finish**.

5. Right-click the **Chapter5** organizational unit, point to **New**, and click **User**. In the New Object—User dialog box, tab down to the Full name field and type **Lab 4 User 2**. Tab down to the User logon name field and type **lab4user2**. Click **Next**. Type **Password01** in both the Password and Confirm password fields. Click to clear the **User must change password at next logon** check box. Click to select the **User cannot change password** check box. Click **Next** and click **Finish**.

6. Close Active Directory Users and Computers.

7. Click **Start**, click **Run**, type **cmd**, and click **OK**.

8. In the command prompt window, type **net share /?** and press **Enter**. The syntax for the NET SHARE command displays. Review the syntax before continuing on with the next step in this lab activity.

9. Type **cd** and press **Enter**.

10. Type **md Chapter5** and press **Enter**

11. Right-click **Start** and click **Explore**.

12. Click **Local Disk (C:)**. The Chapter5 folder that you have just created appears.

13. In the command prompt window, type **net share lab4=c:\chapter5** and press **Enter**. The command executes, and the message lab4 was shared successfully appears.

14. Click **Start**, point to **Administrative Tools**, and click **Computer Management**.

15. In the Computer Management console window, double-click to expand **System Tools** if necessary. Click **Shared Folders** and then double-click **Shares** in the details pane.

16. Under the Share Name field, double-click **lab4**. In the lab4 Properties dialog box, the User limit field is configured to Maximum allowed. Click **Offline Settings**. By default, the option "Only the files and programs that users specify will be available offline" is selected. Click **Cancel** to exit the Offline Settings dialog box.

17. Click the **Share Permissions** tab. The default configuration assigns Read permission to Everyone. Click **Cancel** to exit the lab4 Properties dialog box.

5

18. In the command prompt window, type **net share lab4 /delete** and press **Enter**. The command executes, and the message lab4 was deleted successfully appears (as shown in Figure 5-16).

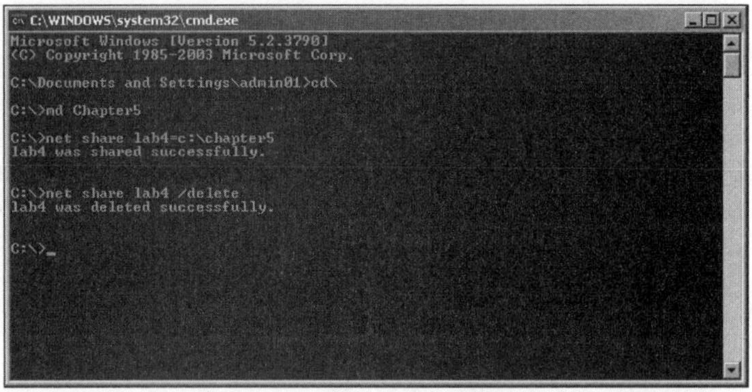

Figure 5-16   Using NET SHARE to create and delete shares

19. Switch to the Computer Management console, right-click **lab4** in the Share Name field, and click **Refresh**. The lab4 share no longer appears in the list of shares.

20. In the command prompt window, type **net share lab4=c:\chapter5 /grant:lab4user1,read /grant:lab4user2,change /users:5 /cache:none**, and press **Enter**. The command executes, and the message lab4 was shared successfully appears (as shown in Figure 5-17).

Figure 5-17   Using NET SHARE to configure permissions, user limits, and caching settings

21. Switch to the Computer Management console window. Right-click **Shares** and click **Refresh**.

22. Double-click the **lab4** share. In the lab4 Properties dialog box, the User limit field is now configured to allow five users to connect to the share (as shown in Figure 5-18). Click **Offline Settings**. The "Files or programs from the share will not be available offline" option is now selected (as shown in Figure 5-19). Click **Cancel** to exit the Offline Settings dialog box.

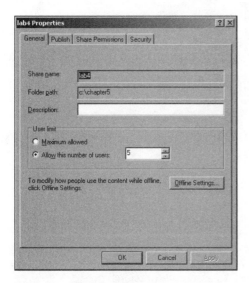

Figure 5-18 Viewing the results of the NET SHARE command

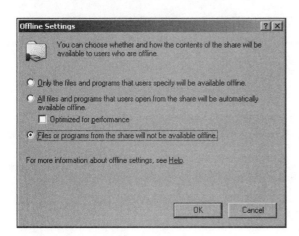

Figure 5-19 Results of using NET SHARE to modify Offline Settings

23. Click the **Share Permissions** tab. Lab 4 User 1 has been granted Read permission to the share. Click the **Lab 4 User 2** account. Lab 4 User 2 has been granted Change permission to the share (as shown in Figure 5-20). Click **Cancel** to exit the lab4 Properties dialog box.

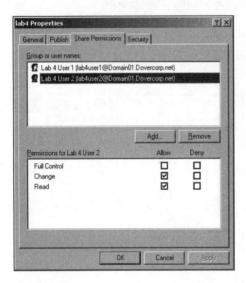

Figure 5-20   Results of using NET SHARE to assign permissions

24. Close the Computer Management console window.

25. Close the command prompt window and then close Windows Explorer.

26. Log off as **AdminX**.

Certification Objectives

Objectives for Microsoft Exam #70-290: Managing and Maintaining a Microsoft Windows Server 2003 Environment:

■ Configure access to shared folders.

■ Manage shared folder permissions.

REVIEW QUESTIONS

1. Which of the following are recommended practices for shared folder permissions? (Choose all that apply.)

   a. Assign permissions to users rather than groups.

   b. Assign users the most restrictive permission that still enables them to access resources as required.

   c. Use NTFS permissions to control access to resources on a terminal server.

   d. All of the above.

2. The default share permission to the Everyone group is:

   a. Read

   b. Change

   c. Full Control

   d. Deny Full Control

3. In order to use the Shared Folders utility, to which group(s) must you belong? (Choose all that apply.)

   a. Power Users

   b. Server Operators

   c. Administrators

   d. None of the above

4. When do share permissions apply to a user?

   a. When gaining access to a resource from across the network

   b. When gaining access to resources on a terminal server

   c. When gaining access to a resource locally on that computer

   d. All of the above

5. Which of the following are true about shared folder permissions?

   a. Deny permission should be used to override specific permissions that are already assigned.

   b. They apply to all files and folders in a shared resource.

   c. They are the only way to secure resources on FAT and FAT32 volumes.

   d. All of the above.

5

LAB 5.5 TROUBLESHOOTING ACCESS TO FILES AND SHARED FOLDERS

Objective

The goal of this lab activity will be to use the tools provided by Windows Server 2003 when troubleshooting access to resources.

Materials Required

This lab will require the following:

- Windows Server 2003 installed and configured according to the instructions at the beginning of this lab manual

Estimated completion time: **60 minutes**

Activity Background

As an Administrator, you will have several tools at your disposal. The steps you take to resolve issues on your network will not always be the same when troubleshooting permission problems.

Earlier in this chapter, you were introduced to Effective Permissions. This tool will prove to be invaluable when determining exactly what permissions a user or group has on an NTFS partition or volume. Effective Permissions analyzes both explicit and inherited permissions and takes into account all local group memberships. If you use the Special Identities groups when assigning permissions to resources on your network, be aware that these groups are not taken into consideration when effective permissions are calculated.

Finally, shared permissions are not involved when effective permissions are calculated, and will also therefore need to be taken into consideration.

ACTIVITY

Activity

1. This lab activity assumes that you have completed Lab 5.4 in this lab manual. If you have not completed this lab activity, you will need to complete that lab before proceeding with this lab activity. Log on as **AdminX** to the **DomainX** domain (where *X* is your assigned student number) with a password of **Password01**.

2. Click **Start**, point to **Administrative Tools**, and click **Active Directory Users and Computers**.

3. If necessary, double-click to expand the **DomainX.Dovercorp.net** domain (where *X* is your assigned student number). Right-click the **Chapter5** organizational unit, point to **New**, and click **Group**.

4. In the New Object—Group dialog box, type **Lab 5.5** and click **OK**.

5. Right-click the **Lab 4 User 2** account and click **Add to a group**.

6. In the Select Group dialog box, click **Advanced**. Under Common Queries, click in the **Name** field, type the letter **l**, and click **Find Now**. In the Search results field, click **Lab 5.5** and then click **OK**. Click **OK** to close the Select Group dialog box.

7. The Add to Group operation was successfully completed message appears. Click **OK** to close the message box.

8. Close Active Directory Users and Computers.

9. Right-click **Start** and click **Explore**.

10. Click **Local Disk (C:)**. The Chapter5 folder should still be shared from Lab 5.4. Right-click the **Chapter5** folder and click **Sharing and Security**. The Chapter5 Properties dialog box appears with the Sharing tab visible. The Chapter5 folder is shared as lab4. Click the **Security** tab. Click **Add**.

11. In the Select Users, Computers, or Groups dialog box, click **Advanced**. Under Common Queries, click in the **Name** field, type the letter **l**, and click **Find Now**. In the Search results field, several names appear. Click to select the **Lab 4 User 1** account (if necessary). Then, holding down the **Ctrl** key on your keyboard, click to select the **Lab 4 User 2** account and then the **Lab 5.5** group. (Lab 4 User 1, Lab 4 User 2, and Lab 5.5 should all be selected.) Click **OK**. Click **OK** to close the Select Users, Computers, or Groups dialog box.

12. In the Chapter5 Properties dialog box, click **Lab 4 User 1** and then click the **Allow** check box for the **Full Control** permission.

13. Click the **Lab 4 User 2** account and then click the **Allow** check box for the **Full Control** permission.

14. Click the **Lab 5.5** group and then click the **Deny** check box for the **Write** permission. Click **Apply**. On the message that appears indicating that you are setting a deny permission entry and that deny entries take precedence over allow entries, click **Yes**. Click **OK** to close the Chapter5 Properties dialog box. Close Windows Explorer.

15. Log off as **AdminX**.

16. Log on as **lab4user1** (the Lab 4 User 1 account) to the **DomainX.Dovercorp.net** domain (where *X* is your assigned student number) with a password of **Password01**.

17. Click **Start**, click **Run**, type **\\serverX** (where *X* is your assigned student number), and press **Enter**.

18. In the **serverX** window, double-click the **lab4** share. Click **File**, point to **New**, and click **Text Document**. The Unable to create file error message appears, indicating Access is denied. Click **OK**.

19. Close the lab4 on serverX window.

20. Right-click **Start** and click **Explore**.

21. Click **Local Disk (C:)**. Right-click **Chapter5** and click **Properties**.

22. In the Chapter5 Properties dialog box, click the **Security** tab. Click the **Lab 4 User 1** account. The Allow check box for the Full Control permission is selected for this account. Next, you are going to check the Effective Permissions tab to verify the NTFS permissions that are applying to this user account for this resource. Click **Advanced**.

23. In the Advanced Security Settings for Chapter5 dialog box, click the **Effective Permissions** tab. Click **Select**.

24. In the Select User, Computer, or Group dialog box, click **Advanced**. Under Common Queries, click in the **Name** field and type the letter **l**. Click **Find Now**. In the Search results field, click the **Lab 4 User 1** account and click **OK**. Click **OK** to close the Select User, Computer, or Group dialog box.

25. The Effective Permissions for Lab 4 User 1 are displayed. This account has the NTFS permissions necessary to create a file in this folder. Therefore, the share permissions must be preventing this user account from creating the file. Before changing the share permissions for this user account, you are going to log on as Lab 4 User 2 and try to create a file in this same folder. Click **Cancel** to exit the Advanced Security Settings for Chapter5 dialog box. Click **OK** to close the Chapter5 Properties dialog box. Close Windows Explorer.

26. Log off as **lab4user1**.

27. Log on as **lab4user2** (the Lab 4 User 2 account) to the **DomainX** domain (where X is your assigned student number) with a password of **Password01**.

28. Click **Start**, click **Run**, type **\\serverX** (where X is your assigned student number), and click **OK**.

29. Double-click the **lab4** share in the serverX window. Click **File** on the menu bar, point to **New**, and click **Text Document**. The Unable to create file message appears, indicating that access is denied. Click **OK**.

30. Close the lab4 on serverX window.

31. Right-click **Start** and click **Explore**.

32. Click **Local Disk (C:)**. Right-click the **Chapter5** folder and click **Properties**.

33. In the Chapter5 Properties dialog box, click the **Security** tab. Click the **Lab 4 User 2** account. The Allow check box for the Full Control permission is selected for this account. Next, you are going to check the effective permissions that apply to this user account on this resource. Click **Advanced**.

34. In the Advanced Security Settings for Chapter5 dialog box, click the **Effective Permissions** tab and then click **Select**.

35. In the Select User, Computer, or Group dialog box, click **Advanced**. Under Common Queries, click in the **Name** field and type the letter **l**. Click **Find Now**. In the Search results field, click the **Lab 4 User 2** account and click **OK**. Click **OK** to close the Select User, Computer, or Group dialog box.

36. The Effective Permissions for Lab 4 User 2 are displayed (as shown in Figure 5-21). The Create and Write permissions for this user account are not available. However, the Lab 4 User 2 account was assigned Full Control to this resource. Click **Cancel** to exit the Advanced Security Settings for Chapter5 dialog box. Click **OK** to close the Chapter5 Properties dialog box.

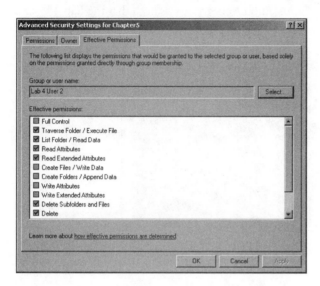

Figure 5-21   Effective Permissions for Lab 4 User 2

37. Click **Start**, click **Run**, type **cmd**, and click **OK**.

5

38. In the command prompt window, type **dsget user "cn=lab 4 user 2,ou=chapter5,dc=domainX,dc=dovercorp,dc=net" –memberof –expand**, (where *X* is your assigned student number) and press **Enter**. The command executes, and the results are displayed in the command prompt window (as shown in Figure 5-22). The Lab 4 User 2 account belongs to the Lab 5.5, Domain Users, and Users groups. Recall that the Lab 4 User 2 account was added to the Lab 5.5 group at the beginning of this exercise.

Figure 5-22   Using DSGET user to view group memberships

39. In Windows Explorer, right-click the **Chapter5** folder and click **Properties**. Click the **Security** tab. Click the **Lab 5.5** group. The Deny check box for the Write permission has been selected. Click **OK** to close the Chapter5 Properties dialog box. Close the command prompt window, and then close Windows Explorer.

40. Log off as **lab4user2**.

41. Log on as **AdminX** to the **DomainX** domain (where *X* is your assigned student number) with a password of **Password01**.

42. First, you are going to fix the problem that is preventing lab4user1 from creating new files in the Chapter5 shared folder. Right-click **Start** and click **Explore**. Click **Local Disk (C:)**. Right-click the **Chapter5** folder and click **Sharing and Security**.

43. On the Sharing tab, click **Permissions**. Click the **Lab 4 User 1** account and then click to select the **Allow** check box for the **Change** permission (as shown in Figure 5-23). Click **Apply**. Click **OK** to close the Permissions for lab4 dialog box. Click **OK** to close the Chapter5 Properties dialog box.

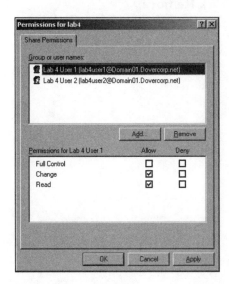

Figure 5-23   Granting the Change share permission to Lab 4 User 1

44. Click **Start**, point to **Administrative Tools**, and click **Active Directory Users and Computers**.

45. Double-click to expand **DomainX.Dovercorp.net** (where *X* is your assigned student number), if necessary. Click the **Chapter5** organizational unit. Right-click the **Lab 5.5** group and click **Properties**. Click the **Members** tab. The Lab 4 User 2 account appears as a member (as shown in Figure 5-24). Click the **Lab 4 User 2** account and click **Remove**.

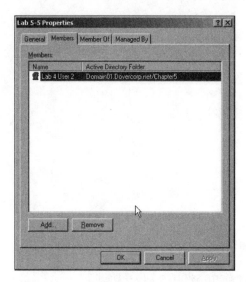

Figure 5-24   Removing the Lab 4 User 2 account from the Lab 5-5 group

46. When asked if you want to remove the selected member(s) from the group, click **Yes**. Click **OK** to close the Lab 5.5 Properties dialog box.

47. Close Active Directory Users and Computers. Close Windows Explorer.

48. Log off as **AdminX**.

49. Log on as **lab4user1** to the **DomainX.Dovercorp.net** domain (where *X* is your assigned student number) with a password of **Password01**.

50. Click **Start**, click **Run**, type **\\serverX** (where *X* is your assigned student number), and click **OK**.

51. In the serverX window (where *X* is your assigned student number), double-click the **lab4** share. Click **File** on the menu bar, point to **New**, and then click **Text Document**. A new text document appears. Type **New1** and press **Enter**. The Lab 4 User 1 account now has the ability to write documents to the lab4 share. Close the lab4 on ServerX window.

52. Log off as **lab4user1**.

53. Log on as **lab4user2** to the **DomainX** domain (where *X* is your assigned student number) with a password of **Password01**.

54. Click **Start**, click **Run**, type **\\serverX** (where *X* is your assigned student number), and click **OK**.

55. In the serverX window (where *x* is your assigned student number), double-click the **lab4** share. Click **File** on the menu bar, point to **New**, and then click **Text Document**. A new text document appears. Type **New2** and press **Enter**. The Lab 4 User 2 account now has the ability to write documents to the lab4 share. Close the lab4 on ServerX window.

56. Log off as **lab4user2**.

57. Log on as **AdminX** to the **DomainX** domain (where *X* is your assigned student number) with a password of **Password01**.

58. Click **Start**, point to **Administrative Tools**, and click **Active Directory Users and Computers**. If necessary, double-click to expand the **DomainX.Dovercorp.net** domain.

59. Right-click the **Chapter5** organizational unit and click **Delete**. When asked if you are sure you want to delete this object, click **Yes**. A message appears indicating that Chapter5 is a container and contains other objects. When asked if you are sure you want to delete object Chapter5 and the objects it contains, click **Yes**.

60. Close Active Directory Users and Computers.

61. Right-click **Start** and click **Explore**.

62. Click **Local Disk (C:)**. Right-click the **Chapter5** folder and click **Delete**. When asked if you are sure you want to remove the Chapter5 folder and move all its contents to the Recycle Bin, click **Yes**. On the message that appears indicating that you are sharing the folder and that others may be using files in this folder, are you sure you want to delete it, click **Yes**. Close Windows Explorer.

63. Log off as **AdminX**.

Certification Objectives

Objectives for Microsoft Exam #70-290: Managing and Maintaining a Microsoft Windows Server 2003 Environment:

- Configure access to shared folders.

- Manage shared folder permissions.

- Configure file system permissions.

- Troubleshoot access to files and shared folders.

- Find domain groups in which a user is a member.

- Manage group memberships.

REVIEW QUESTIONS

1. Which character is appended onto the end of hidden shares?

   a. $

   b. %

   c. &

   d. *

2. Which of the following share names is used for the directory in which the operating system is installed?

   a. Admin$

   b. IPC$

   c. Netlogon

   d. Sysvol

3. Which default shares are only found on domain controllers? (Choose all that apply.)

   a. Admin$

   b. Print$

   c. Netlogon

   d. Sysvol

4. Which of the following are true with regards to shares?

   a. It is not recommended to deny permissions to the Everyone group.

   b. Fixed disks on your computer are shared by default and do not appear with the hand icon in My Computer or Windows Explorer.

   c. Offline access is allowed by default.

   d. All of the above.

5. Which of the following is NOT true?

    a. To use the DSGET user command-line utility, you need to have administrative credentials.

    b. Shared folders are not taken into consideration when determining effective permissions.

    c. Special Identities groups are not taken into consideration when determining effective permissions.

    d. All of the above.

5

MANAGING DISK AND DATA STORAGE

Labs included in this chapter:

♦ Lab 6.1 Creating Primary Partitions, Extended Partitions, and Logical Drives Using DISKPART

♦ Lab 6.2 Creating Mount Points Using Mountvol

♦ Lab 6.3 Using DISKPART to Convert from Basic to Dynamic Disks

♦ Lab 6.4 Using DISKPART to Create, Extend, and Delete Volumes on a Dynamic Disk

♦ Lab 6.5 Using DISKPART to Script the Creation of Volumes

Microsoft MCSE Exam #70-290 Objectives	
Objective	Lab
Manage basic disks and dynamic disks.	6.1, 6.2, 6.3, 6.4, 6.5

Lab 6.1 Creating Primary Partitions, Extended Partitions, and Logical Drives Using DISKPART

Objective

The goal of this lab activity is to create a partition on a basic disk. After completing this lab activity, you will be able to create both a primary and an extended partition using the DISKPART command-line utility, and create a logical drive within an extended partition using the DISKPART command-line utility.

Materials Required

This lab will require the following:

- Windows Server 2003 installed and configured according to the instructions at the beginning of this lab manual

Estimated completion time: **15 minutes**

Activity Background

A basic disk contains primary partitions, extended partitions, and logical drives. These are known as basic volumes and can only be created on basic disks, which are the default on a Windows Server 2003 install. New partitions can be created on basic disks using one of two methods:

- Disk Management in the Computer Management console

- DISKPART command-line utility

In this lab activity, you will be investigating DISKPART. DISKPART is a text-mode command interpreter that can be used to manage disks, partitions, and volumes on a Windows Server 2003 system. When using DISKPART, it is critical that you follow the correct syntax for the command. One of the most important steps in using the DISKPART command is using select to give focus to the object that is being manipulated. When using the list command, the object that has focus will appear with an asterisk next to it.

Activity

1. If necessary, log on as **AdminX** to the **DomainX** domain (where *X* is your assigned student number) with a password of **Password01**.

2. Click **Start**, point to **Administrative Tools**, and click **Computer Management**.

3. In the Computer Management console window, click **Disk Management**. Unless you have created other partitions or volumes, you will have two primary partitions and some unallocated space remaining in the Disk Management window (as shown in Figure 6-1). If you have more than one hard drive installed, the hard drives will be numbered Disk 0, and then Disk 1, and so forth. If you have only one hard drive, it will be Disk 0. In this lab activity, you will be creating primary and extended volumes on Disk 0. If you have already converted your disk from basic to dynamic in the main text exercises, you will not be able to complete this lab activity.

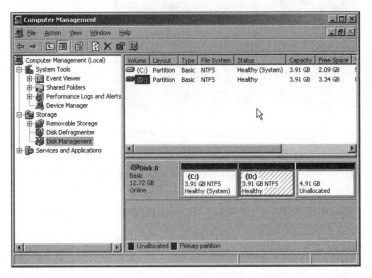

Figure 6-1   Current disk configuration at beginning of this lab

4. Click **Start**, click **Run**, type **cmd**, and click **OK**.

5. In the command prompt window, type **diskpart** and press **Enter**.

6. At the DISKPART prompt, type **list** and press **Enter**. The focus of the DISKPART command can be set to either a disk, a partition, or a volume.

7. At the DISKPART prompt, type **list disk** and press **Enter**. If you have only one hard drive on your computer, your command prompt window will now appear (as shown in Figure 6-2). If you have more than one hard drive on your computer, you will see Disk 0, Disk 1, etc.

Figure 6-2 Using DISKPART to list the hard drives installed on your computer

8. At the DISKPART prompt, type **select** and press **Enter**. Note that you can choose to select either a disk, a partition, or a volume.

9. At the DISKPART prompt, type **select disk 0** and press **Enter**. The message Disk 0 is now the selected disk appears.

10. At the DISKPART prompt, type **create** and press **Enter**. You can use this command to create either a partition or a volume.

11. At the DISKPART prompt, type **create partition** and press **Enter**. There are several options available. You are going to create a primary partition.

12. At the DISKPART prompt, type **create partition primary size=50** and press **Enter**. The message DiskPart succeeded in creating the specified partition appears (as shown in Figure 6-3).

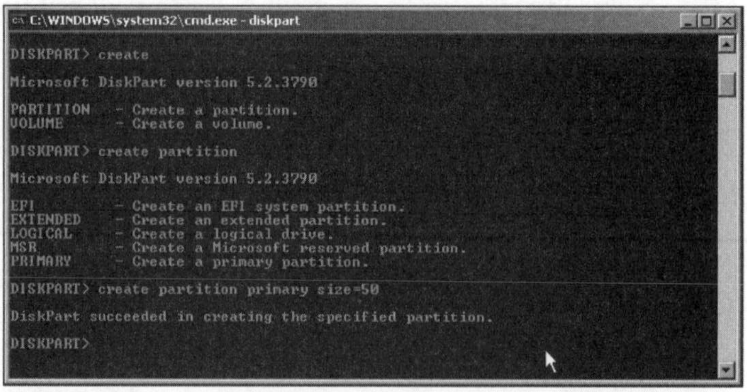

Figure 6-3 Using DISKPART to create a primary partition

13. At the DISKPART prompt, type **list partition** and press **Enter**. Note that an asterisk appears next to the partition that you just created. The asterisk denotes the partition that now has focus. If you started this lab activity with only two primary partitions on Disk 0, the command prompt window will now appear (as shown in Figure 6-4). Partition 3 now has focus.

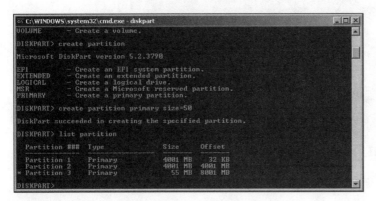

Figure 6-4   An asterisk indicates which partition has focus

14. As Partition 3 now has focus, you do not have to use the select command at this time. Type **assign letter=p** and press **Enter**. The message DiskPart successfully assigned the drive letter or mount point appears.

15. Switch back to the Computer Management console. A primary partition now appears that has been assigned the drive letter P. You are now going to create an extended partition and then create a logical drive within the extended partition.

16. Switch to the command prompt window and type **create partition extended size=100** and press **Enter**. The message DiskPart succeeded in creating the specified partition appears.

17. Type **create partition logical size=50** and press **Enter**. The message DiskPart succeeded in creating the specified partition appears.

18. Type **list partition** and press **Enter**. If your disk had only two primary partitions when you started this lab activity, you will now see Partitions 1 through 5. Partition 5 is now the partition with focus (as shown in Figure 6-5).

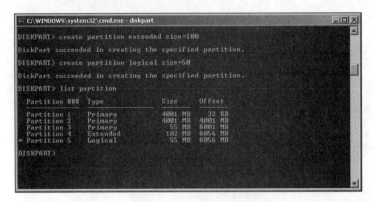

Figure 6-5   Using DISKPART to create a logical drive in an extended partition

19. Type **assign letter=x** and press **Enter**. The message DiskPart successfully assigned the drive letter or mount point appears.

20. Switch to the Computer Management console. The extended partition and the logical drive X: now appear.

21. Switch back to the command prompt window, type **exit**, and press **Enter**.

22. Next, you are going to format the partition and logical drive that you just created. In the command prompt window, type **format p:/fs:fat** and press **Enter**. A message appears indicating that the type of the file system is RAW and the new file system is FAT. You will be prompted with WARNING, ALL DATA ON NON-REMOVABLE DISK DRIVE P: WILL BE LOST! Proceed with Format (Y/N)? Type **y** and press **Enter**. If prompted to enter a volume label, press **Enter**.

23. In the command prompt window, type **format x:/fs:ntfs** and press **Enter**. A message appears indicating that the type of the file system is RAW and the new file system is NTFS. You will be prompted with WARNING, ALL DATA ON NON-REMOVABLE DISK DRIVE X: WILL BE LOST! Proceed with Format (Y/N)? Type **y** and press **Enter**. If prompted to enter a volume label, press **Enter**. Close the command prompt window.

24. Switch to the Computer Management console. The File System column now indicates that drive P: is formatted as FAT and that drive X: is formatted as NTFS (as shown in Figure 6-6). Close the Computer Management console.

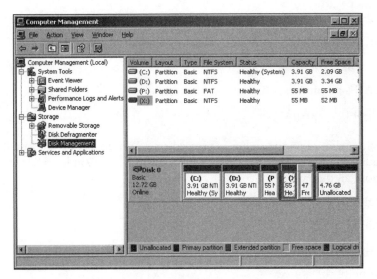

Figure 6-6   Viewing the changes in Disk Management

Certification Objectives

Objectives for Microsoft Exam #70-290: Managing and Maintaining a Microsoft Windows Server 2003 Environment:

■ Manage basic disks and dynamic disks.

REVIEW QUESTIONS

1. What type of partition can be created on a basic disk?

   a. Primary partition

   b. Extended partition

   c. Logical drive

   d. All of the above

2. In order to extend a simple volume, which file system must it be formatted with?

   a. FAT

   b. FAT32

   c. NTFS

   d. All of the above

3. Which of the following features are not supported on basic disks?

   a. Striped volumes

   b. Mirrored volumes

   c. RAID-5 volumes

   d. All of the above

4. Which of the following volumes created on a Windows NT 4.0 installation would be supported by Windows XP Professional or Windows Server 2003? (Choose all that apply.)

   a. Volume sets or stripe sets

   b. Mirror sets

   c. Stripe sets with parity

   d. None of the above

5. When using the DISKPART command-line utility, which of the following characters is used to indicate which disk, partition, or volume has focus?

   a. @

   b. *

   c. %

   d. #

LAB 6.2 CREATING MOUNT POINTS USING MOUNTVOL

Objective

The goal of this lab activity will be to create and delete a mount point on a basic disk.

Materials Required

This lab will require the following:

- Windows Server 2003 installed and configured according to the instructions at the beginning of this lab manual

Estimated completion time: **10 minutes**

Activity Background

Mounted volumes provide administrators with a way of creating additional volumes once all available drive letters have been assigned. Mounted volumes require an empty folder on a partition or volume formatted with the NTFS file system. Rather than being designated by a drive letter, mounted volumes are referred to by their drive paths. In this lab activity, you will be creating mount points using the DISKPART command-line utility.

Activity

6

1. If necessary, log on as **AdminX** to the **DomainX** domain (where *X* is your assigned student number) with a password of **Password01**.

2. Click **Start**, click **Run**, type **cmd**, and click **OK**.

3. In the command prompt window, type **cd** and press **Enter**.

4. In the command prompt window, type **md mount** and press **Enter**.

5. In the command prompt window, type **mountvol /?** and press **Enter**. Part way down in the display, you will see the heading Possible values for Volume-Name along with current mount points are:. Beneath this are a list of all the volumes you currently have created on your system (as shown in Figure 6-7).

Figure 6-7   Possible values for VolumeName along with current mount points

6. Click the **Command Prompt icon** in the upper-left corner of the command prompt window and click **Properties**. On the Options tab under Edit Options, click to select the **QuickEdit Mode** check box. Click **OK**. When asked whether you want to apply these properties to the current window only, or to future windows with the same title, click to select the **Save properties for future windows with same title** option. Click **OK**.

7. In the command prompt window, click the beginning text for the value of volume X. Drag your mouse until you have highlighted the rest of the value (as shown in Figure 6-8) and then right-click your selected text. The text that was selected and appeared white does not appear to be selected any longer. It is on your clipboard.

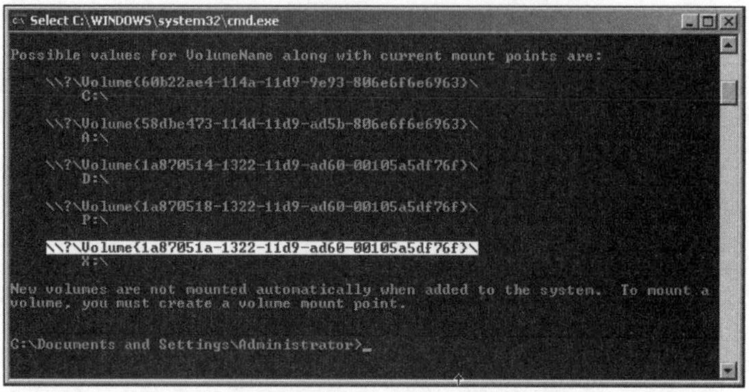

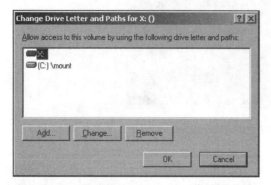

Figure 6-8   Selecting the VolumeName for drive X:

8. In the command prompt window, type **mountvol c:\mount**, press the **spacebar**, and then **right-click**. The text that you copied from the command prompt window for the value of volume X should now be pasted behind the text you just typed. Press **Enter**. The command executes.

9. Click **Start**, right-click **My Computer**, and click **Manage**. The Computer Management console opens. In the Computer Management console, right-click **Drive X:** and click **Change Drive Letter and Paths**. In the Change Drive Letter and Paths for X: () dialog box, drive X: now has both a drive letter X assigned as well as the path (C:)\mount (as shown in Figure 6-9). Click **Cancel**.

Figure 6-9   Drive X: now has both a drive letter and a path

10. In the command prompt window, type **mountvol c:\mount /d** and press **Enter**.

11. Switch to the Computer Management console. Right-click **Drive X:** and click **Change Drive Letter and Paths**. The path to (C:)\mount no longer appears. Click **Cancel**.

12. Close the Computer Management console.

13. Close the command prompt window.

Certification Objectives

Objectives for Microsoft Exam #70-290: Managing and Maintaining a Microsoft Windows Server 2003 Environment:

■ Manage basic disks and dynamic disks.

6

REVIEW QUESTIONS

1. Which of the following can be used to create a new mounted drive?

   a. Disk Management

   b. DISKPART

   c. Both Disk Management and DISKPART

   d. None of the above

2. When formatting a mounted drive, what file systems are available?

   a. FAT

   b. FAT32

   c. NTFS

   d. All of the above

3. When using mountvol to create a mounted drive, how would you find the VolumeName?

   a. Right-click the drive in Disk Management and click **Properties**.

   b. Mountvol /v

   c. Mountvol /?

   d. None of the above

4. Which of the following are true with regards to changing drive letters and paths?

    a. A computer can use up to 26 drive letters.

    b. You cannot change the drive letter of the system volume.

    c. You cannot change the drive letter of the boot volume.

    d. All of the above.

5. Which of the following are requirements for creating a mounted drive? (Choose all that apply.)

    a. The disk must be basic.

    b. The disk must be dynamic.

    c. The folder must be located on an NTFS volume.

    d. The folder must be empty.

Lab 6.3 Using DISKPART to Convert from Basic to Dynamic Disks

Objective

The goal of this lab activity will be to convert a disk from basic to dynamic.

Materials Required

This lab will require the following:

- Windows Server 2003 installed and configured according to the instructions at the beginning of this lab manual

Estimated completion time: **15 minutes**

Activity Background

Dynamic disks offer features that are not supported on basic disks. Multidisk volumes, which include spanned, striped, and fault tolerant volumes (such as mirrored and RAID-5 volumes), are not available on basic disks. In this lab activity, you will be using the DISKPART command-line utility to convert the hard drive from basic to dynamic.

ACTIVITY

Activity

1. If necessary, log on as **AdminX** to the **DomainX** domain (where *X* is your assigned student number) with a password of **Password01**.

2. Click **Start**, click **Run**, type **cmd**, and click **OK**.

3. In the command prompt window, type **diskpart** and press **Enter**.

4. At the DISKPART prompt, type **list disk** and press **Enter**. Your hard drives are listed in the command prompt window. If you have only one hard drive, you will see it numbered as Disk 0.

5. Type **select disk 0** and press **Enter**. You are going to convert this drive from basic to dynamic.

6. At the DISKPART prompt, type **convert dynamic** and press **Enter** (as shown in Figure 6-10). The message You must reboot your computer to complete this operation appears.

Figure 6-10   Using DISKPART to convert to dynamic disk

7. Close the command prompt window.

8. Click **Start** and click **Shutdown**. Under What do you want the computer to do?, click the **drop down arrow** and click **Restart**. Click in the **Comment** field, type **convert to dynamic**, and click **OK**.

9. Log on as **AdminX** to the **DomainX** domain (where X is your assigned student number) with a password of **Password01**.

10. A message appears indicating that Windows has finished installing new devices. The software that supports your device requires that you restart your computer. You must restart your computer before the new settings will take effect. Click **Yes**.

11. Log on as **AdminX** to the **DomainX** domain (where X is your assigned student number) with a password of **Password01**.

12. Click **Start**, point to **Administrative Tools**, and click **Computer Management**.

13. In the Computer Management console, click **Disk Management**. What were previously partitions and logical drives now appear as simple volumes (as shown in Figure 6-11).

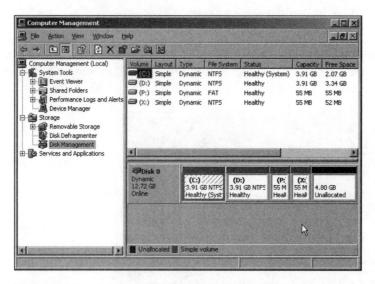

Figure 6-11   A dynamic disk with simple volumes

14. Close the Computer Management console and log off.

Certification Objectives

Objectives for Microsoft Exam #70-290: Managing and Maintaining a Microsoft Windows Server 2003 Environment:

■ Manage basic disks and dynamic disks.

REVIEW QUESTIONS

1. Which of the following steps should be taken if you want to convert a dynamic disk back to a basic disk?

a. Back up, or move, data to another volume.

b. Delete all volumes.

c. Use the Convert to basic disk option in Disk Management.

d. All of the above.

2. Which of the following operating systems have the ability of using dynamic disks?

   a. Windows 2000

   b. Windows XP

   c. Windows Server 2003

   d. All of the above

3. Which of the following are not true?

   a. It is not recommended to convert disks to dynamic if you have a dual-boot configuration.

   b. For the conversion to dynamic disks to complete, the computer must be restarted.

   c. If desired, volumes can be converted back to partitions on a dynamic disk.

   d. Shared folders on dynamic disks are accessible across the network to operating systems such as MS-DOS, Windows 95, Windows 98, and Windows NT.

4. How much drive space must be free or unallocated in order to convert a drive from basic to dynamic?

   a. 1 MB

   b. 2 MB

   c. 5 MB

   d. 10 MB

5. When a basic disk is converted to a dynamic disk, what does the boot, or system partition, become?

   a. A simple volume

   b. A spanned volume

   c. A striped volume

   d. None of the above

LAB 6.4 USING DISKPART TO CREATE, EXTEND, AND DELETE VOLUMES ON A DYNAMIC DISK

Objective

The goal of this lab activity will be to create, extend, and delete simple volumes on a dynamic disk.

Materials Required

This lab will require the following:

- Windows Server 2003 installed and configured according to the instructions at the beginning of this lab manual

---

Estimated completion time: **15 minutes**

Activity Background

Simple volumes are the only type of volumes that can be created on systems having only one dynamic disk. As this is the most probable configuration for computers in this course, you will focus on simple volumes. When a disk is converted from basic to dynamic, all partitions and logical drives become simple volumes.

Extending a volume is a way of increasing the capacity of the volume. If a volume has been formatted with the NTFS file system, it can be extended. Once a volume has been extended, no part of the volume can be deleted without deleting the entire volume. Spanned volumes may contain areas of unallocated space from more than one physical drive. For the purposes of this course, you will only be extending simple volumes.

Additionally, in this lab activity you will be deleting simple volumes on a dynamic disk. In general, all volumes may be deleted on a dynamic disk unless they are the system volume, the boot volume, or a volume that contains an active paging file.

Activity

1. If necessary, log on as **AdminX** to the **DomainX** domain (where *X* is your assigned student number) with a password of **Password01**.

2. Click **Start**, click **Run**, type **cmd**, and click **OK**.

3. In the command prompt window, type **diskpart** and press **Enter**.

4. At the DISKPART prompt, type **list disk** and press **Enter**.

5. At the DISKPART prompt, type **select disk 0** and press **Enter**.

6. At the DISKPART prompt, type **list volume** and press **Enter** (as shown in Figure 6-12). If you started Lab 6.1 with only two primary partitions, C: and D:, you will now have four volumes listed. The extended partition that was created on the basic disk will not appear as a volume on your dynamic disk. Take note of the volume number that has been assigned to the X: drive.

Figure 6-12   Listing the volumes on a dynamic disk

7. Next you are going to extend volume X. In the example, drive X: has been assigned Volume 1. If the volume number that has been assigned to your X: drive is a different value, you will need to type that value into the following command. At the DISKPART prompt, type **select volume 1** and press **Enter**. The message Volume 1 is the selected volume appears.

8. At the DISKPART prompt, type **extend** and press **Enter**. The message DiskPart successfully extended the volume appears.

9. Click **Start**, point to **Administrative Tools**, and click **Computer Management**.

10. In the Computer Management console, click **Disk Management**. You did not specify the size of the extended volume, and therefore, all the remaining space on the drive has been used to create the extended volume.

11. You are now going to delete the extended volume using the DISKPART command. In the command prompt window, type **list volume** and press **Enter**. Volume 1 (drive X:) is still the selected volume.

12. At the DISKPART prompt, type **delete volume** and press **Enter**. The message DiskPart successfully deleted the volume appears (as shown in Figure 6-13).

Figure 6-13   Using DISKPART to delete volumes on a dynamic disk

13. Switch back to the Computer Management console. Drive X: no longer appears.

14. In the command prompt window, type **list volume** and press **Enter**. Volume 1 no longer appears.

15. Take note of the volume number that has been assigned to the P: drive. If a different volume number has been assigned than the one used in this example, you will need to type that number when executing the following command. At the DISKPART prompt, type **select volume 0** and press **Enter**. (Note, this should be the P: drive. Drive P: is formatted with the FAT file system.) Volumes formatted as FAT cannot be extended.

16. At the DISKPART prompt, type **extend size=25** and press **Enter**. The message DiskPart failed to extend the volume. Please make sure the volume is valid for extending appears. This is because the volume is formatted with FAT.

17. At the DISKPART prompt, type **exit** and press **Enter**.

18. Type **convert p: /fs:ntfs** and press **Enter**. When the Conversion complete message appears, type **diskpart** and press **Enter**.

19. At the DISKPART prompt, type **list volume** and press **Enter**. Volume 0 should be drive P: as before. If the volume number that has been assigned to your P: drive is different than the number used in this example, you will need to type that number when executing the following commands.

20. At the DISKPART prompt, type **select volume 0** and press **Enter**. The message Volume 0 is the selected volume appears.

21. At the DISKPART prompt, type **extend size=25** and press **Enter**. The message DiskPart successfully extended the volume appears (as shown in Figure 6-14).

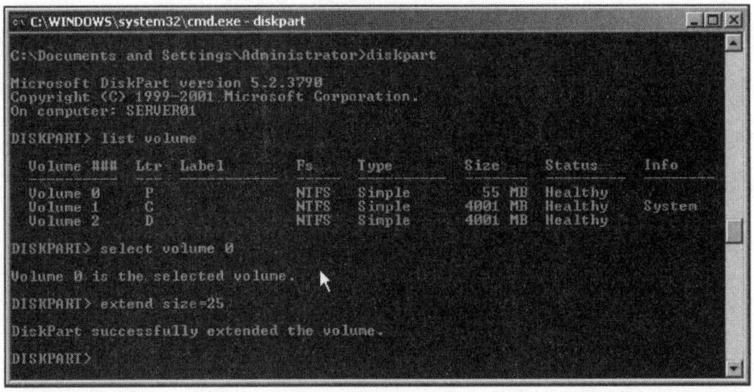

Figure 6-14   Using DISKPART to extend a simple volume on a dynamic disk

22. Switch to the Computer Management console window. Drive P: now appears as an extended volume with a size of 80 MB.

23. You are now going to delete the P: drive. Switch back to the command prompt window. At the DISKPART prompt, type **list volume** and press **Enter**.

24. At the DISKPART prompt, type **delete volume** and press **Enter**. The message DiskPart successfully deleted the volume appears.

25. Type **exit** and press **Enter**.

26. Close the command prompt window.

27. Switch to the Computer Management console. Drive P: no longer appears. If you started out with only drive C: and drive D: at the beginning of Lab 6.1, you will now have two simple volumes, C: and D:. Close the Computer Management console and log off.

Certification Objectives

Objectives for Microsoft Exam #70-290: Managing and Maintaining a Microsoft Windows Server 2003 Environment:

- Manage basic disks and dynamic disks.

REVIEW QUESTIONS

1. Which of the following can be created on a system with only one dynamic disk?

    a. Simple volumes

    b. Striped volumes

    c. Spanned volumes

    d. All of the above

2. Which of the following simple volumes can be deleted?

    a. System volume

    b. Boot volume

    c. Volume with an active paging file or crash dump

    d. None of the above

3. Which of the following are true of simple volumes? (Choose all that apply.)

    a. They can only be created on dynamic disks.

    b. All simple volumes can be extended.

    c. Simple volumes are fault tolerant.

    d. All of the above.

4. Which of the following are true?

    a. Dynamic disks support the creation of fault-tolerant volumes.

    b. Dynamic disks are not supported on portable computers.

    c. Dynamic volumes cannot be converted back to partitions.

    d. All of the above.

5. Which of the following do not support dynamic disks? (Choose all that apply.)

    a. Removable disks

    b. Disks that use USB interfaces

    c. Disks that use IEEE 1394 interfaces

    d. Disks connected to shared SCSI buses

Lab 6.5 Using DISKPART to Script the Creation of Volumes

Objective

The goal of this lab activity will be to automate the creation of volumes using the DISKPART command-line utility.

Materials Required

This lab will require the following:

- Windows Server 2003 installed and configured according to the instructions at the beginning of this lab manual

Estimated completion time: 15 minutes

Activity Background

In addition to creating volumes on a dynamic disk, DISKPART scripts can also be used to convert disks from basic to dynamic. You may want to incorporate DISKPART scripts when automating the deployment of the Windows Server 2003 operating system to new computers.

ACTIVITY

Activity

1. If necessary, log on as **AdminX** to the **DomainX** domain (where *X* is your assigned student number) with a password of **Password01**.

2. Click **Start**, point to **All Programs**, point to **Accessories**, and click **Notepad**.

3. In Notepad, type the following lines.

   select disk 0

   create volume simple size=50

   assign letter=s

   extend size=25

   extend size=30

   exit

4. Click **File** on the menu bar and click **Save As**. In the Save As dialog box, click to save in **Local Disk (C:)**. Click in the **File name** field, type **diskpartscript**, and click **Save**. The diskpartscript.txt file should appear (as shown in Figure 6-15). Close Notepad.

Figure 6-15   Creating a script file to use with DISKPART

5. Click **Start**, click **Run**, type **cmd**, and click **OK**.

6. In the command prompt window, type **diskpart /s c:\diskpartscript.txt** and press **Enter**. Once the command has executed, the message Leaving DiskPart... appears (as shown in Figure 6-16).

Figure 6-16   Using DISKPART /s to create volumes on a dynamic disk

7. Click **Start**, point to **Administrative Tools**, and click **Computer Management**.

8. In the Computer Management console, click **Disk Management**. Drive S: now appears as 105 MB. There are three parts involved in this extended volume; one that is 50 MB, another that is 25 MB, and a third that is 30 MB.

9. In the command prompt window, type **diskpart** and press **Enter**.

10. At the DISKPART prompt, type **select disk 0** and press **Enter**.

11. At the DISKPART prompt, type **list volume** and press **Enter** (as shown in Figure 6-17). Look at the volume number for the S: drive. If you started out with just two primary partitions at the beginning of the lab exercises for Chapter 6, your drive S: will be volume 1.

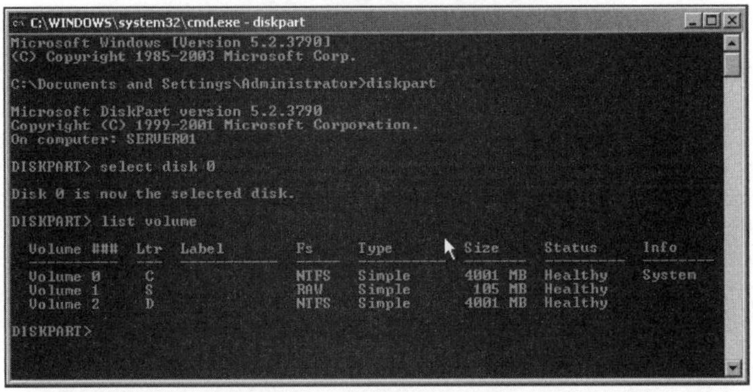

6

Figure 6-17   Using list volume to find the volume number

12. Type **select volume 1** and press **Enter**. The message Volume 1 is the selected volume appears.

13. At the DISKPART prompt, type **delete volume** and press **Enter**. The message DiskPart successfully deleted the volume appears.

14. At the DISKPART prompt, type **exit** and press **Enter**.

15. Close the command prompt window.

16. Switch to the Computer Management console. The simple volume S: no longer appears. Close the Computer Management console and log off.

Certification Objectives

Objectives for Microsoft Exam #70-290: Managing and Maintaining a Microsoft Windows Server 2003 Environment:

- Manage basic disks and dynamic disks.

REVIEW QUESTIONS

1. Volumes formatted with which of the following file systems can be extended?

   a. FAT

   b. FAT32

   c. NTFS

   d. All of the above

2. Which of the following volumes can be extended? (Choose all that apply.)

   a. Simple volume

   b. System or boot volume

   c. Striped volume

   d. Fault-tolerant volumes

3. Which of the following would you use to script the creation of volumes using the DISKPART command-line utility?

   a. DISKPART /v

   b. DISKPART /c

   c. DISKPART /s

   d. None of the above

4. Which of the following are true with regards to spanned volumes?

   a. Spanned volumes can only be created on dynamic disks.

   b. Spanned volumes require a minimum of two dynamic disks.

   c. A spanned volume can be extended onto a maximum of 32 disks.

   d. All of the above.

5. What is the equivalent of a Windows NT 4.0 volume set on the Windows Server 2003 operating system?

   a. Mirrored volume

   b. Striped volume

   c. Spanned volume

   d. RAID-5 volume

ADVANCED FILE SYSTEM MANAGEMENT

Labs included in this chapter:

♦ Lab 7.1 Compressing Files and Folders with COMPACT and Windows Explorer

♦ Lab 7.2 Encrypting Files and Folders with CIPHER and Windows Explorer

♦ Lab 7.3 Implementing Disk Quotas

♦ Lab 7.4 Implementing Stand-alone DFS Roots

♦ Lab 7.5 Implementing Domain-based DFS Roots

Microsoft MCSE Exam #70-290 Objectives	
Objective	Lab
Configure access to shared folders.	7.4, 7.5
Troubleshoot access to files and shared folders.	7.2, 7.3, 7.4, 7.5
Monitor disk quotas.	7.3
Manage a server by using available support tools.	7.1, 7.2

Lab 7.1 Compressing Files and Folders with COMPACT and Windows Explorer

Objective

- In this lab, you will be compressing folders and files on an NTFS volume using Windows Explorer and the COMPACT command-line utility.

Materials Required

This lab will require the following:

- Windows Server 2003 installed and configured according to the instructions at the beginning of this lab manual

Estimated completion time: **20 minutes**

Activity Background

To reduce the amount of space used by files and folders on a given NTFS volume, Windows Server 2003 provides the NTFS compression feature. As the term implies, NTFS compression can only be applied to files and folders on a volume that is formatted with the NTFS file system. There are two ways that a folder or file can be compressed; using Windows Explorer, and using a command-line utility called COMPACT.

Activity

1. If necessary, log on as **AdminX** to the **DomainX** domain (where X is your assigned student number) with a password of **Password01**.

2. Right-click **Start** and click **Explore**. Click **Tools** and then click **Folder Options**. In the Folder Options dialog box, click to clear the Hide extensions for known file types check box. Click **OK** to close the Folder Options dialog box.

3. Click **Local Disk (C:)**.

4. Click **File** on the menu bar, point to **New**, and click **Folder**.

5. Type **Compressed** and press **Enter**.

6. Click the **Compressed** folder in the Folders pane (left pane).

7. Click **File** on the menu bar, point to **New**, and click **Text Document**.

8. Type **File1.txt** and press **Enter**.

9. Right-click the **Compressed** folder and click **Properties**.

10. On the General tab of the Compressed Properties dialog box, click **Advanced**.

11. In the Advanced Attributes dialog box, under Compress or Encrypt attributes, click to select the **Compress contents to save disk space** check box (as shown in Figure 7-1). Click **OK** to close the Advanced Attributes dialog box.

Figure 7-1   Compress contents to save disk space

12. Click **OK** to close the Compressed Properties dialog box.

13. In the Confirm Attribute Changes dialog box, you are asked whether you want to apply this change to this folder only, or if you want it to apply to all subfolders and files as well. If this folder were empty, this dialog box would not appear. Click to select the **Apply changes to this folder only** option button (as shown in Figure 7-2). You are going to apply the compression attribute to the folder, but not to the existing files in this folder. Click **OK** to close the Confirm Attribute Changes dialog box.

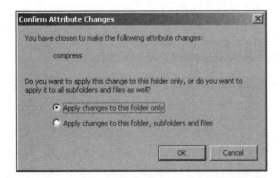

Figure 7-2   Apply changes to this folder only

14. Click **Local Disk (C:)**. The Compressed folder now appears in blue text. This is the default setting for compressed folders on Windows Server 2003.

15. Click **Tools** on the menu and click **Folder Options**.

16. In the Folder Options dialog box, click the **View** tab. Scroll down to the bottom of the tab and notice the second to last entry. Show encrypted or compressed NTFS files in color has been selected by default (as shown in Figure 7-3). Click **Cancel** to exit the Folder Options dialog box.

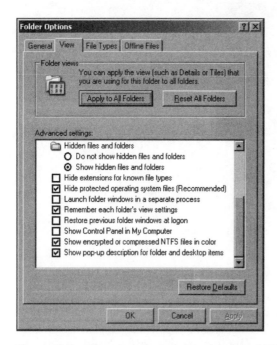

Figure 7-3   Show encrypted or compressed NTFS files in color

17. Click the **Compressed** folder. Click **File** on the menu, point to **New**, and click **Folder**.

18. Before you type a name for the folder, notice that the File1.txt information is shown in black. The Type and Date Modified fields for the folder you are creating are now blue. Type **SubFolder** and press **Enter**.

19. Click the **Compressed** folder. Click **File** on the menu, point to **New**, and click **Text Document**. Type **File2.txt** and press **Enter**. All new folders and files in the Compressed folder will inherit the compression attribute from the Compressed folder (as shown in Figure 7-4).

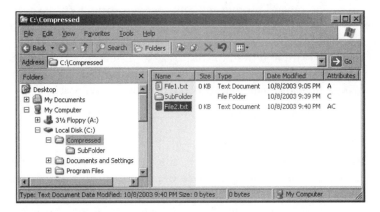

Figure 7-4   New folders and files inherit the compression attribute

20. Click **Start**, click **Run**, type **cmd**, and click **OK**.

21. In the command prompt window, type **compact /?** and press **Enter**. This utility displays or alters the compression of files on NTFS partitions. Take note of the syntax for this command-line utility (as shown in Figure 7-5).

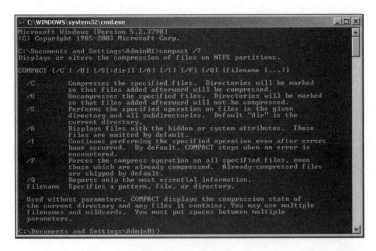

Figure 7-5   The COMPACT command-line utility parameters

22. Type **compact /u c:\compressed\file2.txt** and press **Enter**. After you see the message indicating that 1 files within 1 directories were uncompressed, switch to Windows Explorer. Both File1.txt and File2.txt are now uncompressed.

23. Switch to the command prompt window, type **compact /c c:\compressed\file1.txt** and press **Enter**. When the operation has completed, switch to Windows Explorer and note that File1.txt has now been compressed.

24. Switch to the command prompt window, type **compact /u c:\compressed** and press **Enter**. When you see the message 1 files within 1 directories were uncompressed, switch to Windows Explorer, click **Local Disk (C:)**, and press **F5** on your keyboard to refresh the display. The Compressed folder is no longer compressed. Click the **Compressed** folder. Note that the contents of the folder have retained their original compressed or uncompressed state.

25. Right-click the **SubFolder** folder and click **Properties**.

26. In the SubFolder Properties dialog box, click **Advanced**.

27. In the Advanced Attributes dialog box, the compress option is selected. Click to select **Encrypt contents to secure data**. The check has been removed from the Compress contents to save disk space check box. This is because compression and encryption are mutually exclusive features. You cannot apply both attributes to a file or a folder at the same time.

28. Click **Cancel** to exit the Advanced Attributes dialog box. Click **Cancel** to exit the SubFolder Properties dialog box.

29. Switch to the command prompt window. Type **cd** and press **Enter**.

30. In the command prompt window, type **cd compressed** and press **Enter**.

31. In the command prompt window, type **compact** and press **Enter**. Under Listing C:\Compressed\, the text New files added to this directory will not be compressed appears. The letter C appears next to File1.txt and SubFolder indicating that they are compressed. At the bottom of the output for this command, the compression ratio is also listed (as shown in Figure 7-6).

Figure 7-6   Using COMPACT to view compression attributes

32. Type **compact /u /s** and press **Enter**. When you receive the message 3 files within 3 directories were uncompressed, switch to Windows Explorer. You have just uncompressed File1.txt and the subfolder. The folders and files no longer appear blue.

33. Close the command prompt window.

34. Right-click the **Compressed** folder and click **Delete**.

35. A message appears asking if you are sure you want to remove the Compressed folder and move all its contents to the Recycle Bin. Click **Yes**.

36. Close all windows.

Certification Objectives

Objectives for Microsoft Exam #70-290: Managing and Maintaining a Microsoft Windows Server 2003 Environment:

■ Manage a server by using available support tools.

REVIEW QUESTIONS

1. Which of the following are true regarding compression?

   a. Reduces amount of space used by files and folders to which it is applied

   b. Available with FAT, FAT32, and NTFS file systems

   c. Available for both folders and individual files

   d. All of the above

2. Which of the following are possible with NTFS compression?

   a. The compression attribute can be applied to a folder, but not its contents.

   b. By default, compressed files appear blue in Windows Explorer.

   c. Compressed files can be encrypted.

   d. All of the above.

3. Which of the following cannot be done with NTFS compression?

   a. Compressing a folder without compressing the contents of the folder

   b. Encryption of a compressed file

   c. Working with NTFS compressed files without decompressing them first

   d. All of the above

4. When used without the corresponding parameters, COMPACT will display:

a. The compression state of the current folder and all of its subfolders and files

b. The compression state of the current folder and all of its subfolders

c. The compression state of the files within the current folder only

d. The compression state of the current folder

5. If you wanted to apply the compression attribute to all subdirectories using the COMPACT command-line utility, which of the following parameters would you use?

a. /a

b. /i

c. /f

d. /s

Lab 7.2 Encrypting Files and Folders with CIPHER and Windows Explorer

Objectives

In this lab activity, you will investigate encrypting folders and files using Windows Explorer and the CIPHER command-line utility. You will also investigate a new feature that allows a person who encrypted a file to permit others to access that resource once it has been encrypted.

Materials Required

This lab will require the following:

- Windows Server 2003 installed and configured according to the instructions at the beginning of this lab manual

Estimated completion time: **40 minutes**

Activity Background

In order to secure sensitive data stored on a server, you may wish to utilize another feature available with the NTFS file system: encryption. Encrypting File System can be used to encrypt and decrypt files stored on an NTFS volume (with the exception of those files in the system root directory, and files having the system attribute).

Once a file has been encrypted, only the user who encrypted the file has access to the file (other than the designated Recovery Agent). A new feature on Windows Server 2003 is the ability of the person who has encrypted a file to grant access to that resource to other user accounts. You will also investigate this aspect of the NTFS file system in this lab activity.

Activity

1. If necessary, log on as **AdminX** to the **DomainX** domain (where X is your assigned student number) with a password of **Password01**.

2. Click **Start**, point to **Administrative Tools**, and click **Active Directory Users and Computers**. Double-click **DomainX.Dovercorp.net** to expand, if necessary.

3. Right-click the **Users** container, point to **New**, and click **User**.

4. In the New Object—User dialog box, tab down to the Full name field and type **Encryption Account 1**, then tab down to the User logon name field and type **e1**. Click **Next**.

5. In the Password and Confirm password fields, type **Password01**. Click to clear the **User must change password at next logon** check box. Click **Next** and click **Finish**.

6. Close Active Directory Users and Computers.

7. Right-click **Start** and click **Explore**.

8. Click **Local Disk (C:)**.

9. Click **File** on the menu, point to **New**, and click **Folder**.

10. Type **Encrypted** and press **Enter**.

11. Right-click the **Encrypted** folder and click **Properties**.

12. In the Encrypted Properties dialog box, click **Advanced** on the General tab.

7

13. In the Advanced Attributes dialog box, click to select **Encrypt contents to secure data** (as shown in Figure 7-7) and click **OK**.

Figure 7-7   Encrypt contents to secure data

14. Click **OK** to close the Encrypted Properties dialog box. Unlike the previous exercise where the folder was not empty, you were not prompted as to whether you wanted the encryption attribute to apply only to the folder or to subdirectories and files as well. The Encrypted folder now appears in green text. This is the default setting on Windows Server 2003 for encrypted files and directories.

15. Click the **Encrypted** folder. Click **File** on the menu, point to **New**, and click **Folder** in the Folders pane (left pane).

16. Type **SubFolder** and press **Enter**. The new subdirectory also appears in green text.

17. Click the **Encrypted** folder. Click **File** on the menu, point to **New**, and click **Text Document** in the Folders pane (left pane). Type **File3.txt** and press **Enter**. The new file also appears in green text (as shown in Figure 7-8).

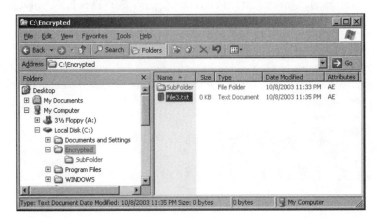

Figure 7-8   Encrypted files and folders in Windows Explorer

18. Double-click **File3.txt**. In Notepad, type **Unless you are listed under Users Who Can Transparently Access This File, you cannot read this text.** Click **Format** and click **Word Wrap**, then click **File** on the menu and click **Save**.

19. Right-click **File3.txt** and click **Properties**. Click **Advanced**.

20. In the Advanced Attributes dialog box, click **Details**.

7

21. The Encryption Details for C:\Encrypted\File3.txt dialog box appears. Under Users Who Can Transparently Access This File, the AdminX (AdminX@DomainX.Dovercorp.net) account appears (where *x* is your assigned student number). Under Data Recovery Agents For This File As Defined By Recovery Policy, the Administrator account is listed in the Recovery Agent Name field. This would be the domain administrator account, as your server is a domain controller and does not have a local administrator account. Presently, AdminX (the account that created the folder and its contents) and the domain administrator account are the only two accounts that have access to this encrypted file (as shown in Figure 7-9). Click **Add**.

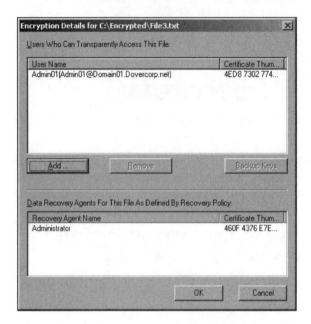

Figure 7-9   Encryption Details for C:\Encrypted\File3.txt

22. In the Select User dialog box, click **Find User**. Click **Advanced** and click **Find Now**.

23. In the Search results field, click to select the **Encryption Account 1** and click **OK**.

24. Click **OK** to close the Select User dialog box.

25. A message appears indicating that no appropriate certificates correspond to the selected user (as shown in Figure 7–10). Click **OK**.

Figure 7-10   No appropriate certificates correspond to the selected user

26. Click **Cancel** to exit the Select User dialog box. Click **Cancel** again.

27. Click **Cancel** to exit the Encryption Details for C:\Encrypted\File3.txt dialog box.

28. Click **Cancel** to exit the Advanced Attributes dialog box.

29. Click **Cancel** to exit the File3.txt Properties dialog box. Close Windows Explorer.

30. Log off as **AdminX**.

31. Log on as **e1** to the **DomainX** domain (where *X* is your assigned student number) with a password of **Password01**.

32. Right-click **Start** and click **Explore**.

33. Click the **Encrypted** folder. Double-click **File3.txt**. You receive the Access is denied message. Click **OK**. Notepad has opened; however, you cannot see the contents of the actual file that you entered earlier in this lab activity. Close Notepad.

34. Click **Local Disk (C:)**, click **File** on the menu, point to **New**, and click **Folder**.

35. Type **Encrypted2** and press **Enter**.

36. Right-click the **Encrypted2** folder and click **Properties**. Click **Advanced**.

37. In the Advanced Attributes dialog box, click to select the **Encrypt contents to secure data** check box. Click **OK**.

38. Click **OK** to close the Encrypted2 Properties dialog box.

39. Close Windows Explorer and log off.

40. Log on as **AdminX** to the **DomainX** domain (where *X* is your assigned student number) with a password of **Password01**.

41. Right-click **Start** and click **Explore**.

42. Click **Local Disk (C:)** and click the **Encrypted** folder. Right-click **File3.txt** and click **Properties**.

43. In the File3.txt Properties dialog box, click **Advanced**.

7

44. In the Advanced Attributes dialog box, click **Details**.

45. In the Encryption Details for C:\Encrypted\File3.txt dialog box, click **Add**. A certificate now appears that has been issued to the e1 user account. Click the **e1** certificate (as shown in Figure 7–11) and click **OK**.

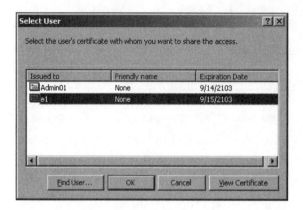

Figure 7-11   File encryption certificates are created when a user encrypts a file

46. Under Users Who Can Transparently Access This File, both AdminX (where *X* is your assigned student number) and e1 now appear (as shown in Figure 7–12). Click **OK** to close the Encryption details for C:\Encrypted\File3.txt dialog box.

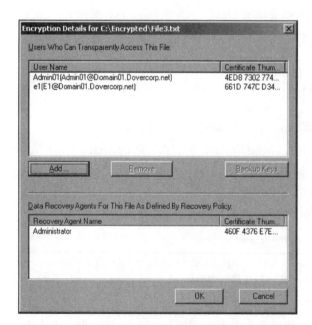

Figure 7-12   Both AdminX and e1 can now transparently access File3.txt

47. Click **OK** to close the Advanced Attributes dialog box. Click **OK** to close the File3.txt Properties dialog box.

48. Close Windows Explorer. Log off as **AdminX**.

49. Log on as **e1**.

50. Right-click **Start** and click **Explore**. Click **Local Disk (C:)**.

51. Double-click the **Encrypted** folder and then double-click **File3.txt**. The file opens, and you are now able to read the contents of the file that you added earlier.

52. Close Notepad, then close Windows Explorer and log off.

53. Log on as **AdminX** (where *X* is your assigned student number). Click **Start**, click **Run**, type **cmd**, and click **OK**.

54. In the command prompt window, type **cipher /?** and press **Enter**. Review the syntax for this command-line utility before completing the next step.

55. Type **cd** and press **Enter**. Type **cd encrypted** and press **Enter**.

56. Type **cipher** and press **Enter**. Both File3.txt and SubFolder have an E beside them. This indicates that the encryption attribute has been set on these objects (as shown in Figure 7-13).

Figure 7-13   Using CIPHER to view encryption attributes

57. Type **cd** and press **Enter**.

58. Close Windows Explorer (if open) before performing this next step. If the encrypted folder is currently being accessed, the following command will not execute properly. Type **cipher /d /a /s:c: \encrypted** and press **Enter**. The command executes, and the message 3 file(s) [or directorie(s)] within 3 directorie(s) were decrypted appears.

59. Close the command prompt window.

60. Right-click **Start** and click **Explore**. Click the **Encrypted** folder. The folder and its contents no longer appear in green text.

61. Right-click the **Encrypted** folder and click **Delete**. When asked if you are sure you want to remove the Encrypted folder and move all its contents to the Recycle Bin, click **Yes**.

62. Right-click the **Encrypted2** folder and click **Delete**. When asked if you are sure you want to remove the Encrypted2 folder and move all its contents to the Recycle Bin, click **Yes**.

63. Close Windows Explorer.

64. Click **Start**, point to **Administrative Tools**, and click **Active Directory Users and Computers**.

65. Click the **Users** container. Right-click **Encryption Account 1** and click **Delete**. When asked if you are sure you want to delete this object, click **Yes**.

66. Close Active Directory Users and Computers and log off.

Certification Objectives

Objectives for Microsoft Exam #70-290: Managing and Maintaining a Microsoft Windows Server 2003 Environment:

- Manage a server by using available support tools.

- Troubleshoot access to files and shared folders.

REVIEW QUESTIONS

1. Which of the following cannot be encrypted on Windows Server 2003?

   a. Files and folders on an NTFS volume

   b. Files with the System attribute

   c. Files in the system root folder

   d. All of the above

2. Which of the following file systems support encryption?

   a. FAT

   b. FAT32

   c. NTFS

   d. All of the above

3. Which of the following would have access to an encrypted folder and its contents?

    a. The account that applied the encryption attribute

    b. The data recovery agents for the file defined by the recovery policy

    c. Accounts listed under Users Who Can Transparently Access This File

    d. All of the above

4. In this lab activity, which account was listed under the Data Recovery Agents For This File As Defined By Recovery Policy field on the Encryption Details dialog box for the encrypted file?

    a. Administrator

    b. Admin01

    c. Enterprise Admins

    d. None of the above

5. Which of the following are true with regards to encryption? (Choose all that apply.)

    a. By default, remote encryption is enabled in a domain environment.

    b. Microsoft recommends that you encrypt at the folder level rather than at the file level.

    c. Encryption is transparent to the user who encrypted the file.

    d. When an encrypted file is opened across the network, the transmitted data is unencrypted.

7

LAB 7.3 IMPLEMENTING DISK QUOTAS

Objectives

In this lab activity, you will be enabling quotas and configuring and testing quota limits. You will also learn how to create quota entries and use Event Viewer to view Quota Events.

Materials Required

This lab will require the following:

- Windows Server 2003 installed and configured according to the instructions at the beginning of this lab manual

Estimated completion time: **30 minutes**

Activity Background

Windows Server 2003 allows administrators to track and control the amount of disk space a user can utilize on NTFS formatted volumes. Members of the Administrators group have the ability to enable quotas on NTFS partitions and volumes. Once enabled, the system will track the amount of disk space used according to the user accounts that have stored files and folders on that volume. Earlier in this chapter, you investigated compressing files and folders on NTFS partitions and volumes. With regard to quotas, administrators should keep in mind that the size of the original, uncompressed file will count towards a user's quota limit, and therefore, compressing folders and files on an NTFS volume will not rectify a situation where a user has exceeded their quota limit.

Administrators can configure warning levels and quota limits. Once a user has reached or exceeded these values, an event can be logged to the System log in Event Viewer.

ACTIVITY

Activity

1. If necessary, log on as **AdminX** of the **DomainX** domain (where *X* is your assigned student number) with a password of **Password01**.

2. Right-click **Start**, and click **Explore**.

3. Right-click **Local Disk (D:)** and click **Properties**.

4. Click the **Quota** tab. By default, disk quotas are disabled. If you enabled disk quotas in a previous lab, click to deselect the Enable quota management check box and click **Apply**. Then click to select the **Enable quota management** check box. All other options on this tab are now available.

5. Click to select the **Deny disk space to users exceeding quota limit** check box.

6. Click to select the **Limit disk space to** option button. Tab to the Limit disk space to field and type **50**. Click the **drop-down arrow** next to KB and click **MB**.

7. Tab down to the Set warning level to field and type **40**. Click the **drop-down arrow** next to KB and click **MB**.

8. Under Select the quota logging options for this volume, click to select both the **Log event when a user exceeds their quota limit** and the **Log event when a user exceeds their warning level** check boxes. Your Quota tab settings should now resemble Figure 7-14. Click **Apply**.

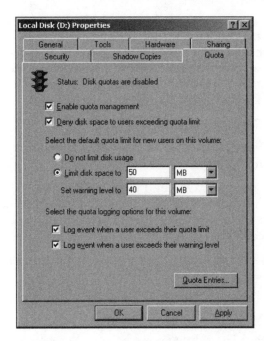

Figure 7-14 Configuring Quota management settings

9. The Disk Quota message box appears, indicating that you should enable the quota system only if you intend to use quotas on this disk volume (as shown in Figure 7-15). Click **OK** to enable the quota system now.

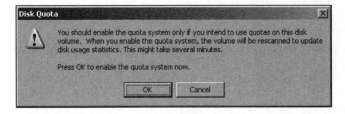

Figure 7-15 Enabling disk quotas

10. Click **Quota Entries**. Unless you have written information to this drive, the only quota entry that appears is the BUILTIN\Administrators group. No Limit appears in both the Quota Limit and Warning Level fields. By default, the Administrators group will not be affected by disk quota settings.

11. Next, you will create a new user account in Active Directory to which you will assign a quota entry for Local Disk (D:). Click **Start**, point to **Administrative Tools**, and click **Active Directory Users and Computers**.

12. Right-click the **Users** container, point to **New**, and click **User**.

13. In the New Object—User dialog box, tab down to the Full name field and type **Quota Test**. Then tab down to the User logon name field and type **Quota**. Click **Next**. In the Password and Confirm password fields, type **Password01**. Click to clear the **User must change password at next logon** check box. Click to select the **User cannot change password** check box. Click **Next**. Click **Finish**.

14. Close Active Directory Users and Computers.

15. Switch to the Quota Entries for Local Disk (D:) window. Click **Quota** on the menu and click **New Quota Entry**.

16. In the Select Users dialog box, click **Object Types**. Under Select the types of objects you want to find, the only object types listed are Users. New quota entries can only be created for user accounts. Click **Cancel**. In the Select Users dialog box, click **Advanced**.

17. Under Common Queries, type the letter **Q** in the Name Starts with field. Click **Find Now**.

18. The Quota Test account will appear in the Search results field. Click the **Quota Test** account and click **OK**.

19. Click **OK** to close the Select Users dialog box.

20. In the Add New Quota Entry dialog box, the quota entry settings you applied previously are now applied to this new quota entry. You will modify these settings. Tab to the Limit disk space to field and type **20**. Tab to the Set warning level to field and type **10**. (See Figure 7-16.) Click **OK**.

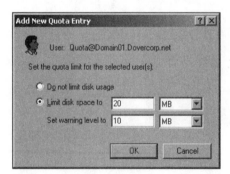

Figure 7-16   Adding a new quota entry

21. Close the Quota Entries for Local Disk (D:) window.

22. Click **OK** to close the Local Disk (D:) Properties dialog box. Close Windows Explorer.

23. Log off.

24. Log on as **Quota** to the **DomainX** domain (where *X* is your assigned student number) with a password of **Password01**.

25. Right-click **Start** and click **Explore**.

26. Click **Local Disk (C:)**. Double-click **Program Files**. Right-click the **Support Tools** directory and click **Properties**. In the Support Tools Properties dialog box, note that the size of the directory is greater than the 20 MB limit that you have configured for this user account. Click **Cancel** to exit the Support Tools Properties dialog box. Right-click the **Support Tools** directory and click **Copy**.

27. Right-click **Local Disk (D:)** and click **Paste**, and file copying begins.

28. The Error Copying File or Folder dialog box appears, indicating that there is not enough free disk space. Click **OK**.

29. Click **Start**, right-click **My Computer**, and click **Manage**. In the Computer Management console, double-click **Event Viewer**.

30. Under Event Viewer, right-click **System** and click **Properties**. Click the **Filter** tab.

31. Click the **drop-down arrow** in the Event source field and click **ntfs**. Click the **drop-down arrow** in the Category field and click **Disk**. (See Figure 7-17.) Click **OK** to close the System Properties dialog box.

7

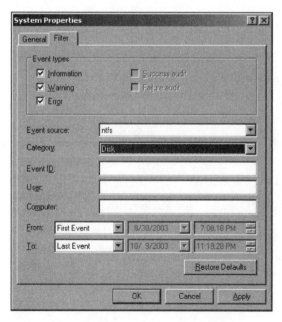

Figure 7-17   Filtering the System log

32. Double-click to open the event with **37** in the Event field. In the Event Properties dialog box, the User field indicates DomainX\Quota (where *X* is your assigned student number). The description for this event indicates that a user hit their quota limit on volume D: (as shown in Figure 7-18).

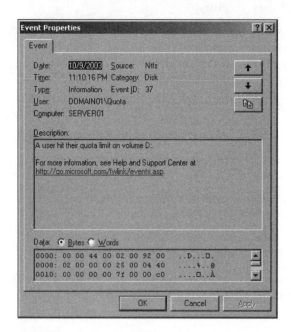

Figure 7-18   Event ID 37

33. Click **OK** to close the Event Properties dialog box.

34. Click **View** on the menu and click to select **All Records**. You have now removed the filter on the System log in Event Viewer.

35. Close all windows and log off.

36. Log on as **AdminX** to the **DomainX** domain (where *X* is your assigned student number) with a password of **Password01**.

37. Right-click **Start** and click **Explore**.

38. Right-click **Local Disk (D:)** and click **Properties**.

39. In the Local Disk (D:) Properties dialog box, click the **Quota** tab.

40. Click **Quota Entries**. Double-click the quota entry for
Quota@DomainX.Dovercorp.net (where *X* is your assigned student num-
ber), which is flagged with a yellow triangle with an exclamation mark. The
Quota Settings for Quota Test dialog box appears (as shown in Figure 7-19).

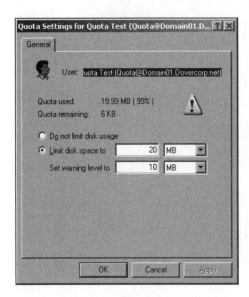

Figure 7-19   Quota settings for the Quota Test account

7

41. In the Quota Settings for Quota Test dialog box, notice the Quota used and the Quota remaining fields. Tab to the Limit disk space to field and type **50**. Tab down to the Set warning level to field and type **40**. Click **Apply**. The icon for this entry has now changed (as shown in Figure 7-20).

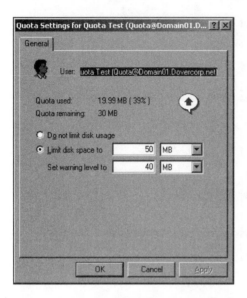

Figure 7-20 Modified quota settings for the Quota Test account

42. Click **OK** to close the Quota Settings for Quota Test dialog box.

43. Close the Quota Entries for Local Disk (D:) window.

44. On the Local Disk (D:) Properties dialog box, click to deselect the **Enable quota management** check box. Click **Apply**.

45. A message will appear notifying you that you should disable the quota system only if you do not intend to use quotas on this disk volume (as shown in Figure 7-21). Click **OK** to disable the quota system now.

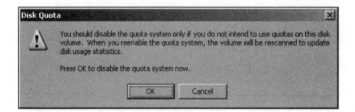

Figure 7-21 Disabling quotas

46. The traffic light icon should now appear red. Click **OK** to close the Local Disk (D:) Properties dialog box.

47. Close Windows Explorer.

Certification Objectives

Objectives for Microsoft Exam #70-290: Managing and Maintaining a Microsoft Windows Server 2003 Environment:

- Troubleshoot access to files and shared folders.

- Monitor disk quotas.

REVIEW QUESTIONS

1. Which of the following are true with regards to quotas and Windows Server 2003?

   a. By default, the built-in Administrators group has no quota limit.

   b. Quotas are only available on NTFS formatted drives.

   c. To enable quotas, you must be a member of the Administrators group.

   d. All of the above.

2. Which of the following logs would an event be written to if a quota limit were exceeded?

   a. Application

   b. Security

   c. System

   d. Active Directory

3. New quota entries can be created for which of the following?

   a. User accounts

   b. Global groups

   c. Domain local groups

   d. All of the above

4. The Quota tab is not displayed in a volume's properties dialog box. Which of the following could explain this occurrence?

   a. The volume has not been formatted with the NTFS file system.

   b. Quotas are only available on computers that have accounts in an Active Directory domain.

   c. You are not logged on as a member of the Administrators group.

   d. All of the above.

5. Which of the following are true with regards to quotas and compression?

   a. The size of the compressed file counts towards a user's quota limit.

   b. The size of the uncompressed file counts towards a user's quota limit.

   c. Once a user has exceeded their quota limit, they should compress all files and folders on the partition or volume.

   d. None of the above.

LAB 7.4 IMPLEMENTING STAND-ALONE DFS ROOTS

Objective

In this lab activity, you will be implementing a stand-alone Distributed File System (DFS) root, configuring links, and disabling referrals.

Materials Required

This lab will require the following:

- Windows Server 2003 installed and configured according to the instructions at the beginning of this lab manual

Estimated completion time: **30 minutes**

Activity Background

DFS is an administrative utility available on Windows Server 2003 that can make access to network resources easier for those who need to find them. There are two types of DFS roots: stand-alone and domain-based. This activity focuses on stand-alone. DFS can make resources that reside on multiple servers appear as though they are all in one directory on one server. By implementing DFS, users will no longer have to remember the physical location of resources they need to access.

ACTIVITY

Activity

1. If necessary, log on as **AdminX** to the **DomainX** domain (where *X* is your assigned student number) with a password of **Password01**.

2. Click **Start**, right-click **My Computer**, and click **Manage**.

3. In the Computer Management window, double-click **Shared Folders**.

4. Right-click **Shares** and click **New Share**.

5. In the Welcome to the Share a Folder Wizard page, click **Next**.

6. On the Folder Path page, click **Browse**. In the Browse for Folder dialog box, click **Local Disk (D:)**. Click **Make New Folder**, type **StandAlone**, and click **OK**.

7. The Folder Path page should now indicate D:\StandAlone as the Folder path. Verify that this has been configured properly and click **Next**.

8. On the Name, Description, and Settings page, review the default settings and click **Next**.

9. On the Permissions page, click to select **Administrators have full access**; **other users have read-only access**. Click **Finish**.

10. On the Sharing was Successful page, click to select the **When I click Close, run the wizard again to share another folder** check box. Click **Close**.

11. Following the same steps that were taken in creating the stand-alone share, create three other shares with the same permissions on Local Disk (D:) called **Link1**, **Link2**, and **Link3**. When you are creating the last share (Link3), click to clear the **When I click Close, run the wizard again to share another folder** check box. Click **Close**.

12. Close the Computer Management window.

13. Click **Start**, point to **Administrative Tools**, and click **Distributed File System**.

14. In the Distributed File System console, right-click **Distributed File System** and click **New Root**.

15. In the Welcome to the New Root Wizard page, review the information provided and click **Next**.

16. On the Root Type page, click the **Stand-alone root** option button (as shown in Figure 7-22). Click **Next**.

7

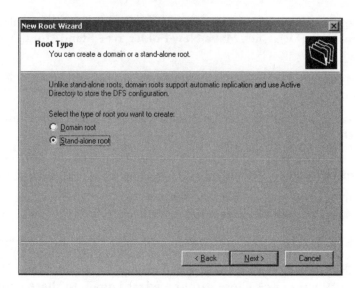

Figure 7-22 Creating a stand-alone root

17. On the Host Server page, type **ServerX** (where *X* is your assigned student number) and click **Next**.

18. On the Root Name page, type **StandAlone** in the Root name field. The Preview of UNC path to the root field updates to reflect \\ServerX\StandAlone (where *X* is your assigned student number). See Figure 7-23. Click **Next**.

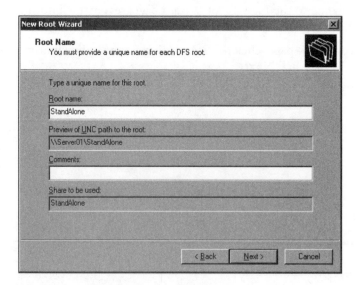

Figure 7-23 The Root Name page

19. On the Completing the New Root Wizard page, click **Finish**. The Distributed File System console now displays \\ServerX\StandAlone (where *X* is your assigned student number).

20. Right-click **\\ServerX\StandAlone** in the Details pane (left pane) and click **New Link**.

21. In the New Link dialog box, type **Folder One** in the Link name field. In the Path to target field, click **Browse**.

22. In the Browse for Folder dialog box, double-click **Entire Network**. Double-click **Microsoft Windows Network**. Double-click **DomainX** (where *X* is your assigned student number). Double-click **ServerX** (where *X* is your assigned student number). Click **Link1** and click **OK**.

23. In the New Link dialog box, verify that the Path to target (shared folder) field now reflects \\ServerX\Link1 (as shown in Figure 7-24). Click **OK** to close the New Link dialog box.

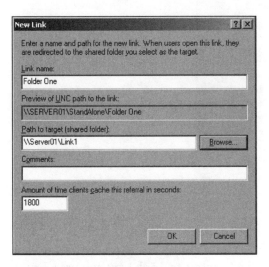

Figure 7-24   The New Link dialog box

24. Right-click **\\ServerX\StandAlone** and click **New Link**.

25. In the New Link dialog box, type **Folder Two** in the Link name field. Click **Browse**.

26. In the Browse for Folder dialog box, double-click **Entire Network**. Double-click **Microsoft Windows Network**. Double-click **DomainX**. Double-click **ServerX**, click **Link2**, and click **OK**.

27. In the New Link dialog box, verify that the Path to target (shared folder) field now displays \\ServerX\Link2. Click **OK** to close the New Link dialog box.

28. In the Distributed File System console, note that the target for Folder Two is pointing to \\ServerX\Link2. In the Distributed File System console, right-click **Folder Two** and click **New Target**.

29. In the New Target dialog box, note that when users open the link they will be redirected to the shared folder you select as the target. Click **Browse** next to the Path to target (shared folder) field.

30. In the Browse for Folder dialog box, double-click **Entire Network**. Double-click **Microsoft Windows Network**. Double-click **DomainX** (where *X* is your assigned student number). Double-click **ServerX** (where *X* is your assigned student number), click **Link3**, and click **OK**.

31. In the New Target dialog box, the Path to target (shared folder) field should now display \\ServerX\Link3. The Add this target to the replication set option is not available. This option is available to domain-based DFS roots only. Click **OK** to close the New Target dialog box. Folder Two now has two targets (as shown in Figure 7-25).

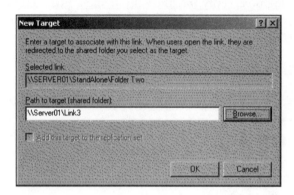

Figure 7-25   Target for Folder Two

32. Right-click **Start** and click **Explore**.

33. Click **Local Disk (D:)**.

34. Click the **Link2** folder. Click **File** on the menu, point to **New**, and click **Text Document**. Type **Redirected to Link2.txt** and press **Enter**. If you are redirected to Link2, you will see this text document.

35. Click the **Link3** folder. Click **File** on the menu, point to **New**, and click **Text Document**. Type **Redirected to Link3.txt** and press **Enter**. If you are redirected to Link3, you will see this text document.

36. Click **Start**, click **Run**, type **\\ServerX\StandAlone** (where *X* is your assigned student number), and click **OK**. Folder One and Folder Two appear as subdirectories. Double-click **Folder Two**. Which text file do you see? Have you been redirected to Link2 or Link3? (Your window will appear similar to Figure 7-26) Take note of which target you have been redirected to, as you will be using this information in the next step.

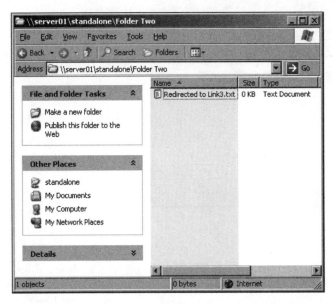

Figure 7-26   What users see when connecting to the share

37. Switch to the Distributed File System console. Click **Folder Two**. Right-click the **\\ServerX\LinkY** target (where *X* is your assigned student number and where *Y* is the number of the link that you were redirected to in the previous step) and click **Enable or Disable Referral**. The DFS Referral field now appears as Disabled (as shown in Figure 7-27).

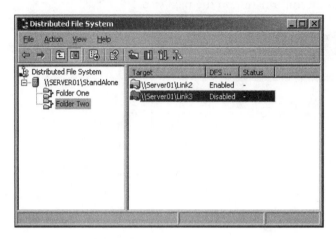

Figure 7-27   DFS referral disabled

38. Switch to the Folder Two window and press **F5** to refresh the display. Even though you have disabled the referral for LinkY (where *Y* is the number of the link you were redirected to earlier in this lab activity), it has been cached on your system. The default amount of time that clients will cache a referral is 1,800 seconds. In order to test this, you will stop sharing the LinkY directory.

39. Switch to Windows Explorer.

40. Click the **D:\LinkY** directory (where *Y* is the number of the link you were redirected to). Right-click **LinkY** and click **Sharing and Security**. On the Sharing tab, click **Do not share this folder**. Click **OK**. If you get a message indicating that there are files open by users connected to LinkY and if you stop sharing the folder, the files will close and users may lose data, click **Yes** to continue. The hand now disappears from underneath the Link2 folder in Windows Explorer.

41. Switch to the Folder Two window and press **F5** to refresh the display. You have now been redirected to the other target for Folder Two. With a stand-alone DFS root, you must manually copy the contents into all target directories. Otherwise, when users are redirected to different targets, they will not be able to view the same information as you are observing in this lab activity.

42. Close the **Folder Two** window.

43. In the Distributed File System console, right-click **\\ServerX\StandAlone** (where *X* is your assigned student number) and click **Properties**.

44. Click the **Publish** tab. This root can be published to Active Directory. Click to select the **Publish this root in Active Directory** check box (as shown in Figure 7–28). Click **OK**.

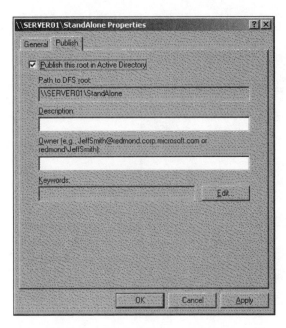

Figure 7-28   Publishing the stand-alone root in Active Directory

45. Click **Start**, point to **Administrative Tools**, and click **Active Directory Users and Computers**.

46. In the Active Directory Users and Computers console, click **View** on the menu and click **Users, Groups, and Computers as containers**.

47. Click **DomainX.Dovercorp.net** (where *X* is your assigned student number) and then double-click the **Domain Controllers** organizational unit.

48. Double-click **ServerX** (where *X* is your assigned student number). The StandAlone shared folder has been published to Active Directory (as shown in Figure 7-29).

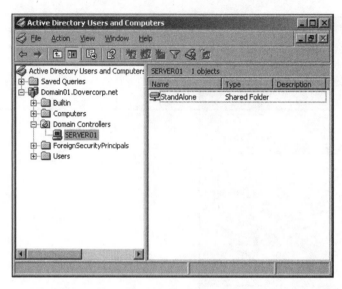

Figure 7-29   How published folders appear in Active Directory

49. Close Active Directory Users and Computers.

50. Switch to the Distributed File System console. Right-click **\\ServerX\StandAlone** (where *X* is your assigned student number) and click **Delete Root**.

51. A message appears indicating that this will delete the DFS root \\ServerX\StandAlone, and that clients will not be able to access this DFS again. Click **Yes** to indicate that you are sure you want to continue.

52. Close the Distributed File System console.

53. Close all windows and log off.

Certification Objectives

Objectives for Microsoft Exam #70-290: Managing and Maintaining a Microsoft Windows Server 2003 Environment:

■ Configure access to shared folders.

■ Troubleshoot access to files and shared folders.

REVIEW QUESTIONS

1. Which of the following are advantages of implementing a distributed file system?

   a. Users do not need to know the physical location of resources.

   b. Resources appear to reside in one location on the network.

   c. A DFS helps to balance server load.

   d. All of the above.

2. On a stand-alone DFS root, how would you ensure that multiple targets for a link contained the same content?

   a. Configure a replication set between the targets.

   b. Manually copy information into all target folders.

   c. Stand-alone DFS roots do not offer the ability to configure multiple targets for DFS links.

   d. None of the above.

3. During this lab activity, you were able to access a resource after the referral for that target had been disabled. Which of the following best explains that occurrence?

   a. The DFS service must be restarted for these changes to take effect.

   b. You did not have the necessary permissions to disable the referral.

   c. Your computer had cached the initial referral for that resource.

   d. None of the above.

7

4. Which of the following are true with regard to DFS referral?

   a. When disabled for a target, users will not be directed to the target folder until it is enabled again.

   b. If a user has been directed to a target folder and the referral for that target is disabled, the user can still access the target using the cached referral.

   c. The default referral time is 1,800 seconds.

   d. All of the above

5. Which of the following are true with regard to targets? (Choose all that apply.)

   a. They must be an existing shared folder.

   b. It is recommended that you use NTFS permissions to secure the folder.

   c. Deleting a target will delete the associated shared folders.

   d. Deleting a target will reset both NTFS and shared folder permissions.

LAB 7.5 IMPLEMENTING DOMAIN-BASED DFS ROOTS

Objectives

In this lab activity, you will be implementing a domain-based DFS root.

Materials Required

This lab will require the following:

- Windows Server 2003 installed and configured according to the instructions at the beginning of this lab manual

Estimated completion time: **30 minutes**

Activity Background

This activity focuses on using a domain-based DFS to create links, configure an initial master, and check link status.

Activity

1. If necessary, log on as **AdminX** to the **DomainX** domain (where *X* is your assigned student number) with a password of **Password01**.

2. Click **Start**, right-click **My Computer**, and click **Manage**.

3. In the Computer Management console, click **Shared Folders**.

4. Right-click **Shares** and click **New Share**.

5. On the Welcome to the Share a Folder Wizard page, click **Next**.

6. On the Folder Path page, click **Browse**.

7. In the Browse For Folder dialog box, click **Local Disk (D:)**. Click **Make New Folder**, type **DomainX Root** (where *X* is your assigned student number), and press **Enter**. Click **OK** to close the Browse For Folder dialog box.

8. On the Folder Path page, the Folder path field should now show D:\DomainX Root. Click **Next**.

9. On the Name, Description, and Settings page, click **Next**.

10. On the Permissions page, click to select **Administrators have full access; other users have read-only access**, and click **Finish**.

11. On the Sharing was Successful page, click to select the **When I click Close, run the wizard again to share another folder** check box. Click **Close**.

12. On the Folder Path page, click **Browse**. In the Browse For Folder dialog box, click **Local Disk (D:)**, then click **LinkY** (where *Y* is the number of the folder that is no longer shared). Click **OK**. On the Folder Path page, verify that the Folder path field displays D:\LinkY and click **Next**. On the Name, Description, and Settings page, click **Next**. On the Permissions page, click to select **Administrators have full access; other users have read-only access** and click **Finish**. On the Sharing was Successful page, click to deselect the **When I click Close, run the wizard again to share another folder** check box and click **Close**.

13. Click **Start**, point to **Administrative Tools**, and click **Distributed File System**.

14. In the Distributed File System console, right-click **Distributed File System** and click **New Root**.

15. On the Welcome to the New Root Wizard page, click **Next**.

16. On the Root Type page, verify that Domain root is selected and click **Next**.

7

17. On the Host Domain page, verify that your domain is the selected Domain name (as shown in Figure 7-30). Click **Next**.

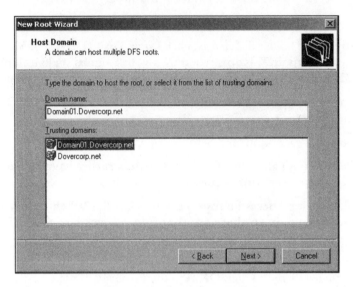

Figure 7-30 Selecting the host domain

18. On the Host Server page, click **Browse**.

19. In the Find Computers dialog box, click **ServerX** in the Search results field (where X is your assigned student number) and click **OK**.

20. The Host Server page should now display ServerX.DomainX.Dovercorp.net in the Server name field (where X is your assigned student number). Click **Next**.

21. On the Root Name page, type **DomainX Root** (where X is your assigned student number). Both the Preview of UNC path to the root and the Share to be used fields are filled in using the information you entered. Click **Next**.

22. On the Completing the New Root Wizard page, click **Finish**.

23. In the Distributed File System console, right-click **\\DomainX.Dovercorp.net\DomainX Root** (where X is your assigned student number) and view the shortcut menu. In addition to creating new links below the root, you also have the capability of creating a new root target. This is one of the major differences between stand-alone DFS roots and domain-based DFS roots. You have the ability of having a duplicate of the DFS structure stored on an entirely different server in your domain. As you only have one server in your domain, you will not be able to create a new root target.

24. From the shortcut menu that appears when you right-click **\\DomainX.Dovercorp.net\DomainX Root** (where X is your assigned student number), click **New Link**.

25. In the New Link dialog box, type **Folder One** in the Link name field. Click **Browse**. In the Browse For Folder dialog box, double-click **Entire Network**. Double-click **Microsoft Windows Network**. Double-click **DomainX** (where *X* is your assigned student number). Double-click **ServerX** (where *X* is your assigned student number), click **Link1**, and click **OK**.

26. In the New Link dialog box, verify that the Path to target (shared folder) field displays \\ServerX\Link1 and click **OK**. Folder One now appears in the Distributed File System console.

27. Right-click **\\DomainX.Dovercorp.net\DomainX Root** (where *X* is your assigned student number) and click **New Link**.

28. In the New Link dialog box, type **Folder Two** in the Link name field. Click **Browse**. In the Browse For Folder dialog box, double-click **Entire Network**. Double-click **Microsoft Windows Network**. Double-click **DomainX** (where *X* is your assigned student number). Double-click **ServerX** (where *X* is your assigned student number), click **Link2**, and click **OK**.

29. In the New Link dialog box, verify that the Path to target (shared folder) field displays \\ServerX\Link2 (where *X* is your assigned student number) and click **OK**.

30. Right-click **Folder Two** and click **New Target**.

31. In the New Target dialog box, note that the Add this target to the replication set check box is selected. This option was not available on our stand-alone root that we created in the previous lab activity. Click **Browse**.

32. In the Browse For Folder dialog box, double-click **Entire Network**. Double-click **Microsoft Windows Network**. Double-click **DomainX** (where *X* is your assigned student number). Double-click **ServerX** (where *X* is your assigned student number), click **Link3**, and click **OK**. Click **OK** to close the New Target dialog box.

33. A message appears indicating that the target cannot be replicated until replication is configured. Click **Yes**.

34. Another message appears indicating that you have more than one target on the same computer and that only one of them will be selected to join the replication. Click **Yes**.

35. Review the information provided on the Welcome to the Configure Replication Wizard page (as shown in Figure 7-31) and click **Next**.

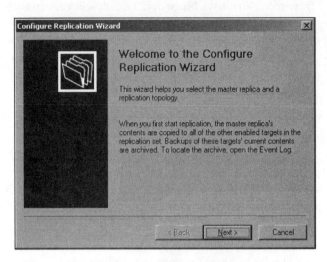

Figure 7-31   The Configure Replication Wizard

36. On the Configure Replication Wizard page, note that you need to select one target as the initial master. Its contents will be replicated to other targets for the first replication. (See Figure 7-32.) Click **Next**. An error occurs indicating that a replication set needs at least two members (as shown in Figure 7-33). Click **OK**.

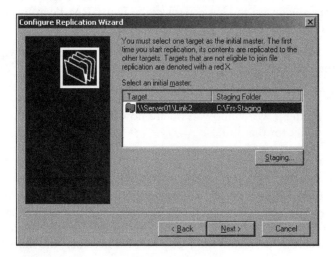

Figure 7-32   Selecting an initial master

Figure 7-33   Requirements for configuring replication

37. Click **Cancel** to exit the Configure Replication Wizard. Unlike with the stand-alone root, the domain-based DFS root would have automatically copied the contents of the Link2 folder to the Link3 folder. This ensures that when clients are redirected to either target they will be able to access the same content.

38. Click **Start**, click **Run**, type **\\ServerX\DomainX Root** (where *X* is your assigned student number), and click **OK**. Double-click **Folder Two**. Take note of which target you have been redirected to.

39. Switch to the Distributed File System console. Right-click the **\\ServerX\LinkY** target for Folder Two (where *X* is your assigned student number, and where *Y* is the number of the folder that you have been redirected to) and click **Remove Target**.

40. A message appears indicating that if this is the only target of this DFS link, then the link will also be deleted. Click **Yes** to indicate that you want to continue.

41. Switch to the Folder Two window. Even though the target has been deleted, the referral has been cached on your local machine for a period of 30 minutes.

42. Switch to the Computer Management console and double-click **Shared Folders**. Click **Shares**. Right-click **LinkY** (where *Y* is the number of the folder that you have been redirected to) and click **Stop Sharing**. A message appears asking if you are sure you want to stop sharing the folder. Click **Yes**.

43. Right-click **Link1** and click **Properties**. Click the **Share Permissions** tab. Click the **Everyone** group and click to select the **Deny Read** permission check box. Click **OK** to close the Link1 Properties dialog box.

44. The Security dialog box appears, indicating that you are setting a deny permissions entry and that it will take precedence over allow entries. Click **Yes**.

45. Close the Computer Management console.

46. Switch to the Folder Two window. You are now being redirected to what is now the only target for that link.

47. Switch back to the Distributed File System console. Next, you will test the permissions you just modified on Link1 and Link3.

48. Click **Folder One**. Right-click the **\\ServerX\Link1** target (where *X* is your assigned student number) and click **Check Status**. The Status appears as Offline (as shown in Figure 7-34). Recall that the folder is still shared; however, you changed the Everyone permission to Deny Read. Therefore, the share permissions are not allowing DFS to access the folder.

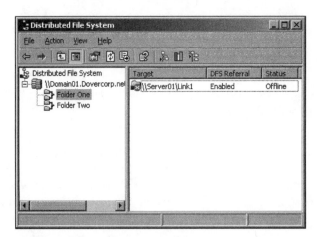

Figure 7-34 Status Offline

49. Click **Folder Two**. Right-click the **\\ServerX\Link3** target (where *X* is your assigned student number) and click **Check Status**. Note that the Status appears as Online.

50. Right-click **\\DomainX.Dovercorp.net\DomainX Root** (where *X* is your assigned student number) and click **Check Status**. Note that the Status field indicates Online.

51. Right-click **\\DomainX.Dovercorp.net\DomainX Root** (where *X* is your assigned student number) and click **Properties**. Click the **Publish** tab. Both types of DFS roots can be published to Active Directory. Click **Cancel**.

52. Right-click **\\DomainX.Dovercorp.net\DomainX Root** (where *X* is your assigned student number) and click **Delete Root**.

53. A message appears indicating that this will delete the DFS root and that clients will not be able to access this DFS again. Click **Yes**.

54. Close the Distributed File System console.

55. In Windows Explorer, click **Local Disk (D:)**. If the folders are not currently visible, click **View** on the menu, point to the **Explorer Bar**, and click **Folders**. Right-click **DomainX Root** and click **Delete**. When asked if you are sure you want to remove the folder and move all its contents to the Recycle Bin, click **Yes**. When a message appears indicating that you are sharing the folder and if you delete the folder it will no longer be shared, click **Yes**. Use the procedure as outlined above to delete the **Link1**, **Link2**, **Link3**, and **StandAlone** shared folders.

56. Close all open windows.

Certification Objectives

Objectives for Microsoft Exam #70-290: Managing and Maintaining a Microsoft Windows Server 2003 Environment:

- Configure access to shared folders.

- Troubleshoot access to files and shared folders.

REVIEW QUESTIONS

1. Which of the following is true with regards to automatic file replication and DFS?

   a. It is only available with stand–alone DFS roots.

   b. It is only available with domain-based DFS roots.

   c. A root or link must have at least two targets before replication can begin.

   d. None of the above.

2. Which of the following permissions apply to users accessing resources on a DFS root?

   a. Share permissions

   b. NTFS permissions

   c. DFS permissions

   d. All of the above

3. Which of the following are true about stand-alone DFS roots? (Choose all that apply.)

   a. Cannot have more than one root-level target

   b. Can have more than one root-level target

   c. Do not support automatic file replication using the File Replication Service

   d. Must be hosted on a domain member server

4. Which of the following are true with regards to fault-tolerant options for stand–alone DFS roots? (Choose all that apply.)

   a. Fault tolerance is not supported.

   b. Fault tolerance is supported through Server Clusters.

   c. Fault tolerance is supported through FRS.

   d. Fault tolerance is supported through both Server Clusters and FRS.

5. When checking the status of a DFS root or link, a yellow exclamation mark appears. What does this indicate?

   a. The root or link can be reached and all of its targets can be reached.

   b. The root or link can be reached, but not all of its targets can be reached because DFS referral is disabled, or some other problem is preventing access to the target.

   c. The root or link cannot be reached.

   d. None of the above.

7

IMPLEMENTING AND MANAGING PRINTERS

Labs included in this chapter:

♦ Lab 8.1 Configuring Printer Priority and Availability

♦ Lab 8.2 Reviewing Print Server Properties

♦ Lab 8.3 Configuring Printing Preferences

♦ Lab 8.4 Managing Printers Using PRNMNGR.VBS and PRNJOBS.VBS

Microsoft MCSE Exam #70-290 Objectives	
Objective	Lab
Troubleshoot print queues.	8.1, 8.4
Monitor print queues.	8.1, 8.4

Lab 8.1 Configuring Printer Priority and Availability

Objective

The goal of this lab activity is to configure printer priority and availability settings of the Advanced tab in the properties of an installed printer.

Materials Required

This lab will require the following:

- Windows Server 2003 installed and configured according to the instructions at the beginning of this lab manual

Estimated completion time: **15 minutes**

Activity Background

Printer priority settings control the order in which documents are printed to a specific print device, with higher priority documents taking precedence. Printer availability settings control the times of the day when a certain printer can be used. If documents are sent to a printer outside of its available hours, those documents are held (spooled) until the printer becomes available.

ACTIVITY

Activity

1. Log on to Windows Server 2003 using your **AdminXX** account (where *XX* is your assigned student number). Click **Start** and then click **Printers and Faxes**.

2. In the Printers and Faxes window, double-click the **Add Printer** icon.

3. At the Add Printer Wizard Welcome screen, click **Next**.

4. At the Local or Network Printer screen, ensure that **Local printer attached to this computer** is selected and uncheck the **Automatically detect and install my Plug and Play printer** check box, if necessary. Click **Next**.

5. At the Select a Printer Port screen, ensure that **LPT1: (Recommended Printer Port)** is selected in the Use the following port section and click **Next**.

6. At the Install Printer Software screen, click **HP** in the Manufacturer column and then click **HP LaserJet 6P** in the Printers column. Click **Next**. If the Use Existing Driver screen appears, ensure that the **Keep existing driver (recommended)** option button is selected and click **Next**.

7. At the Name Your Printer screen, type **6P Low Priority** in the Printer name field and click **Next**.

8. At the Printer Sharing screen, click **Do not share this printer** (if necessary) and click **Next**.

9. At the Print Test Page screen, click the **No** option button (if necessary) and then click **Next**.

10. At the Completing the Add Printer Wizard screen, click **Finish**.

11. In the Printers and Faxes window right-click the **6P Low Priority** printer icon and click **Properties**.

12. Click the **Advanced** tab (as shown in Figure 8-1). Note the default settings for printer availability (Always available) and Priority 1 (the lowest priority).

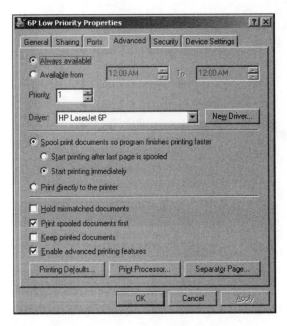

Figure 8-1   The Advanced tab of the properties of a local printer

13. Click the **Available from** option button. In the first text box, select **5:00 PM**. In the second text box, select **9:00 AM**. This makes this particular printer available from 9 AM to 5 PM. If a user sends a job to this printer outside of these hours, the job will be held (spooled) until the time that the printer becomes available. This is an excellent option for large print jobs that can be printed at nonpeak hours. Click **OK**.

14. Repeat steps 2 through 10 to create another printer named **6P High Priority** that also uses port LPT1. This creates a new printer object that prints to the same print device on LPT1, but will represent a different print queue that can have different properties configured.

15. In the Printers and Faxes window, right-click the **6P High Priority** printer icon and click **Properties**.

16. Click the **Advanced** tab. Type **99** in the Priority text box (as shown in Figure 8-2) and then click **OK**. Because this printer is always available, any jobs sent to it will be spooled and then printed immediately. However, when jobs are printed to this printer after 5:00 PM, these jobs will have a higher priority than those sent or waiting for the 6P Low Priority printer, which uses the same print device.

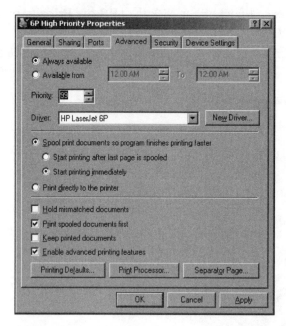

Figure 8-2   Configuring the printer priority setting

17. Close all open windows.

Certification Objectives

Objectives for Microsoft Exam #70-290: Managing and Maintaining a Microsoft Windows Server 2003 Environment:

- Troubleshoot print queues.

- Monitor print queues.

REVIEW QUESTIONS

1. What is the default printer priority value for a printer installed on a Windows Server 2003 system?

   a. 1

   b. 99

   c. 100

   d. 0

2. What will happen to a print job that is sent to a printer outside of its available hours?

   a. The print job will be lost.

   b. The print job will be spooled and held until the printer becomes available.

   c. The print job will print immediately.

   d. Access to the printer will be denied.

3. True or False? More than one printer can be configured to use the same physical print device.

4. Which of the following is the default availability setting for a new printer installed on a Windows Server 2003 system?

   a. Always available

   b. Available from 9 AM to 5 PM

   c. Never available

   d. None of the above

5. By default, the highest available priority for a printer is _____, the default priority value is 1, and the lowest available printer priority is _____.

LAB 8.2 REVIEWING PRINT SERVER PROPERTIES

Objective

The goal of this lab activity is to view print server properties on a Windows Server 2003 system.

Materials Required

This lab will require the following:

- Windows Server 2003 installed and configured according to the instructions at the beginning of this lab manual

Estimated completion time: **10 minutes**

Activity Background

The properties of a print server allow an administrator to configure form settings, view and configure the ports associated with installed print devices, view and change installed drivers, and configure advanced settings, such as the location of the print spooler folder, logging, and notification options.

Activity

1. Click **Start** and then click **Printers and Faxes**.

2. Click **File** and then click **Server Properties**. The Print Server Properties window opens (as shown in Figure 8-3). The screens displayed in this activity may be slightly different than those on your system, depending on which previous activities you have completed.

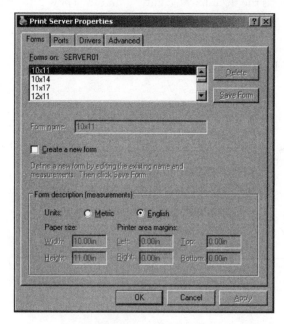

Figure 8-3   The Print Server Properties window

3. Review the settings on the Forms tab, which displays existing forms available on the print server and also allows custom forms to be defined. Forms are added to a Windows Server 2003 system according to the drivers installed for configured printers.

4. Click the **Ports** tab (as shown in Figure 8-4). This tab lists all available ports on the print server and displays the printers configured on each port. Ports can also be added, deleted, and configured from this tab.

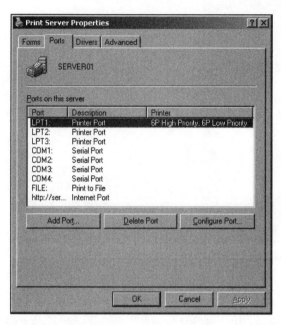

Figure 8-4   Viewing port configuration settings for a print server

5. Click the **Drivers** tab (as shown in Figure 8-5). This tab lists all installed printer drivers, as well as information on supported processors and Windows versions that the driver supports. This tab can be used to add, remove, reinstall, or view the properties of a selected driver on the list.

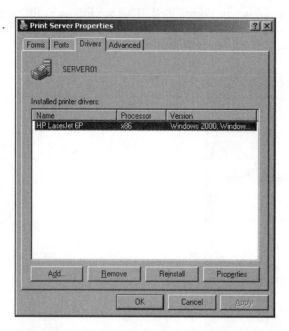

Figure 8-5　Viewing installed drivers for a print server

6. Click any available driver in the Installed printer drivers list and click **Properties**. This displays more information about an installed driver, including data type, the driver path, and information about associated files (as shown in Figure 8-6). Click **Close**.

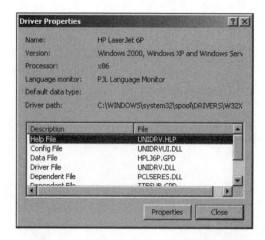

Figure 8-6　Viewing the properties of an installed driver

7. Click the **Advanced** tab (as shown in Figure 8-7). This tab allows an administrator to configure a new location for the spool folder, configure spooler logging options, and control settings related to beeps and notification settings when documents are printed on both Windows Server 2003 and other client operating systems. Click **OK**.

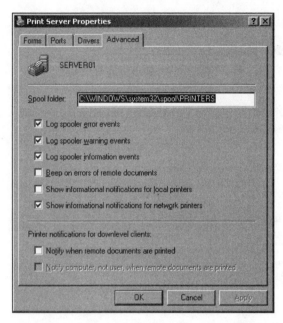

Figure 8-7   Viewing advanced settings for a print server

8. Close all open windows.

REVIEW QUESTIONS

1. Selecting the _____ option from the File menu in the Printers and Faxes window accesses the properties of a print server.

2. The Ports tab in the Print Server Properties window will allow you to do which of the following? (Choose all that apply.)

   a. Add a port

   b. Delete a port

   c. Configure a port

   d. Disable a port

3. The location of a print server's spool folder can be configured from the _____ tab of the Print Server Properties window.

4. True or False? Windows Server 2003 does not support the configuration of printer notifications for downlevel (Windows NT 4.0, Windows 95/98/ME) clients.

5. True or False? The driver associated with a printer can be deleted using the Print Server Properties window.

LAB 8.3 CONFIGURING PRINTING PREFERENCES

Objective

The goal of this lab activity is to view and configure printing preference settings for a printer installed on a Windows Server 2003 system.

Materials Required

This lab will require the following:

- Windows Server 2003 installed and configured according to the instructions at the beginning of this lab manual

Estimated completion time: **5 minutes**

Activity Background

Printing preferences allow an administrator to control many of the advanced settings associated with a particular printer and its installed driver. For example, some print devices can be configured to print in a draft mode, allow an administrator to configure page orientation settings, select a paper source, and more. It is important to remember that available printer preference settings can often be very different for different print device models, since the capabilities associated with the driver dictate what an administrator can configure.

Activity

1. Click **Start** and then click **Printers and Faxes**.

2. Right-click the **6P Low Priority** printer icon (created in Lab 8-1) and click **Printing Preferences**. This opens the 6P Low Priority Printing Preferences window (as shown in Figure 8-8).

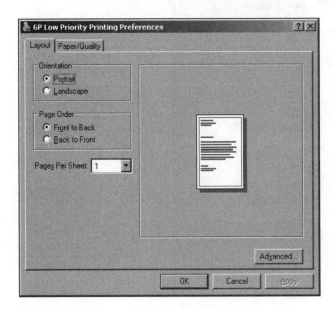

Figure 8-8   The Printing Preferences window

3. In the Orientation section, notice the default setting of Portrait. By default, all documents sent to this printer print using this orientation, unless specified differently by the user sending the print job. Click the **Landscape** option button. Notice that the preview page changes to show a page in Landscape orientation (as shown in Figure 8-9).

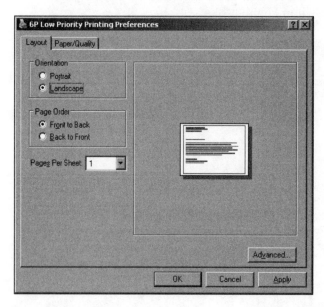

Figure 8-9   Configuring landscape orientation for a printer

4. Review the Page Order section. These settings control the order in which pages are output, either Front to Back (default) or Back to Front. When Front to Back is configured, the top page of any completed output will be page 1.

5. Notice the setting for the Pages Per Sheet drop-down box. By default, each page prints on its own sheet. Click the **Pages Per Sheet** drop-down box and select **2**. Notice that the preview pane changes to show that 2 pages will be printed on a single sheet (as shown in Figure 8-10).

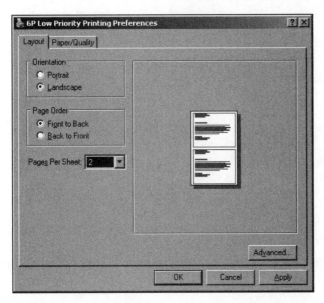

Figure 8-10   Configuring a printer to print multiple pages per sheet

8

6. Click the **Paper/Quality** tab. This tab allows you to configure paper source settings for the printer (as shown in Figure 8-11). The Paper Source setting is configured to Automatically Select by default for the HP LaserJet 6P.

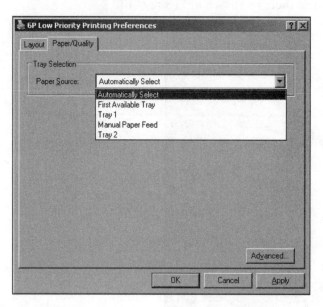

Figure 8-11 Configuring Paper Source settings

7. Click the **Advanced** button. This opens the HP LaserJet 6P Advanced Options window (as shown in Figure 8-12). From this window, paper options, graphics settings, document options, and printer features specific to the HP LaserJet 6P can be configured.

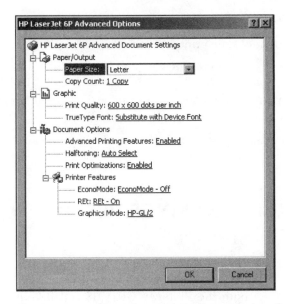

Figure 8-12 The Advanced Options window for a printer

8. In the Printer Features section, click the **EconoMode – Off** link. In the drop-down box that appears, select **EconoMode – On**. This ensures that all documents are output using EconoMode, a configurable setting on many HP printers that prints documents in draft quality (using less toner). Click **OK** to close the HP LaserJet 6P Advanced Options dialog box. Click **OK** to close the 6P Low Priority Printing Preferences dialog box.

9. Close all open windows.

REVIEW QUESTIONS

1. True or False? The driver installed for a printer dictates the configurable options available in the Printing Preferences settings for that printer.

2. Which of the following preference options can be configured from the Printing Preferences settings on an HP LaserJet 6P printer?

   a. Orientation

   b. Pages Per Sheet

   c. Advanced Document Settings

   d. All of the above

3. Which of the following represent potential reasons why an administrator might choose to configure printing preferences to print multiple pages per sheet? (Choose all that apply.)

   a. To reduce the amount of paper consumed

   b. To reduce the amount of toner consumed

   c. To increase the amount of time print jobs require

   d. To reduce the amount of time print jobs require

4. True or False? An administrator can control the print quality settings for graphics in the Advanced Options window for an HP LaserJet 6P.

5. The option to print in draft quality on an HP printer is commonly referred to as _____.

LAB 8.4 MANAGING PRINTERS USING PRNMNGR.VBS AND PRNJOBS.VBS

Objectives

The goal of this lab activity is to use both the PRNMNGR.VBS and PRNJOBS.VBS scripts included with Windows Server 2003 to manage printers and print jobs from the command line, rather than through the standard Printers and Faxes graphical interface.

Materials Required

This lab will require the following:

- Windows Server 2003 installed and configured according to the instructions at the beginning of this lab manual

Activity Background

Using PRNMNGR.VBS and PRNJOBS.VBS scripts is a new and useful capability included with Windows Server 2003 that makes the management of printers from the command line (or from within a remote telnet session, for example) much more flexible.

Estimated completion time: **10 minutes**

ACTIVITY

Activity

1. Click **Start** and then click **Run**. In the Open text box, type **cmd** and click **OK**.

2. At the command line, type **cd** and press **Enter**. This returns you to the C: prompt.

3. At the command line, type **cd \windows\system32** and press **Enter**. Both the PRNMNGR.VBS and PRNJOBS.VBS commands require the use of the command-line Windows Script Host (CSCRIPT.EXE), which is found in the \WINDOWS\system32 directory.

4. At the command line, type **cscript prnmngr.vbs –l** and press **Enter**. This displays a list of all printers configured on the local computer (as shown in Figure 8-13).

Figure 8-13   Using PRNMNGR.VBS to view installed printers from the command line

5. At the command line, type **cscript prnmngr.vbs –g** and press **Enter**. This displays the default printer configured on the local computer.

6. At the command line, type **cscript prnmngr.vbs –d –p "6P Low Priority"** and press **Enter**. This deletes the existing 6P Low Priority printer created in Lab 8-1. Administrators should be very careful with this command, as you will not be prompted to confirm the printer deletion.

7. At the command line, type **cscript prnmngr.vbs** and press **Enter**. When no switches are specified, this command displays help settings associated with the PRNMNGR.VBS script.

8. At the command line, type **cscript prnjobs.vbs** and press **Enter**. When no switches are specified, this command displays help settings associated with the PRNJOBS.VBS script.

9. At the command line, type **cscript prnjobs.vbs –l** and press **Enter**. This will display a list of all print jobs in the print queue for all printers on the server.

10. Click **Start** and then click **Run**. In the Open text box, type **notepad.exe** and click **OK**.

11. Type **test** in the Notepad window, click **File**, and then click **Save**. In the Save As dialog box, type **text.txt** in the File name text box and click **Save**.

12. Click **File** and then click **Print**. In the Print window, click the **6P High Priority** icon, if necessary, and then click **Print**. Close Notepad.

13. At the command prompt window, type **cscript prnjobs.vbs –l –p "6P High Priority"** and press **Enter**. This displays the contents of the print queue for the 6P High Priority printer (as shown in Figure 8-14).

```
Command Prompt                                                    _ □ X
C:\WINDOWS\system32>cscript prnjobs.vbs -l -p "6P High Priority"
Microsoft (R) Windows Script Host Version 5.6
Copyright (C) Microsoft Corporation 1996-2001. All rights reserved.


Job id 2
Printer 6P High Priority
Document test.txt - Notepad
Data type NT EMF 1.008
Driver name HP LaserJet 6P
Description 6P High Priority, 2
Machine name \\SERVER01
Notify admin01
Owner admin01
Pages printed 0
Parameters
Size 20
Status An error is associated with the job Job is printing
Time submitted 10/13/2003 16:29:36

Number of print jobs enumerated 1

C:\WINDOWS\system32>    01
```

Figure 8-14   Viewing the contents of a print queue using PRNJOBS.VBS

14. Close all open windows.

For more information on using the PRNMNGR.VBS and PRNJOBS.VBS scripts to manage printers from the command line, see their associated topics in the Windows Server 2003 Help and Support Center.

NOTE

Certification Objectives

Objectives for Microsoft Exam #70-290: Managing and Maintaining a Microsoft Windows Server 2003 Environment:

- Troubleshoot print queues.

- Monitor print queues.

REVIEW QUESTIONS

1. In order to use both the PRNMNGR.VBS and PRNJOBS.VBS scripts, an administrator should be within the \WINDOWS\ _____ directory at the command line.

2. Which of the following commands must be issued at the beginning of the PRNMNGR.VBS command in order for it to function correctly?

   a. Cscript

   b. Script

   c. Wscript

   d. Batch

3. Which of the following switches will display a list of all printers configured on the local computer when used in conjunction with the cscript prnmngr vbs command?

   a. –A

   b. –L

   c. –S

   d. –List

4. Which of the following commands will display the command line help associated with the PRNJOBS.VBS script?

   a. Cscript prnjobs.vbs

   b. Cscript prnjobs.vbs –help

   c. Cscript prnjobs.vbs –a

   d. Cscript prnjobs.vbs –h

5. The PRNJOBS.VBS and PRNMNGR.VBS scripts both rely on which of the following in order to be properly executed from the command line?

   a. The Windows installer service

   b. The Windows script host

   c. The Windows printer host

   d. The Windows diagnostics host

8

9

IMPLEMENTING AND USING GROUP POLICY

Labs included in this chapter:

♦ Lab 9.1 Configuring System Service Settings Using Group Policy

♦ Lab 9.2 Configuring Folder Redirection Settings Using Group Policy

♦ Lab 9.3 Determining Group Policy Settings Using GPRESULT

♦ Lab 9.4 Assigning an Application to Computers Using Group Policy

♦ Lab 9.5 Configuring Group Policy Software Removal

Lab 9.1 Configuring System Service Settings Using Group Policy

Objective

The goal of this lab is to learn how system service settings can be configured for computers using Group Policy. In this lab, you will configure system service settings in a Group Policy object applied at the domain level.

Materials Required

This lab will require the following:

- Windows Server 2003 installed and configured according to the instructions at the beginning of this lab manual

Estimated completion time: **10 minutes**

Activity Background

The ability to control how services are configured on domain computers is an important and powerful capability of Group Policy. For example, an administrator might decide to reduce the risk of junior administrators, unknowingly or accidentally enabling the services that might represent a potential security threat by disabling these services via policy settings. Once complete, these settings would be applied to all computers that fall under the scope of the Group Policy object.

Activity

1. If necessary, log on to your domain using your **AdminXX** account (where *XX* is your assigned student number). Click **Start**, select **Administrative Tools**, and then click **Active Directory Users and Computers**.

2. Right-click the **DomainXX.Dovercorp.net** icon (where *XX* is your assigned student number) and click **Properties**.

3. Click the **Group Policy** tab. Click **New** and then name the new policy **Service Restrictions**. Once complete, click the **Edit** button.

4. In the Computer Configuration section, click the **plus sign (+)** next to Windows Settings to expand it. Click the **plus sign (+)** next to Security Settings to expand it.

5. Click the **System Services** node to view its contents (as shown in Figure 9-1).

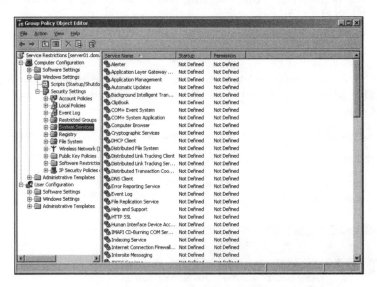

Figure 9-1   The System Services node of a Group Policy object

6. Right-click **ClipBook** and click **Properties**.

7. Check the **Define this policy setting** check box, and ensure that **Disabled** is selected (as shown in Figure 9-2).

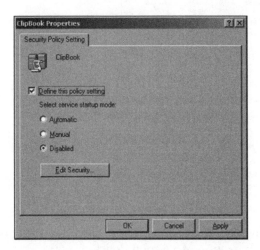

Figure 9-2   Configuring the properties of the ClipBook service in a Group Policy object

8. Click the **Edit Security** button, and review the security settings assigned to the Administrators group. These permissions control how administrators can interact with this service after the policy settings are applied. Click **OK**. Click **OK** to close the ClipBook Properties window.

9. Right-click **Routing and Remote Access** and click **Properties**.

10. Check the **Define this policy setting** check box, ensure that **Disabled** is selected, and click **OK**.

11. Close the Group Policy Object Editor window. In the DomainXX.Dover-corp.net Properties window, click the **Options** button.

12. In the Service Restrictions Options window, check the **No Override** check box. This will stop policies applied after this one from overriding the settings in this policy. Click **OK**.

13. Click **Close** and then close the Active Directory Users and Computers window.

14. Restart your server. Once complete, log on using your **AdminXX** account.

15. Click **Start**, select **Administrative Tools**, and then click **Services**. The Services console is shown in Figure 9-3.

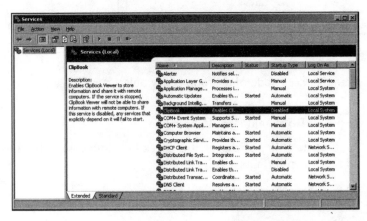

Figure 9-3   Viewing service settings after the application of a Group Policy object

16. Review the Startup Type column settings for both the ClipBook and Routing and Remote Access Service services, confirming that they are both now set to Disabled.

17. Close all open windows.

Review Questions

1. Service configuration settings are found under which of the following nodes of the Computer Configuration section of a Group Policy object?

   a. Computer Configuration > Windows Settings > Security Settings

   b. User Configuration > Windows Settings > Security Settings

   c. Computer Configuration > Administrative Templates

   d. User Configuration > Administrative Templates

2. True or False? Service settings cannot be configured in the User Configuration section of Group Policy.

3. System Service settings can be configured in Group Policy objects applied to which of the following? (Choose all that apply.)

 a. Local computer

 b. Domain

 c. Site

 d. OU

4. To configure service security settings using Group Policy, click the _____ button after defining the policy setting.

5. True or False? When Group Policy settings are applied at the site level with the No Override option, they cannot be overridden at the domain or OU level.

LAB 9.2 CONFIGURING FOLDER REDIRECTION SETTINGS USING GROUP POLICY

Objective

The goal of this lab activity is to learn how the location of local folders, such as My Documents, can be redirected through the use of Group Policy settings.

Materials Required

This lab will require the following:

- Windows Server 2003 installed and configured according to the instructions at the beginning of this lab manual

Estimated completion time: **10 minutes**

Activity Background

Redirecting user folders provides an excellent way to ensure that all user data files are saved to a server location, rather than on the local computer. Ultimately, this makes it easier for administrators to back up user data files without the need to worry that users may be saving them on local systems, which may not be backed up regularly.

ACTIVITY

Activity

1. If necessary, log on to your domain using your **AdminXX** account (where *XX* is your assigned student number). Click **Start** and then click **My Computer**.

2. Open drive **D:**, and create a new folder named **Shared2**.

3. Right-click the **Shared2** folder and click **Properties**. Click the **Sharing** tab, click the **Share this folder** option button, and then click **OK**. Close My Computer.

4. Click **Start**, select **Administrative Tools**, and then click **Active Directory Users and Computers**.

5. Right-click the **Marketing** OU and click **Properties**.

6. Click the **Group Policy** tab, click **New**, and name the new policy **Folder Redirection**.

7. Ensure that the **Folder Redirection** policy is selected and then click **Edit**.

8. Under User Configuration, click the **plus signs (+)** next to Windows Settings and then Folder Redirection to expand them (as shown in Figure 9-4).

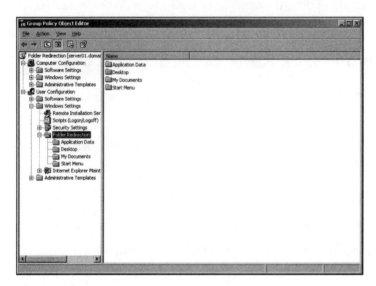

Figure 9-4   The Folder Redirection node of a Group Policy object

9. Right-click **My Documents** and click **Properties**.

10. In the Setting list box, click **Basic – Redirect everyone's folder to the same location** (as shown in Figure 9–5).

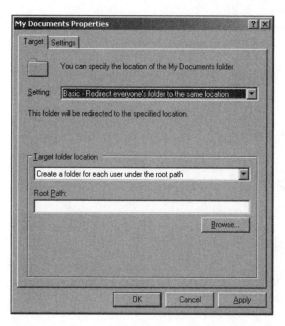

Figure 9-5 Configuring Folder Redirection settings

11. In the Root Path text box, type **\\serverXX\shared2** (where *XX* is your assigned student number). Note the full path to which user folders will be redirected at the bottom of the window, and click **OK**.

12. Close the **Group Policy Object Editor** window, as well as the Properties of the Marketing OU.

13. Close **Active Directory Users and Computers** and then reboot.

14. Log on as user **jhsmith** using the password **Password01**.

15. Click **Start**, select **All Programs**, select **Accessories**, and then click **Windows Explorer**.

16. Right-click the **My Documents** folder and then click **Properties**. Verify that the Target folder location for the user jhsmith now points to \\serverXX\shared2\jhsmith\My Documents (where *XX* is your assigned student number).

17. Close all open windows.

REVIEW QUESTIONS

1. Once folder redirection is implemented for a user's My Documents folder, any documents saved to that folder will ultimately be saved to which of the following locations?

   a. C:\Documents and Settings

   b. C:\Windows

   c. \\Servername\Sharename

   d. \\Servername\c$

2. The _____ Setting option will redirect everyone's folder to the same location.

3. True or False? Folder redirection settings are located in the User Configuration section of a Group Policy object.

4. Which of the following folders can be redirected using Group Policy? (Choose all that apply.)

   a. Application Data

   b. Desktop

   c. My Documents

   d. Start Menu

5. True or False? It is not possible to remove folder redirection settings and have users go back to using local folders using Group Policy.

LAB 9.3 DETERMINING GROUP POLICY SETTINGS USING GPRESULT

Objective

The goal of this lab activity is to learn how Resultant Set of Policy (RSoP) data can be gathered by using the GPRESULT command-line utility.

Materials Required

This lab will require the following:

- Windows Server 2003 installed and configured according to the instructions at the beginning of this lab manual

Estimated completion time: **5 minutes**

Activity Background

In order to gather information on effective Group Policy settings, an administrator can use either the Resultant Set of Policy MMC snap-in or the GPRESULT tool from the command line. The GPRESULT command-line tool gives an administrator additional flexibility when the need exists to generate results from the command line. A good example would be when an administrator is remotely managing a server from within a Telnet session.

Activity

1. If necessary, log on to your domain using your **AdminXX** account (where *XX* is your assigned student number). Click **Start** and then click **Run**. In the Open text box, type **cmd** and click **OK**.

2. At the command prompt, type **gpresult /?** and press **Enter**. Review the switches associated with the gpresult command and their purposes.

3. To view the Group Policy settings applied to the Administrator user account, type **gpresult /user administrator** and press **Enter**.

4. Scroll through the output provided by the GPRESULT tool (as illustrated in Figure 9-6). Review the information provided by the gpresult command, including which policies are applied to the Administrator user account.

9

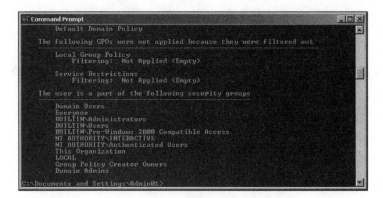

Figure 9-6 Viewing the output of the GPRESULT tool

5. Close the command prompt window.

REVIEW QUESTIONS

1. Which of the following are valid switches when using the GPRESULT command? (Choose all that apply.)

   a. /?

   b. /user

   c. /computer

   d. /system

2. Which of the following represents the correct syntax for determining the Group Policy settings applied to a user named John on the local computer using the GPRESULT command?

   a. gpresult /u:john

   b. gpresult /user john

   c. gpresult −a:john

   d. gpresult /all

3. True or False? The GPRESULT command can be used to determine the Group Policy settings that will apply to a particular user on a different computer.

4. Which of the following represents the correct syntax for determining the Group Policy settings applied to a user named John on a computer named DESKTOP3 using the GPRESULT command?

   a. gpresult /user:john /computer:desktop3

   b. gpresult /user john /s desktop3

   c. gpresult /all

   d. gpresult /c:desktop3 user:john

5. True or False? Issuing the GPRESULT command for a particular user will refresh the Group Policy settings of that user if the user is currently logged on to the network.

LAB 9.4 ASSIGNING AN APPLICATION TO COMPUTERS USING GROUP POLICY

Objective

The goal of this lab activity is to configure and view the results of assigning an application to computers using Group Policy. When assigned to a computer, software packages are installed the next time that a system is restarted.

Materials Required

This lab will require the following:

- Windows Server 2003 installed and configured according to the instructions at the beginning of this lab manual

---

Estimated completion time: **10 minutes**

Activity Background

When software applications need to be installed on multiple client or server systems, assigning the software to computers via Group Policy is often the most efficient and effective method that can be used. When assigned to a computer, software is installed the next time the system reboots and made available to all users of that computer.

Activity

1. If necessary, log on to your domain using your **AdminXX** account (where *XX* is your assigned student number).

2. Click **Start**, select **Administrative Tools**, and then click **Active Directory Users and Computers**.

3. Right-click the **DomainXX.Dovercorp.net** icon (where *XX* is your assigned student number) and then click **Properties**.

4. Click the **Group Policy** tab.

5. Click **New**, and name the new policy **Assigned Software**. Once complete, click **Edit**.

6. In the Computer Configuration section, click the **plus sign (+)** next to Software Settings.

7. Right-click the **Software Installation** icon, select **New**, and then click **Package**.

8. In the Open dialog box, type **\\serverXX\shared\suptools.msi** (where *XX* is your assigned student number) in the File name text box and click **Open**.

9

9. In the Deploy Software dialog box, ensure that the **Assigned** option button is selected (as shown in Figure 9-7) and click **OK**.

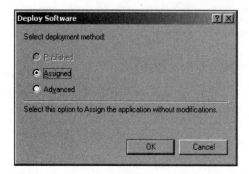

Figure 9-7   Assigning an application to computers using Group Policy

10. Close the Group Policy Object Editor window, and then click **Close** at the DomainXX.Dovercorp.net Properties window. Close Active Directory Users and Computers.

11. Reboot your server. Once complete, log on to your domain using your **AdminXX** account (where *XX* is your assigned student number).

12. Click **Start**, and select **All Programs** to confirm that the Windows Support Tools are installed and available. Once complete, continue on to the next lab activity, or log off.

REVIEW QUESTIONS

1. An application can be assigned to computers at which of the following levels? (Chose all that apply.)

   a. Site

   b. Domain

   c. OU

   d. Group

2. True or False? Applications cannot be published to computers.

3. Which of the following could be used to stop an application from being assigned to a specific computer that is part of an OU when that application is assigned via a Group Policy object applied to that OU?

   a. Block Inheritance

   b. No override

   c. Security permissions

   d. This is not possible.

4. Which of the following options are available when attempting to assign an application to computers using Group Policy?

   a. Assigned

   b. Published

   c. Advanced

   d. Simple

5. True or False? When assigning an application to computers, a UNC path (rather than a local path) must be provided in order for the application to be made available to network computers.

9

LAB 9.5 CONFIGURING GROUP POLICY SOFTWARE REMOVAL

Objective

The goal of this lab activity is to configure software removal settings for an application originally deployed using Group Policy.

Materials Required

This lab will require the following:

- Windows Server 2003 installed and configured according to the instructions at the beginning of this lab manual

Estimated completion time: **10 minutes**

Activity Background

In the same way that software can be deployed to users and computers via Group Policy, it can also be removed using Group Policy settings. This is useful in cases where an administrator wants to remove software originally deployed via Group Policy with minimal administrative intervention required.

ACTIVITY

Activity

1. If necessary, log on to your domain using your **AdminXX** account (where *XX* is your assigned student number).

2. Click **Start**, select **Administrative Tools**, and then click **Active Directory Users and Computers**. Right-click the **DomainXX.Dovercorp.net** icon (where *XX* is your assigned student number) and then click **Properties**. Click the **Group Policy** tab. Click the **Assigned Software** GPO and then click **Edit**.

3. Under Computer Configuration, click the **plus sign (+)** next to Software Settings to expand it, and click **Software installation** to view deployed packages.

4. Right-click **Windows Support Tools**, select **All Tasks**, and then click **Remove**.

5. In the Remove Software dialog box, ensure that the **Immediately uninstall the software from users and computers** option button is selected (as shown in Figure 9-8) and click **OK**.

Figure 9-8   The Remove Software dialog box

6. Close all open windows and then restart your server. During the startup process, watch for the message stating that the Windows Support Tools software is being removed.

7. Log on using your **AdminXX** account.

8. To confirm that the Windows Support Tools have been uninstalled, click **Start**, click **Control Panel**, and then click **Add or Remove Programs**. Note that the Windows Support Tools are no longer installed.

9. Close all open windows.

REVIEW QUESTIONS

1. True or False? Applications assigned using Group Policy can only be manually removed.

2. Application removal settings are configured by right-clicking on an installed package, selecting _____, and then selecting _____.

3. Which of the following are options available in the Remove Software dialog box? (Choose all that apply.)

   a. Immediately uninstall the software from users and computers.

   b. Remove software immediately.

   c. Allow users to continue to use the software, but prevent new installations.

   d. Do not allow new installations.

4. True or False? A normal user can permanently uninstall an application that was assigned to a computer.

5. True or False? When software is assigned to a computer, it is only installed if a user explicitly installs it via Add or Remove Programs in Control Panel.

9

10

ADMINISTERING A SERVER

Labs included in this chapter:

◆ Lab 10.1 Creating an MMC in Author Mode

◆ Lab 10.2 Using Remote Assistance

◆ Lab 10.3 Using the Remote Desktops MMC Snap-in

◆ Lab 10.4 Using Terminal Services Command-line Utilities

◆ Lab 10.5 Installing and Using the Remote Desktop Web Connection

Microsoft MCSE Exam #70-290 Objectives	
Objective	Lab
Manage a server by using available support tools.	10.1
Manage a server by using Remote Assistance.	10.2
Manage servers remotely.	10.3, 10.4, 10.5
Manage a server by using Terminal Services remote administration mode.	10.3, 10.4
Diagnose and resolve issues related to client access to Terminal Services.	10.4

LAB 10.1 CREATING AN MMC IN AUTHOR MODE

Objective

The goal of this lab is to learn how to create customized Microsoft Management Consoles (MMC) that can be distributed to users and administrators that only require access to limited sections of an MMC snap-in.

Materials Required

This lab will require the following:

- A Windows Server 2003 system installed and configured according to the instructions at the beginning of this lab manual

Estimated completion time: **10 minutes**

Activity Background

The tools included to administer your server can often be confusing to junior administrators and users that only perform a limited subset of the commands available. You can create consoles that limit the resources available to them. You can also save this limited console specifying that the user cannot add new snap-ins, and thereby limit what they are able to access. In this lab, you will create a console for an administrator that only needs access to the users container of the Active Directory Users and Computers MMC.

Activity

1. If necessary, log on as **AdminX** to the **DomainX** domain (where *X* is your assigned student number). Close any open windows.

2. Click **Start**. Click **Run**. Type **mmc**. Click **OK**.

3. Click **File** on the menu bar and click **Add/Remove Snap-in**.

4. In the Add/Remove Snap-in window, click **Add**. Click **Active Directory Users and Computers** and click **Add** (as shown in Figure 10-1). Click **Close**. Click **OK**.

Figure 10-1   Add Active Directory Users and Computers snap-in

10

5. Click the **plus sign [+]** next to Active Directory Users and Computers. Click the **plus sign [+]** next to DomainX.Dovercorp.net (where *X* is your assigned student number).

6. Right-click the **Users** container and click **New Window from Here** (as shown in Figure 10-2).

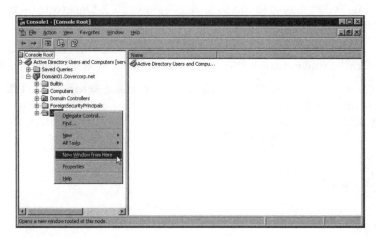

Figure 10-2   Opening new MMC window

7. In the menu bar, click **Window** and then click **Console Root**. Press **Ctrl+F4** to close that window.

8. Click **File**. Click **Options**. In the Options window, type **Users Console** in the text box. Click the **down arrow** and change the Console mode to **User mode – limited access, single window**. Click the **check box** beside Do not save changes to this console. Click **OK** (as shown in Figure 10-3).

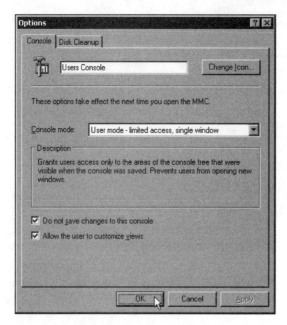

Figure 10-3   Configured console mode

9. Click **File**. Click **Save**. In the Save As window, click **Desktop** and type the file name **Users Console**. Click **Save**.

10. In the open console window, click **File** and note that you can still add snap-ins and make other changes. You are still in Author mode. Close the MMC.

11. Double-click the **Users Console.msc** file on your desktop. Click **File** and note that you no longer have the options to add snap-ins or make other changes to this MMC. This file can be distributed to the administrators that only require access to the Users container. Close Users Console.

Certification Objectives

Objectives for Microsoft Exam #70-290: Managing and Maintaining a Microsoft Windows Server 2003 Environment:

- Manage a server by using available support tools.

REVIEW QUESTIONS

1. Which Console mode are you in when you first start a Microsoft Management Console from the run box?

   a. Author mode

   b. User mode – full access

   c. User mode – limited access, multiple window

   d. User mode – limited access, single window

2. Which Console mode are you in when you first start one of the preconfigured MMC tools from the Administrative Tools menu?

   a. Author mode

   b. User mode – full access

   c. User mode – limited access, multiple window

   d. User mode – limited access, single window

3. In which Console modes are you unable to add or remove snap-ins? (Choose all that apply.)

   a. Author mode

   b. User mode – full access

   c. User mode – limited access, multiple window

   d. User mode – limited access, single window

4. True or False? You can modify the preconfigured MMC tools using a right-click on the shortcut and clicking Author.

5. Which of the following administrative tools cannot be added as a snap-in to an MMC?

   a. Active Directory Users and Computers

   b. Device Manager

   c. Licensing

   d. Services

10

Lab 10.2 Using Remote Assistance

Objective

The goal of this lab is to learn how to use Remote Assistance to access and administer a server.

Materials Required

This lab will require the following:

- Two Windows Server 2003 systems

- A lab partner

Estimated completion time: **15 minutes**

Activity Background

Implementations of Terminal services in Windows NT & 2000 had one great deficiency: they did not allow you to connect to the console session of the remote computer. Accessing the console is important because there are many third-party applications, such as print monitors and backup software, which will only deliver their messages to the console session. This forced many administrators into using third-party applications for remote control of their computers. Windows Server 2003 systems offer three new methods to access the console session of the remote server.

The first method uses the Remote Desktop Connection tool. Chapter 10 Activity 10-7 demonstrated using the Remote Desktop Connection tool from the Start Menu. When initiated from the command line, you can add the /console switch and connect to the console session of the remote computer. The full command is **MSTSC/console**. At that point, it can be used like any other Remote Desktop connection.

Labs 10.2 and 10.3 will examine the other two applications included in Windows Server 2003 to access the console remotely.

Windows Server 2003 and Windows XP include a new application called Remote Assistance (RA). Remote Assistance requires someone physically sitting at the remote server to accept your connection and give you control. Microsoft refers to this person as the Novice and the connecting person as the Expert.

Activity

The following steps are to be completed on the Novice Server:

1. If necessary, log on as **AdminX** to the **DomainX** domain (where *X* is your assigned student number). Close any open windows.

2. Enable **Remote Assistance** on your server. Click **Start**. Right-click **My Computer** and click **Properties**.

3. Click the **Remote** tab. Click **Turn on Remote Assistance and allow invitations to be sent from this computer**.

4. Click the **Advanced** button. In the Invitations section, set the maximum amount of time an invitation can remain open to **1 hour**. Click **OK**, then click **OK**.

5. To send an invitation, click **Start**. Click **Help and Support**. In the Support Tasks section, click the hyperlink called **Remote Assistance** (as shown in Figure 10-4).

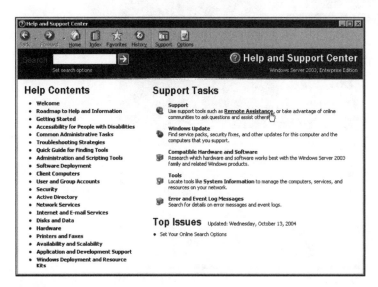

Figure 10-4 Remote Assistance link

6. Click **Invite someone to help you**. Click **Save invitation as a file (Advanced)** on the lower-right corner of the page. Read the instructions and click **Continue**. Type **testpass** in the Type password and Confirm password text boxes. Click **Save Invitation**. In the left pane of the Save As window, click **My Computer**. Double-click **Local Disk (C:)** and then click **Save**.

7. Click **View the status of all my invitations (1)**. This shows the status of outstanding invitations that have been sent. Close **Help and Support Center**.

The following steps are to be completed on the Expert Server:

1. Click **Start**. Click **Run**. Type **\\ServerYY.DomainYY.Dovercorp.net\c$** (where *YY* is your partner's student number). Click **OK**. When asked to authenticate, type **DomainYY/AdminYY** in the User name text box and your partner's password in the Password text box. Press **Enter**.

2. Double-click **RAInvitation.msrcincident**.

3. In the Password text box, type **testpass**. Click **Yes**.

4. Novice: Click **Yes** to accept the offer of remote assistance.

5. Expert: Read the text below the Chat History heading. It indicates that the status of this connection is Screen View Only. Click the **Take Control** button in the upper-left corner.

6. Novice: Click **Yes** to allow the Expert to take control of your computer (as shown in Figure 10-5).

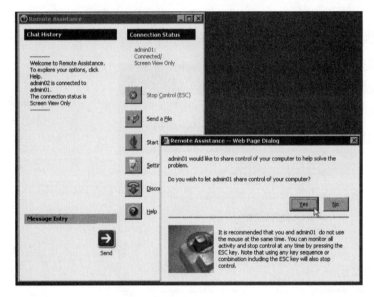

Figure 10-5   Allow remote control

7. Expert: Click **OK** to clear the Remote Assistance dialog box.

8. In your Remote Assistance window, right-click the **task bar** and click **Task Manager**. Click the **Users** tab. You are identified by the status "Shadowing" and a session of "RDP-Tcp#" followed by a number (similar to Figure 10-6). Note that all of your actions appear on your partner's console session, unlike an RDC connection. Close Task Manager.

Figure 10-6   Task Manager Users tab

9. Press **Ctrl+Alt+Delete**. Note that your own Windows Security window appears. Ctrl+Alt+Delete will not work on a remote session. Click **Cancel**.

10. Press **Ctrl+Alt+End**. That brings up your partner's Windows Security window just as if you had pressed Ctrl+Alt+Delete while physically at the server. Click **Cancel**.

11. Press **Esc** to release control of your partner's computer. Click **OK**.

12. Click **Disconnect**. Close all open windows.

13. Novice: Click **OK**. Close **Remote Assistance**.

Certification Objectives

Objectives for Microsoft Exam #70-290: Managing and Maintaining a Microsoft Windows Server 2003 Environment:

■ Manage a server by using Remote Assistance.

REVIEW QUESTIONS

1. Remote Assistance invitations can be sent using which of the following methods? (Choose all that apply.)

   a. Windows Messenger

   b. E-mail

   c. Saved to a file

   d. Internet Explorer

2. Remote Assistance is included in which operating systems? (Choose all that apply.)

   a. Windows 95

   b. Windows XP Home

   c. Windows Server 2003

   d. Windows XP Pro

3. What user rights does the Expert have on the remote computer during a Remote Assistance session?

   a. Local Administrator

   b. The user rights of the logged on user that accepted the connection

   c. Guest

   d. Domain User

4. How many consecutive times can the Expert connect to the Novice computer on one invitation?

   a. Once

   b. Twice

   c. Sixteen

   d. Unlimited connections until the invitation expires

5. Which keyboard shortcut will open the Windows Security window on the remote computer?

   a. Ctrl+Alt+Delete

   b. Ctrl+Alt+End

   c. Ctrl+Alt+Esc

   d. Esc

Lab 10.3 Using the Remote Desktops MMC Snap-in

Objective

The goal of this lab is to learn how to configure and use the Remote Desktops MMC snap-in to connect to and administer your server.

Materials Required

This lab will require the following:

- Two Windows Server 2003 systems

- A lab partner

Estimated completion time: **15 minutes**

Activity Background

The second method to access the console of a remote Windows Server 2003 remotely is using the Remote Desktop snap-in in the Microsoft Management console. It has the additional advantage of enabling you to connect to multiple servers in one window. In this lab, you will connect to the console of your partner's server and to a new terminal session of your own server.

10

Activity

The following steps are to be completed by both partners:

1. If necessary, log on as **AdminX** to the **DomainX** domain (where *X* is your assigned student number). Close any open windows.

2. Click **Start**. Click **Run**. Type **MMC**. Click **OK**.

3. If necessary, maximize the **console root** window then maximize the **Console1** window. The remote desktop will only be as large as your open window.

4. Click **File**. Click **Add/Remove Snap-in**. Click **Add**. Scroll down and click **Remote Desktops**. Click **Add**. Click **Close**. Click **OK**.

5. Click the **Remote Desktops** folder. Right-click the **Remote Desktops** folder and click **Add new connection**.

6. In the Server name or IP address box, type **ServerXX** (where *XX* is your student number). Uncheck **Connect to console**. In the Logon information section, type your **AdminX** account and password. Type your **full domain name** in the Domain box. An example is shown in Figure 10-7. Click **OK**.

Figure 10-7 Remote Desktops connection to your server

7. Click the **plus sign [+]** next to Remote Desktops. Click **ServerXX**. Enter your password, then click **OK** to log on to a terminal session to your server.

8. Right-click the **task bar** and click **Task Manager**. Click the **Users** tab. You see two sessions, similar to Figure 10-8. Close **Task Manager**.

Figure 10-8 Sample Task Manager with one console session and one remote session

9. In the Remote Desktop session, click **Start**. Click **Log Off** and again click **Log Off**. Once your MMC window states "Disconnected from server," click the **Remote Desktops** folder in the left pane of your MMC.

The following steps are to be completed by Partner 1 only:

1. Right-click **Remote Desktops** and click **Add new connection**.

2. In the Server name or IP address box, type
ServerYY.DomainYY.Dovercorp.net (where *YY* is your partner's student
number). Confirm that Connect to console is checked. In the Logon information
section, type your partner's **AdminYY** account and password. Type your
partner's full domain name in the Domain box. An example is shown in Figure
10-9. Click **OK**.

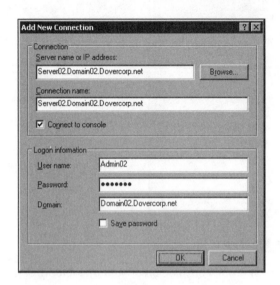

Figure 10-9   Remote Desktops console connection to partner server

3. Before you connect, make sure your partner is ready. Click
ServerYY.DomainYY.Dovercorp.net in your MMC window. When
connected, the window will be exactly as your partner left it. When you connected using the same account name, your partner's screen was locked. Only
one person may be on the console session at one time. If your partner unlocks
the computer, you will be disconnected.

4. In the remote session, right-click the **task bar** and click **Task Manager**. Click the **Users** tab. Note that only one user session exists and, even though you are effectively at the console, you are still listed as an RDP-Tcp session (similar to Figure 10-10). Close **Task Manager**.

Figure 10-10   Users tab of Task Manager with one remote session to console

5. In the left pane of your MMC window, right-click **ServerYY.DomainYY.Dovercorp.net** and click **Disconnect**. Close the **MMC** window. Click **No**.

The following steps are to be completed by Partner 2 only:

1. Do not continue until your partner has completed the steps above. Unlock your computer. Press **Ctrl+Alt+Delete**. Type your password. Press **Enter**.

2. In your MMC window, right-click **Remote Desktops** and click **Add new connection**.

10

3. In the Server name or IP address box, type
ServerYY.DomainYY.Dovercorp.net (where *YY* is your partner's student
number). Confirm that Connect to console is checked. You will log on as a
<u>different user</u> than your partner. In the Logon information section, type your
partner's **Administrator** account and password. Type your partner's **full
domain name** in the Domain box. An example is shown in Figure 10-11.
Click **OK**.

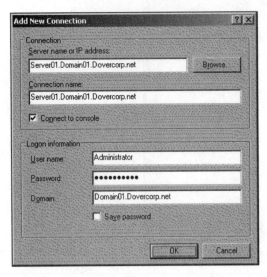

Figure 10-11 Remote Desktops console connection using Administrator account

4. Click **ServerYY.DomainYY.Dovercorp.net** in your MMC window. Read
the dialog box that appears. Only one user can use the console at one time and
you are logging in with a different user name, so your partner will be forced to
log off before you can continue. Click **Yes**.

5. Once connected, click **Start**, click **Log Off**, and again click **Log Off**. Close
the MMC window. Click **No**.

Certification Objectives

Objectives for Microsoft Exam #70-290: Managing and Maintaining a Microsoft Windows
Server 2003 Environment:

- Manage servers remotely.

- Manage a server by using Terminal Services remote administration mode.

REVIEW QUESTIONS

1. What advantage does the Remote Desktops MMC snap-in have that the Remote Desktop Connection tool does not?

   a. Multiple active remote sessions in one window

   b. Allows two users to connect to the console session simultaneously

   c. Ability to access the console session

   d. Does not require anyone to be at the remote server

2. What advantage does the Remote Desktops MMC snap-in have that Remote Assistance does not? (Choose all that apply.)

   a. Multiple active remote sessions in one window

   b. Allows two users to connect to the console session simultaneously

   c. Ability to access the console session

   d. Does not require anyone to be at the remote server

3. What will happen to a user who is logged on to the console session when you log on to the console session with the same account using the Remote Desktops MMC snap-in?

   a. They will be forced to log off.

   b. The computer will be locked.

   c. Nothing, it will not affect the console user.

   d. They will be asked to accept the connection.

4. What will happen to a user who is logged on to the console session when you log on to the console session with a different account using the Remote Desktops MMC snap-in?

   a. They will be forced to log off.

   b. The computer will be locked.

   c. Nothing, it will not affect the console user.

   d. They will be asked to accept the connection.

10

5. Which of the following statements about the Remote Desktops MMC snap-in is false?

   a. If you disconnect from an active remote session, the session will continue on the remote server.

   b. If you log off in an active remote session, the session will close on the remote server.

   c. If you close the MMC while an active remote session exists, the session will continue on the remote server.

   d. You cannot return to a disconnected session, you must start a new session.

Lab 10.4 Using Terminal Services Command-line Utilities

Objective

The goal of this lab is to learn how to use some of the command-line utilities to manage terminal server connections.

Materials Required

This lab will require the following:

- Two Windows Server 2003 systems

- Terminal Services installed as in Chapter 10 Activity 10-8

- A lab partner

Estimated completion time: **15 minutes**

Activity Background

Your server includes several useful command-line utilities to manage connections to your terminal server. As an administrator you can disconnect, log off, or join other users' sessions from the command line. You can also initiate your own connections from the command line.

Activity

The following steps are to be completed by both partners:

1. If necessary, log on as **AdminX** to the **DomainX** domain (where *X* is your assigned student number). Close any open windows.

2. Click **Start**. Click **Help and Support**. In the Search box, type **Managing terminal services from the command line**. Press **Enter**. In the Search Results pane, click **Help Topics**, then click the entry that reads **Managing Terminal Services from the command line : Terminal Services** (as shown in Figure 10-12). The help page lists all of the commands available. As time permits, read through the help page. Close **Help and Support Center**.

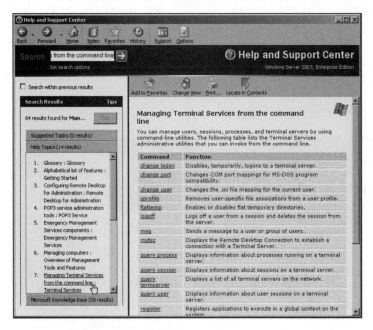

Figure 10-12   Command line help page

3. Click **Start**. Click **Administrative Tools**. Click **Active Directory Users and Computers**. If necessary, click the **plus sign [+]** next to your domain and click the **Users** container. Right-click the **AdminXX** account and click **Properties**. Click the **Remote control** tab. Click to uncheck **Require user's permission**. Click **OK**. Close the Active Directory Users and Computers window.

4. Click **Start**. Click **Administratvie Tools**. Click **Terminal Services Configuration**. Click **Server Settings** then right-click **Restrict each user to one session** and click **No**. Close the Terminal services configuration window.

5. Click **Start**. Click **Run**. Type **mstsc**. Click **OK**.

6. In the Computer text box, type **ServerYY.DomainYY.Dovercorp.net** (where *YY* is your partner's student number). Click **Options**. Type **AdminYY** in the User name text box, and type your partner's password in the Password text box. Type **DomainYY** in the Domain text box. Click the check box beside **Save my password**. Click **Save As**. Type the file name **ServerYY**. Click **Save**. Click **Connect**.

7. In the remote session to your partner's server, click **Start**. Click **Run**. Type **notepad**. Press **Enter**. Leave the connection open in the background.

8. Do not continue until your partner has a session open to your server. At your console, click **Start**. Click **Run**. Type **cmd**. Press **Enter**.

9. Type **query session**. Press **Enter**. You will see three sessions, similar to Figure 10-13. The console session has a greater than symbol [>] before it; this indicates that it is the session you are currently in. The session that has a state of Listen is not a real session. This indicates that your server is listening for connections. The third session is your partner's remote session. Make a note of the session name; it will be rdp-tcp# followed by a number. The session ID can also be used to identify the session; it is a whole number. In Figure 10-13, the session ID of the remote connection is 2.

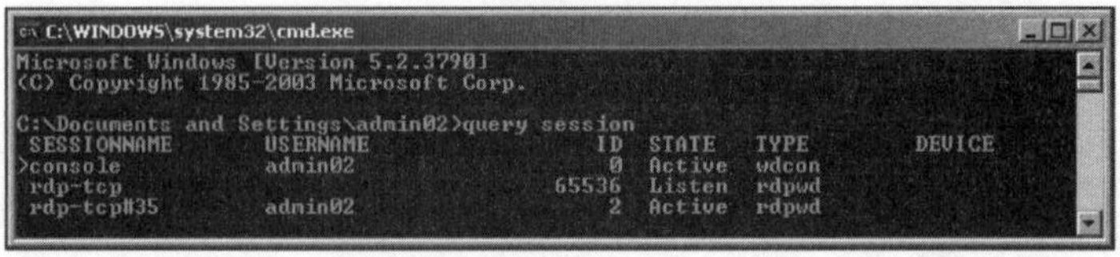

Figure 10-13   Results of query session command

10. Type **query process** *SessionName* (where *SessionName* is the name recorded in Step 8). Press **Enter**. Your results will look similar to Figure 10-14. Make a note of the session ID and the PID for notepad.exe.

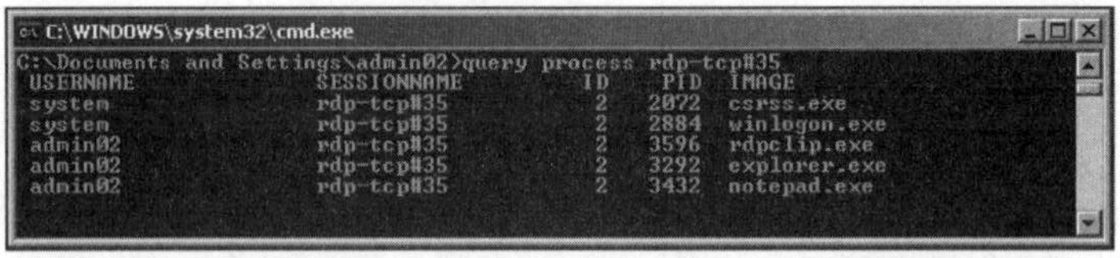

Figure 10-14   Results of query process command

11. Type **tskill** *PID* **/id:***SessionID* **/v** (where *PID* and *SessionID* are the numbers recorded in Step 9). Press **Enter**. For example, to kill the notepad.exe process shown in Figure 10-14, you would type the command shown in Figure 10-15. Note that in your partner's remote connection to your server, Notepad has been terminated.

Figure 10-15   Ending the notepad.exe process with tskill command

12. Type **query process** *SessionName* (where *SessionName* is the name recorded in Step 9) to confirm that notepad.exe is no longer present.

13. Type **msg** *SessionName* **Testing message function** (where *SessionName* is the name recorded in Step 9). Press **Enter**. Your message appears in your partner's remote connection to your server. By default, it will disappear in 60 seconds if your partner does not click **OK**.

14. In order to use the Shadow command, you must open a terminal session to your own server. The Shadow command cannot be completed from the console session. Click **Start**. Click **Run**. Type **mstsc**. Press **Enter**.

15. In the Computer text box, type **ServerXX.DomainXX.Dovercorp.net** (where *XX* is your student number). Click **Options**. Type **AdminXX** in the User name text box, and type your password in the Password text box. Type **DomainXX** in the Domain text box. Click **Save As**. Type the file name **ServerXX**. Click **Save**. Do not connect, click **Cancel**.

16. In your command prompt window, type **cd My Documents**. Press **Enter**. Type **mstsc ServerXX.rdp** (where *XX* is your student number). Press **Enter**. Type your password in the Log On to Windows screen. Click **OK**.

17. In your remote session to your own server, click **Start**. Click **Run**. Type **cmd**. Press **Enter**.

18. Type **shadow** *SessionName* (where *SessionName* is the name recorded in Step 9) as shown in Figure 10-16. Press **Enter**. You will connect to your partner's remote session with your server. While in shadowing mode, you both share control of the mouse and keyboard in this session.

10

Figure 10-16   Shadow command launches a remote desktop connection

19. In this session, click **Start**. Click **Run**. Type **cmd**. Press **Enter**. Type **query session**. Press **Enter**. Your result will be similar to Figure 10-17. The active session, which is your partner's session that you are shadowing, will be indicated by the greater than symbol [>]. Your session will now have a state of RCtrl. Type **Exit**.

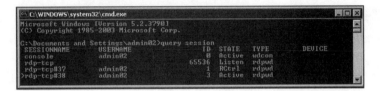

Figure 10-17   Results of query session command while shadowing

20. Right-click the **task bar** and click **Task Manager**. Click the **Users** tab. Your result will be similar to Figure 10-18. Your session has a status of Shadowing. Close Task Manager.

Figure 10-18   Users tab of the Task Manager while shadowing

21. Press **Ctrl+*** (asterisk) to stop shadowing your partner's session. You will return to your session with your server. Click **Start**. Click **Log Off** and again click **Log Off**.

22. In your console, return to your command prompt window. Type **query session**. Press **Enter**. The greater than symbol [>] will be beside the console session, which is your active session. Your partner will still be connected with the same session name as before.

23. Type **tsdiscon** *SessionName* (where *SessionName* is the name recorded in Step 8). Press **Enter**. A dialog box, shown in Figure 10-19, will appear on your partner's console. The same dialog box will appear on your console when your partner completes this step. Click **OK** to close the Remote Desktop Disconnected dialog box when it appears.

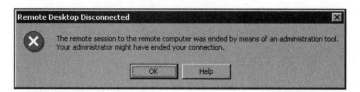

Figure 10-19   Remote Desktop Disconnected dialog box

24. In your command prompt window, type **query session**. Notice that your partner's session still exists but that the session name is blank. Anyone with the correct password for that account could reconnect to the session, and the applications would still be running.

25. You will need the numerical session ID of your partner's disconnected session to log off the session. Type **logoff** *SessionID* (for example, logoff 2). Press **Enter**. Type **query session** and press **Enter** to confirm that the session is deleted. Note that if the session hangs, you can use the "reset session *SessionID*" command to force it to delete.

26. Close all open windows.

Certification Objectives

Objectives for Microsoft Exam #70-290: Managing and Maintaining a Microsoft Windows Server 2003 Environment:

- Manage servers remotely.

- Manage a server by using Terminal Services remote administration mode.

- Diagnose and resolve issues related to client access to Terminal Services.

REVIEW QUESTIONS

1. Which command can be used from the command line to disconnect a remote session but leave it active?

    a. logoff

    b. tsdiscon

    c. tskill

    d. reset session

2. Which command can be used from the command line to end a process in a remote session?

    a. logoff

    b. tsdiscon

    c. tskill

    d. reset session

3. Which command-line utility allows you to share control of a session if the appropriate permissions are configured?

    a. RCTRL

    b. MSTSC

    c. Change logon

    d. Shadow

4. Which tab of Active Directory Users and Computers, User Properties, must be properly configured to allow you to shadow and interact with a user's active session?

    a. Terminal Services Profile

    b. Remote Control

    c. Sessions

    d. Environment

5. Which of the following commands can show you the session name and session ID of a remote session? (Choose all that apply.)

a. Query session

b. Query user

c. Query process

d. Query termserver

LAB 10.5 INSTALLING AND USING THE REMOTE DESKTOP WEB CONNECTION

Objective

The goal of this lab is to learn how to install the Remote Desktop Web Connection utility and access your server from Internet Explorer.

Materials Required

This lab will require the following:

10

- A Windows Server 2003 system installed and configured according to the instructions at the beginning of this lab manual

Estimated completion time: **20 minutes**

Activity Background

The Remote Desktop Web Connection is another useful tool that enables remote administration of your server. It is an ActiveX plug-in that is downloaded to a connecting Web browser. It allows you to connect from any computer with Microsoft Internet Explorer 5 or later (MSIE) without requiring installation of a special client application. It does not allow remote access to the console session. Note also that you do not need to install the utility on all of the servers you wish to access; one installation is enough for a single network. The utility is a component of Internet Information Server 6 (IIS), so that must also be installed in this lab.

ACTIVITY

Activity

1. If necessary, log on as **AdminX** to the **DomainX** domain (where X is your assigned student number). Close any open windows.

2. Click **Start**, click **Control Panel**, and then click **Add or Remove Programs**.

3. Click the **Add/Remove Windows Components** button.

4. At the Windows Components window, double-click **Application Server**.

5. At the Application Server window, double-click **Internet Information Services (IIS)**.

6. At the Internet Information Services (IIS) window, scroll down and double-click **World Wide Web Service**.

7. At the World Wide Web Service window, click **Remote Desktop Web Connection** and click the **check box** next to it. Additional components that are required will automatically be selected (as shown in Figure 10-20). Click **OK** three times until you are back at the Windows Components window. Click **Next**. When prompted for the Windows Server 2003 CD, enter the path to the i386 folder (D:\Source\i386), then click **OK**.

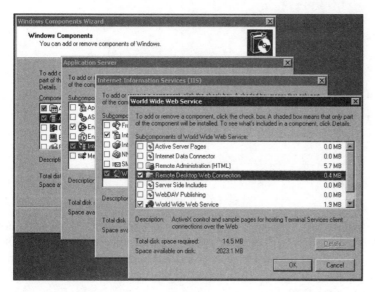

Figure 10-20   Dependencies will be installed when Remote Desktop Web Connection is selected

8. On the Completing the Windows Components Wizard page, click **Finish**.

9. Close the **Add or Remove Programs** window. Click **Start**. Click **Run**. Type **http://serverXX/tsweb** (where *XX* is your student number). Click **OK**.

10. A Security Warning window appears (as shown in Figure 10-21). Click **Yes** to install the Remote Desktop ActiveX Control.

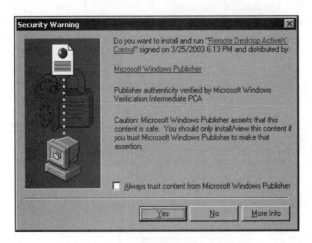

Figure 10-21   Install the ActiveX control

11. Read the Remote Desktop Web Connection page. In the Server text box, type **ServerXX**. Click the **down arrow** and change the size to **800 by 600**. Click to select the **Send logon information for this connection** check box. Type in your **AdminX** account and your **full domain name** (as shown in Figure 10-22). Click **Connect**.

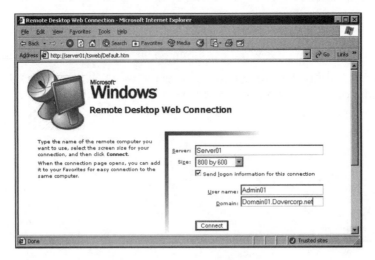

Figure 10-22   Configured Web connection

12. At the Log On to Windows screen, enter your **password** and click **OK**.

13. Once logged on to the terminal session, you can administer your server like any other terminal session. Click **Start**. Click **Log Off** and again click **Log Off**. Close the **Remote Desktop Web Connection** window.

14. Uninstall IIS in preparation for following chapters. Click **Start**. Click **Control Panel**. Click **Add or Remove Programs**.

15. Click **Add/Remove Windows Components**. Double-click **Application Server**. In the Application Server window, uncheck **Internet Information Services (IIS)**, then click **Yes** in the Setup dialog box. Click **OK**. Click **Next**. When complete, click **Finish**.

16. Close the **Add or Remove Programs** window.

Certification Objectives

Objectives for Microsoft Exam #70-290: Managing and Maintaining a Microsoft Windows Server 2003 Environment:

- Manage servers remotely.

REVIEW QUESTIONS

1. Which of the following remote administration utilities allow you to access the console session? (Choose all that apply.)

   a. Remote Desktop Connection

   b. Remote Assistance

   c. Remote Desktops MMC snap-in

   d. Remote Desktop Web Connection

2. What kind of Web component is installed at the client to use Remote Desktop Web Connection?

   a. JavaScript

   b. ActiveX

   c. Flash

   d. XML

3. Which of the following IIS services requires installation to run the Remote Desktop Web Connection utility?

   a. World Wide Web Service

   b. File Transfer Protocol (FTP) Service

   c. SMTP Service

   d. NNTP Service

10

4. What advantage does the Remote Desktop Web Connection utility have over the Remote Desktop Connection tool?

   a. Multiple active remote sessions in one window

   b. Does not require the installation of a client application

   c. Ability to access the console session

   d. Does not require anyone to be at the remote server

5. Which of the following systems can be used to access a Microsoft Terminal Server? (Choose all that apply.)

   a. Windows XP desktop system

   b. Macintosh OS X desktop system

   c. PDA running Windows Pocket PC 2002

   d. Windows 95

11

MONITORING SERVER PERFORMANCE

Labs included in this chapter:

♦ Lab 11.1 Monitoring with Task Manager

♦ Lab 11.2 Manipulating Processes with Task Manager

♦ Lab 11.3 Monitoring with the Event Log

♦ Lab 11.4 Monitoring with the System Monitor

♦ Lab 11.5 Long-term Monitoring with Performance Monitor

Microsoft MCSE Exam #70-290 Objectives	
Objective	Lab
Monitor system performance.	11.1, 11.2, 11.3, 11.4, 11.5
Monitor and optimize a server environment for application performance.	11.1, 11.2
Monitor process performance objects.	11.2
Monitor file and print servers.	11.3, 11.4, 11.5
Monitor and analyze events.	11.3
Monitor print queues.	11.4, 11.5

LAB 11.1 MONITORING WITH TASK MANAGER

Objective

The goal of this lab is to learn about Task Manager and use it to monitor running processes. After completing this lab activity, you will be able to start Task Manager using four different methods and configure Task Manager to show additional data.

Materials Required:

This lab will require the following:

- A Windows Server 2003 system installed and configured according to the instructions at the beginning of this lab manual

Estimated completion time: **10 minutes**

Activity Background

Task Manager is a useful tool to get a quick look at the current environment and performance of your server. It is always available and should be accessible even if your computer has a stalled process.

ACTIVITY

Activity

1. If necessary, log on to your domain using the **AdminXX** account (where *XX* is your assigned student number) with a password of **Password01**.

2. Close any open windows.

3. Use the following four methods to open Task Manager. Close Task Manager after each. Task Manager cannot be opened in separate instances.

   - Click **Start**. Click **Run**. Type **taskmgr** and press **Enter**.
   - Right-click on an open area of the task bar and click **Task Manager**.
   - Use keyboard shortcut **Ctrl+Alt+Delete**.
   - Use keyboard shortcut **Ctrl+Shift+Esc**.

4. Open Task Manager using one of the methods above.

5. Click the **Processes** tab. Note that Taskmgr is itself a listed process.

6. In the menu bar, click **View** and click **Select Columns**. Then select all of the columns (as shown in Figure 11-1). Click **OK**.

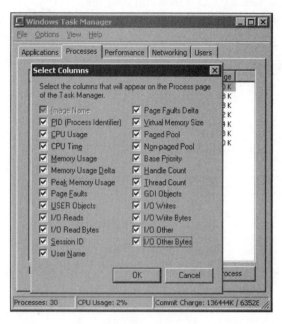

Figure 11-1 Processes column headings

7. Click the **Maximize** button to expand the Task Manager window to full size.

8. The column headings are not self-explanatory, so we need to look in the Help for explanations. Press the **F1** key to activate Help. Minimize your Task Manager window so you can see the Help window.

11

9. In the Help window, double-click **Task Manager**. Double-click **Working with processes**. Click **Process counter column headings** (as shown in Figure 11-2). Click **CPU Time** and read the description. Click **CPU Usage** and read that as well. As time permits, read through the other column descriptions. Close the Help window.

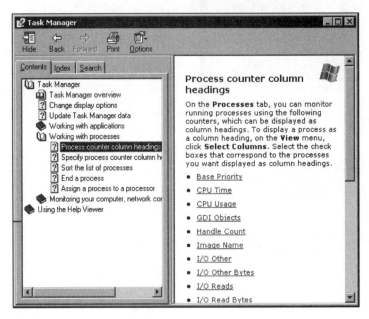

Figure 11-2   Details from Task Manager help

10. Return to Task Manager. Click the **Restore Down** button to return Task Manager to its previous size.

11. Click **View**. Click **Select Columns**. Deselect all columns except the following:

- CPU Usage

- Memory Usage

- User Name

- Base Priority

12. Click **OK** to close the Select Columns window.

13. Click the **Performance** tab.

14. Click **View**. Click **Show Kernel Times**. The specific CPU usage of Kernel Processes (core system) will be shown on your graph in red.

15. To see the effect of this on the graph, type **Alt+F**, then **N**. Type **Explorer** in the Open text box, then press **Enter**. Close the Windows Explorer window.

16. Click the **Networking** tab.

17. Click **View**. Click **Network Adapter History**. Click to turn on **Bytes Sent (Red)**.

18. Click **View**. Click **Network Adapter History**. Click to turn on **Bytes Received (Yellow)**.

19. Click **View**. Click **Select Columns**. Click **Bytes** (as shown in Figure 11-3) and then click **OK**. You may return to the Help application to determine what each column means.

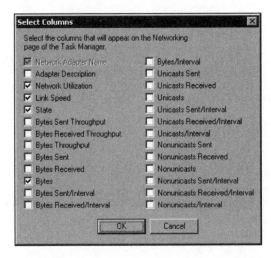

Figure 11-3   Networking columns available

11

20. In the bottom of the window, use the scroll bar to view the number of bytes that each adapter has sent/received.

21. Click **Options**. Note the options available. Click **Reset**. The graph and counters will be reset.

22. Click the **Users** tab.

23. Click **View**. Click **Select Columns**. Note that all columns are selected. Click **Cancel**.

24. Click **Options** and click **Show Full Account Name**.

25. Close Task Manager.

Certification Objectives

Objectives for Microsoft Exam #70-290: Managing and Maintaining a Microsoft Windows Server 2003 Environment:

- Monitor system performance.

- Monitor and optimize a server environment for application performance.

REVIEW QUESTIONS

1. Which of these keyboard shortcuts will open Task Manager?

   a. Ctrl+Shift+Backspace

   b. Ctrl+Alt+Delete

   c. Ctrl+Shift+Esc

   d. Ctrl+Esc

2. To monitor the number of pages currently resident in memory for a running process, you would need which column active in Task Manager?

   a. Memory Usage

   b. Memory Usage Delta

   c. Handle Count

   d. Base Priority

3. You have a nonresponsive application. Which tabs of Task Manager will be able to help you diagnose the problem? (Choose all that apply.)

   a. Applications

   b. Processes

   c. Performance

   d. Networking

   e. Users

4. How can you save Task Manager data for later analysis, or to compare performance over a year-long interval?

   a. TMArchive /plz

   b. Save to SQL server

   c. taskmgr.exe >> archive.xls

   d. None of the above. Task Manager data cannot be archived or saved.

5. Which of these networking counters will show you the current network usage of your server?

   a. State

   b. Link Utilization

   c. Network Utilization

   d. Bytes

LAB 11.2 MANIPULATING PROCESSES WITH TASK MANAGER

Objective

The goal of this lab is to change the priority of processes and end processes in Task Manager, and to investigate the function of listed processes.

Materials Required:

This lab will require the following:

- A Windows Server 2003 system installed and configured according to the instructions at the beginning of this lab manual

Estimated completion time: **10 minutes**

Activity Background

The Processes tab of Task Manager provides the most detailed information about what your server is running. It can also be used to manipulate processes at a basic level. Using Task Manager, you can start processes, stop processes, and modify the base priority of processes.

ACTIVITY

Activity

1. If necessary, log on to your domain using the **AdminXX** account (where *XX* is your assigned student number).

2. Use the keyboard shortcut **Ctrl+Shift+Esc** to open Task Manager.

3. Click the **Processes** tab.

4. Note that the Base Priority column still exists from the previous lab. The Priority for taskmgr.exe is set to High. Thus, if a process hangs that has a priority of Normal or lower, the Task Manager process should have no trouble getting processor cycles so that you can end the hung process.

5. Right-click the process **taskmgr.exe**. Click **Set Priority**. The only priority higher than High is Realtime. If you were to select this priority for taskmgr.exe, then no process could hang without you being able to end it with Task Manager. Click **Realtime**.

11

6. A warning message pops up (as shown in Figure 11-4) to tell you that this change may cause instability. If Task Manager itself were to stall or simply take up a lot of processor cycles, it could cause other core processes to fail and your computer could bluescreen. Click **No**.

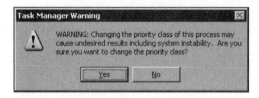

Figure 11-4   Priority change confirmation message

When working directly on a mission-critical server, it may be of benefit to lower the priority of processes that do not contribute to the server's function but still need to be completed.

7. Click **File** in the menu bar. Click **New Task (Run...)**. Type **Notepad**. Click **OK**.

8. Return to the Processes tab of Task Manager. Right-click **notepad.exe**. Click **Set Priority**. Click **BelowNormal**. Click **Yes** to the warning message.

9. With **notepad.exe** still selected, click **End Process**. Read the warning message (as shown in Figure 11-5) and click **Yes**.

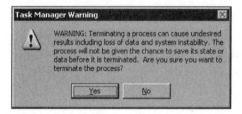

Figure 11-5   End Process confirmation message

10. An important skill in working with Task Manager is the ability to investigate what each listed process does. Note that ctfmon.exe may be in your listed processes. If it is not, press **Alt+F**, then **N**. Type **ctfmon** and press **Enter**. Minimize the Windows Task Manager window.

11. Click **Start**. Click **Search**. In the file name box, type **ctfmon.exe** and click **Search**.

12. Ctfmon.exe will show up in the right pane when it is found. Click **Stop** to stop the search. Note that the executable is in the \WINDOWS\system32 directory. That most likely means that it is part of the operating system and not an installed application.

13. Right-click **ctfmon.exe** and click **Properties**.

14. Click the **Version** tab. Note the Description. In the "Other version information" section, click through all of the item names. This hasn't revealed the executable's purpose. Click **Cancel** to close the Properties window. Close the Search Results window.

15. Click **Start**. Click **Help and Support**. In the Search box, type **ctfmon.exe** and click the **green arrow** to begin the search.

16. In the Microsoft Knowledge Base section, click the item **OFFXP: What is CTFMON And What Does It Do?** In reading the article, you can determine that the executable runs the language bar application. With this information, you can decide whether you need the application to run at all, or perhaps at a lower priority, to tune your server for performance.

17. Close all windows.

Certification Objective

Objectives for Microsoft Exam #70-290: Managing and Maintaining a Microsoft Windows Server 2003 Environment:

- Monitor system performance.

- Monitor and optimize a server environment for application performance.

- Monitor process performance objects.

11

REVIEW QUESTIONS

1. There is a critical task (priority Normal) that needs to be completed. Which of the following would be the most effective step you could take to provide more resources while maintaining system stability?

   a. Use the Services MMC to stop all other running processes.

   b. Using Task Manager, increase the priority to AboveNormal.

   c. Using Task Manager, increase the priority to Realtime.

   d. Using Task Manager, decrease the priority of all other processes to BelowNormal.

2. The server has a hung process (xyz.exe), and the mouse doesn't work. Which of the following sets of keystrokes will allow you to end the process?

a. Ctrl+Alt+Delete. Arrow key to Task Manager button. Enter. Alt+Tab to Processes tab. Tab to processes list. Down arrow to xyz.exe. Shift+E to end process. Enter to confirm.

b. Ctrl+Esc. Arrow Key to Run. Type taskmgr. Enter. Ctrl+Tab to Processes tab. Tab to processes list. Down arrow to xyz.exe. Ctrl+E to end process. Enter to confirm.

c. Ctrl+Shift+Esc. Ctrl+Tab to Processes tab. Tab to processes list. Down arrow to xyz.exe. Alt+E to end process. Enter to confirm.

d. Ctrl+Esc. Arrow Key to Run. Type net stop xyz.exe. Enter.

3. From which tab can you start a new task?

a. Processes

b. Users

c. Performance

d. From all tabs using File menu

4. True or False? The only critical processes are those associated with the user "SYSTEM."

5. Which of the following is not a valid priority?

a. Lowest

b. Normal

c. Realtime

d. AboveNormal

LAB 11.3 MONITORING WITH THE EVENT LOG

Objective

The goal of this lab is to learn how to monitor and manipulate events that are tracked in the event log. After completing this lab activity, you will be able to view events in the event log and filter and save events.

Materials Required:

This lab will require the following:

- A Windows Server 2003 system installed and configured according to the instructions at the beginning of this lab manual

Estimated completion time: **15 minutes**

Activity Background

The event log has the advantage of being always available to you. After a server has experienced any sort of failure, the event log should be the first place an administrator should look to begin troubleshooting. The Event Viewer is quite flexible in the type of events it can log and the way it can filter and present events, but its ability to manipulate events is limited and entries cannot be edited or removed individually.

ACTIVITY

Activity

1. If necessary, log on to your domain using the **AdminXX** account (where *XX* is your assigned student number).

2. We are going to log printer events. First, it will be necessary to install a test printer. Click **Start**. Click **Printers and Faxes**.

3. Click **File**. Click **Add Printer**.

4. In the Welcome to the Add Printer Wizard, click **Next**.

5. Accept the default **Local printer** option. Deselect **Automatically detect and install my Plug and Play printer**. Click **Next**.

6. Select **Create a new port**. Click **Next**. In the Enter a port name text box, type **NUL**. Click **OK**.

7. In the left pane, select the manufacturer **Generic**. In the right pane, select the printer **Generic/Text Only**. Click **Next**.

8. Name the printer **Generic**. Click **Next**.

9. Set the share name to **Generic**. Click **Next**.

10. Click **Next** to leave the Location and Comment fields blank.

11. Select **Yes** to print a test page. Click **Next**.

12. Confirm your settings and click **Finish**. Click **OK** in the Generic dialog box. Close the Printers and Faxes window.

13. Click **Start**. Click **Administrative Tools**. Click **Event Viewer**.

11

14. Click the **System** event log. Note the Print events. Double-click to open the top Print event. If necessary, click the **down arrow** to find the event with Event ID 10 that indicates the test page printed successfully (as shown in Figure 11-6).

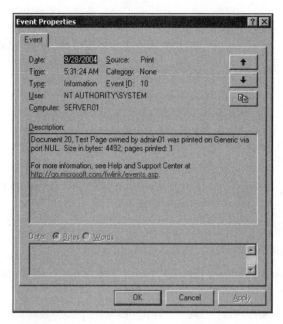

Figure 11-6   Example of a successful print event

15. Click **OK** to close the event.

16. Click **Start**. Click **Run**. Type **cmd** and press **Enter**. A command prompt window starts at C:\Documents and Settings\AdminXX\.

17. Type **dir >> test.txt**. Press **Enter**.

18. Type **print /d:\\serverXX\Generic test.txt** (where *XX* is your assigned student number). Press **Enter**.

19. Return to your event viewer window and press **F5** to refresh. Double-click the **top Printer event** with ID 10. Click **OK** to close the event.

20. In the left pane, right-click the **System** log and click **New Log View**.

21. Right-click **System(2)** and click **Rename**. Rename the log to **Print Log** and press **Enter**.

22. Right-click **Print Log** and click **Properties**. Click the **Filter** tab. Use the drop-down box labeled **Event source** and click **Print**. Click **OK** to see the filtered results.

23. Return to your command prompt window. Use the **up arrow** to recall the last print command and press **Enter**. Type **exit**, then press **Enter** to close the command prompt window.

24. Return to your event log and click the **Print Log** window. Click the **Refresh** button or press **F5**. Note that there is a new event. This event log is configured to show only print events; however, all events are still in the System log.

25. Right-click **Print Log** and click **Export List**. Confirm that the log will be saved in the My Documents folder. In the File name box, type **printlog** and click **Save**.

26. Click **Start**. Click **Windows Explorer**. Click **My Documents**. Double-click **printlog.txt**. Note that only the filtered results were saved to the file. This file can be imported into any database or spreadsheet program for detailed, long-term analysis.

27. Close all windows.

Certification Objectives

Objectives for Microsoft Exam #70-290: Managing and Maintaining a Microsoft Windows Server 2003 Environment:

- Monitor system performance.

- Monitor file and print servers.

- Monitor and analyze events.

11

REVIEW QUESTIONS

1. What is the default action the event viewer takes when the maximum log size is reached?

   a. Overwrite events as needed

   b. Overwrite events older than 7 days

   c. Overwrite events older than 30 days

   d. Do not overwrite events (clear log manually)

2. True or False? Individual events can be deleted within the event log.

3. True or False? Individual events can be copied and then pasted into a text editor.

4. Which of the following logs cannot be cleared without leaving an event that indicates who cleared it?

   a. Application

   b. Security

   c. System

   d. Directory Service

   e. File Replication Service

5. True or False? Log Views can be saved between sessions.

LAB 11.4 MONITORING WITH THE SYSTEM MONITOR

Objective

The goal of this lab is to learn how to monitor performance counters using the System Monitor. After completing this lab activity, you will be able to configure the System Monitor to chart print queue performance counters and understand the relative value of the Graph, Histogram, and Report views.

Materials Required:

This lab will require the following:

- A Windows Server 2003 system installed and configured according to the instructions at the beginning of this lab manual

- A generic printer configured according to lab 11.3

Estimated completion time: **15 minutes**

Activity Background

The System Monitor has a number of options available for the presentation of data, whether captured previously or captured live.

ACTIVITY

Activity

1. If necessary, log on to your domain using the **AdminXX** account (where *XX* is your assigned student number).

2. Click **Start**. Click **Administrative Tools**. Click **Performance**.

3. The System Monitor starts with three counters by default to give you an immediate snapshot of the server. Click the **New Counter Set** icon to clear the default counters.

4. Right-click the **chart display** and click **Properties**. In the Data tab, click **Add** to open the Add Counters window.

5. Using the Performance object drop-down box, click **Print Queue**. In the Select counters from list box, verify that **Jobs** is selected. Click **Explain** for details on the counter. In the Select instances from list box, select **Generic**. Click **Add**.

6. In the Select counters from list box, click **Jobs Spooling**. Hold **Ctrl** and click **Bytes Printed/sec**, **Max. Jobs Spooling**, and **Total Jobs Printed**. Click **Add** (see Figure 11-7). Click **Close**. Click **Apply**.

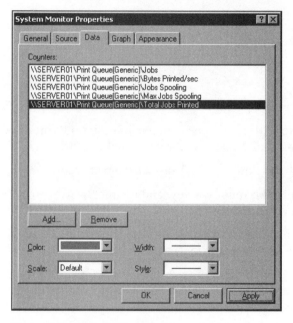

Figure 11-7   Added counters

7. Click the **Graph** tab. In the vertical scale section, enter **10** as the Maximum. Click **OK**.

8. Click **Start**. Click **Run**. Type **cmd** and press **Enter**. A command prompt window starts at C:\Documents and Settings\AdminXX\.

9. Type **dir \ /s >> test2.txt**. Press **Enter**. It will take a moment to complete.

10. Type **Notepad prntest.bat** and press **Enter**. Notepad will open and ask if you wish to create the file. Click **Yes**.

11. Type **print /d:\\serverXX\Generic test2.txt** (where *xx* is your assigned student number). Copy that line and paste it on the next line until you have 10 identical commands, one per line (as shown in Figure 11-8). Close Notepad. Click **Yes** to save.

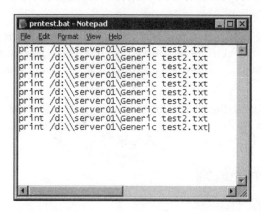

Figure 11-8   prntest.bat

12. Return to your command prompt window. Type **prntest** and press **Enter**.

13. Return to your System Monitor. The counters Jobs, Bytes Printed/sec, and Jobs Spooling produced data that is well represented in a chart.

14. Change your view by clicking on the **View Histogram** icon.

15. Return to the command prompt window and use the up arrow to recall the prntest command. Press **Enter**.

16. Return to the System Monitor. The Histogram is best used for cumulative counters like Max. Jobs Spooling and Total Jobs Printed.

17. Set your view to **Report** and run the test once more. Once again, this view is most useful when either the activity is continuous or it is displaying cumulative or averaged counters.

18. Click the **View Log Data** icon. Click the **General** tab. Notice in the Report and histogram data section that Default is selected. The default is to show current data. Click **Average** (as shown in Figure 11-9). Click **OK**.

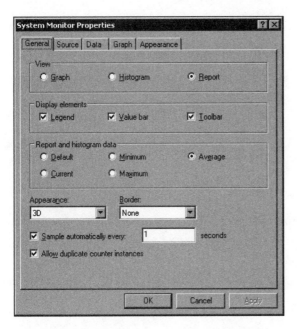

Figure 11-9   System Monitor General tab

19. Run the test a few more times and notice the effect on the data shown in the Report and Histogram views. While the noncumulative counters are represented in a more useful way, the cumulative counters are now inaccurate as they are averaged as well.

20. Close all windows.

Certification Objectives

Objectives for Microsoft Exam #70-290: Managing and Maintaining a Microsoft Windows Server 2003 Environment:

- Monitor system performance.

- Monitor file and print servers.

- Monitor print queues.

REVIEW QUESTIONS

1. Which view is most effective to show counters that are not cumulative or averaged?

   a. Graph

   b. Histogram

   c. Report

2. True or False? Clear Display clears all counters back to zero.

3. In the System Monitor, multiple performance objects of the same type are referred to as a:

   a. Performance object

   b. Performance counter

   c. Performance object instance

   d. Duplicate object

4. What is the best way to view cumulative, averaged, and current data in the System Monitor simultaneously?

   a. Graph view

   b. Histogram with Average selected on the General tab

   c. Report with Average selected on the General tab

   d. In separate System Monitor windows

5. Which of the following indicate that there is a problem? (Choose all that apply.)

   a. Memory – Pages/sec = Average 1.8

   b. Processor – % Interrupt Time = Current 11%

   c. Processor – % Processor Time = Current 100%

   d. Logical Disk – Avg Disk Queue Length = Average 27.2

LAB 11.5 LONG-TERM MONITORING WITH PERFORMANCE MONITOR

Objective

The goal of this lab is to learn how to use the Performance Monitor to set up long-term logging of essential services. After completing this lab activity, you will be able to use counter logs to monitor servers over the long term.

Materials Required:

This lab will require the following:

- A Windows Server 2003 system installed and configured according to the instructions at the beginning of this lab manual

Estimated completion time: **10 minutes**

Activity Background

A key function of the System Administrator is to anticipate and respond to issues before users become aware of them. Monitoring performance means very little if you have nothing to compare it to. An administrator should set focused performance logs to run for months and archive them to a central location to compare performance over time.

Activity

ACTIVITY

1. If necessary, log on to your domain using the **AdminXX** account (where *XX* is your assigned student number) with the password **Password01**.

2. Click **Start**. Click **Administrative Tools**. Click **Performance**.

3. Double-click **Performance logs and Alerts**.

4. Click **Counter Logs**.

5. Right-click **Counter Logs** and click **New Log Settings**.

6. In the New Log Settings box, type **Print ServerXX** (where *XX* is your student number). Click **OK**.

7. Click **Add Objects**. Click **Print Queue**. Click **Add**. Click **Close**.

8. Click the **Log Files** tab.

9. Confirm that the **Binary File type** is selected and click **Configure**. In the Log file size section, click **Limit of** and type **100**. Click **OK**.

10. Click the **Schedule** tab.

11. In the Stop log section, click **When the 100-MB log file is full**. Click the **Start a new log file** check box. Click **OK**.

12. The log begins immediately.

13. Check that the service is set to start automatically. Click **Start**. Click **Administrative Tools**. Click **Services**. Scroll down to Performance Logs and Alerts and check that it is set to run automatically, so that your log will resume after a reboot.

11

14. As we don't really want it to log in this test environment, return to your counter log, right-click **Print ServerXX**, and select **Stop**. Click **Yes** in the confirmation dialog box.

15. Close all windows.

Certification Objectives

Objectives for Microsoft Exam #70-290: Managing and Maintaining a Microsoft Windows Server 2003 Environment:

- Monitor system performance.

- Monitor file and print servers.

- Monitor print queues.

REVIEW QUESTIONS

1. Long-term logging is best accomplished with which of the following?

   a. System Monitor

   b. Trace logs

   c. Counter logs

   d. Task Manager

2. Which log file types overwrite themselves when full?

   a. Binary file

   b. Text file (comma delimited)

   c. Text file (tab delimited)

   d. Binary circular file

3. With which configured startup type would a counter log resume logging following a reboot?

   a. Disabled

   b. Immediate

   c. Automatic

   d. Manual

4. Which of the following services need to be running for Alerts to function? (Choose all that apply.)

    a. Performance Logs and Alerts

    b. Alerter

    c. Messenger

    d. Event log

5. You suspect that there is a memory leak in one of the new applications running on your server. You don't want to use processor cycles and disk writes unnecessarily. Which type of monitoring would most effectively address your needs?

    a. Application event log

    b. A triggered Alert

    c. A triggered trace log

    d. A counter log

11

12

MANAGING AND IMPLEMENTING BACKUPS AND DISASTER RECOVERY

Labs included in this chapter:

- ◆ Lab 12.1 Incremental and Differential Backups
- ◆ Lab 12.2 Incremental and Differential Restore
- ◆ Lab 12.3 Configuring a Backup Schedule
- ◆ Lab 12.4 Preparing for Automated System Recovery
- ◆ Lab 12.5 Using the Boot Logging Feature

Microsoft MCSE Exam #70-290 Objectives	
Objective	Lab
Manage backup procedures.	12.1
Restore backup data.	12.2
Schedule backup jobs.	12.3
Implement Automated System Recovery (ASR).	12.4
Monitor server hardware.	12.5

LAB 12.1 INCREMENTAL AND DIFFERENTIAL BACKUPS

Objectives

The goal of this lab is to learn how to perform incremental and differential backups.

Materials Required

This lab will require the following:

- A Windows Server 2003 system installed and configured according to instructions at the beginning of this lab manual

Estimated completion time: **15 minutes**

Activity Background

The three main backup types are normal (more commonly known as a full backup), incremental, and differential. Normal backups save all files. Incremental backups save all files that have changed since the last normal or incremental backup. Differential backups save all files that have changed since the last normal or incremental backup, even if there have been other differential backups. To implement an efficient backup routine, an administrator must be able to understand and perform each backup type.

ACTIVITY

Activity

1. If necessary, log on to your domain using the **AdminXX** account (where *XX* is your assigned student number). Close any open windows.

2. Click **Start**. Click **Run**. Type **cmd** and click **OK**.

3. At the command prompt, type **d:** and press **Enter**. Type **mkdir Backup\Data** and press **Enter**. Type **cd backup\data** and press **Enter**. Type **notepad text1.txt** and press **Enter**.

4. When prompted by Notepad to create the file, click **Yes**. In Notepad, type **Full backup test**. Click **File**. Click **Exit**. Click **Yes** to save the file. Minimize the command prompt window.

5. Click **Start**. Click **Run**. Enter **ntbackup** and press **Enter**. Click **Next** to start the wizard. Click **Next** to select the default, Back up files and settings. Click the **Let me choose what to back up** option button. Click **Next**.

6. Click the **plus sign [+]** next to My Computer. Click the **plus sign [+]** next to Local Disk [D:]. Click the **plus sign [+]** next to Backup. Click the **check box** next to the Data folder (as shown in Figure 12-1). Click **Next**.

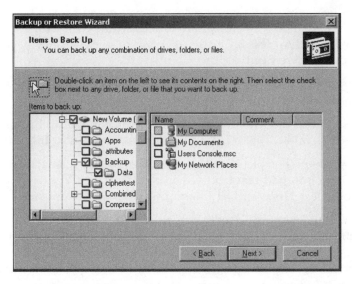

Figure 12-1   Selecting the Data folder

7. Click **Browse** to choose a location to save your backup.

8. In the File name box, type **d:\Backup\Normal.bkf**. Click **Save**. Click **Next** to continue the wizard. Click **Advanced**.

9. Make certain that the backup type is set to Normal, and click **Next**. Click **Next** to accept the defaults. Click **Next** to append the data. Click **Next** to run the job now. Click **Finish**.

10. When the backup is complete, click **Close**.

11. Return to the command prompt window. Type **notepad text2.txt** and press **Enter**. When prompted by Notepad to create the file, click **Yes**. Type **Incremental backup test 1**. Click **File**. Click **Exit**. Click **Yes** to save the file.

12. In the command prompt window, type **ntbackup** and press **Enter**. Minimize the command prompt window.

13. Click **Next** to start the wizard. Click **Next** to select the default, Back up files and settings. Click the **Let me choose what to back up** option button. Click **Next**. As shown in Figure 12-1, place a check mark next to the Data folder. Click **Next**.

14. In the Type a name for this backup box, type **Incremental1**. Click **Next** to continue the wizard. Click **Advanced**.

12

15. Using the drop-down box, change the backup type to **Incremental**. Keep clicking **Next** to accept all the defaults. Click **Finish** to begin the backup. When the backup is complete, click **Close**.

16. Return to the command prompt window. Type **notepad text3.txt** and press **Enter**. When prompted by Notepad to create the file, click **Yes**. Type **Incremental backup test 2**. Use the keyboard to save and close the file. Press **ALT+F**, then **X**. Press **Enter**.

17. In the command prompt window, type **ntbackup** and press **Enter**. Minimize the command prompt window.

18. Click **Next** to start the wizard. Use the same settings as the last Incremental backup, except, in the Type a name for this backup box, type **Incremental2**.

19. Once the backup is completed and closed, return to the command prompt window. Type **notepad text4.txt** and press **Enter**. Click **Yes** to create a new file. Enter the text **Differential1 backup test**. Save and close the file.

20. Type **ntbackup** and press **Enter**. Click **Next** to start the wizard. Click **Next** to select the default, Back up files and settings. Click the **Let me choose what to back up** option button. Click **Next**. Click the **plus sign [+]** next to My Computer. Click the **plus sign [+]** next to Local Disk [D:]. Click the **plus sign [+]** next to Backup.

21. Click the **check box** next to the Data folder. Click **Next**. Name the backup **Differential1** and click **Next**. Click **Advanced**.

22. Select the backup type **Differential**. Click through to the finish and start the backup. Once the differential backup has completed, click **Close**.

23. Return to the command prompt window. Type **notepad text5.txt** and press **Enter**. Click **Yes** to create a new file. Type the text **Differential2 backup test**. Save and close the file.

24. Type **ntbackup** and press **Enter**. Use the same settings as the differential backup above, except name the backup **Differential2**. Once completed (as shown in Figure 12-2), close the backup window.

Figure 12-2 Completed differential backup

25. Return to the command prompt window. Type **cd..** and press **Enter**. At the D:\Backup> prompt, type **dir** and press **Enter**. Note the five backup files you have created. Close the command prompt window.

Certification Objectives

Objectives for Microsoft Exam #70-290: Managing and Maintaining a Microsoft Windows Server 2003 Environment:

- Manage backup procedures.

12

REVIEW QUESTIONS

1. What is the extension for a backup file?

a. .dbf

b. .bkf

c. .bak

d. .bks

2. Which of the following weekly backup routines is likely to use the least storage space?

   a. Mon:Normal; Tues:Normal; Wed:Normal; Thurs:Normal; Fri:Normal

   b. Mon:Normal; Tues:Diff; Wed:Diff; Thurs:Diff; Fri:Diff

   c. Mon:Normal; Tues:Diff; Wed:Diff; Thurs:Inc; Fri:Inc

   d. Mon:Normal; Tues:Inc; Wed:Inc; Thurs:Inc; Fri:Inc

3. Which of the following weekly backup routines would be most convenient if you had to restore files deleted after the Friday backup?

   a. Mon:Normal; Tues:Normal; Wed:Normal; Thurs:Normal; Fri:Normal

   b. Mon:Normal; Tues:Diff; Wed:Diff; Thurs:Diff; Fri:Diff

   c. Mon:Normal; Tues:Diff; Wed:Diff; Thurs:Inc; Fri:Inc

   d. Mon:Normal; Tues:Inc; Wed:Inc; Thurs:Inc; Fri:Inc

4. What is the minimum right a user needs to back up a file?

   a. Read

   b. Read and Execute

   c. Modify

   d. Full Control

5. Which backup types would be suitable for a one-time backup of a file or directory? (Choose all that apply.)

   a. Normal

   b. Incremental

   c. Differential

   d. Daily

   e. Copy

LAB 12.2 INCREMENTAL AND DIFFERENTIAL RESTORE

Objectives

The goal of this lab is to learn how to restore incremental and differential backups.

Materials Required:

This lab will require the following:

■ A Windows Server 2003 system installed and configured according to the instructions at the beginning of this lab manual

Estimated completion time:**10 minutes**

Activity Background

Incremental backups build upon one another. In order to restore an incremental backup, you may have to restore the last full backup, and then every incremental backup in the order they were created. Differential backups are not impacted by any previous ones. In order to restore a differential backup, you will have to restore the most recent normal backup, and then only the most recent differential backup.

ACTIVITY

Activity

1. If necessary, log on to your domain using the **AdminXX** account (where *XX* is your assigned student number).

2. Click **Start**. Click **Run**. Type **cmd**. Click **OK**.

3. Type **d:** and press **Enter**.

4. Type **cd Backup** and press **Enter**.

5. Type **del Data** and press **Enter**. Type **Y** to confirm.

6. Type **ntbackup** and press **Enter**. Click **Next** to start the wizard.

7. Click the **Restore files and settings** option button. Click **Next**.

12

8. Note that your backup indexes are all listed (as shown in Figure 12-3). Double-click the index for Normal.bkf.

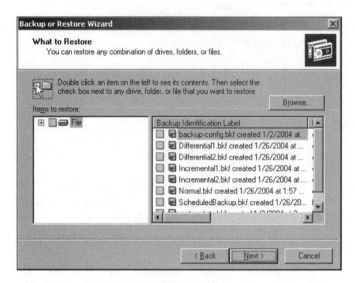

Figure 12-3   Available backup indexes

9. Double-click to expand the **D:** drive. Double-click **Backup**. Click the **Data folder** so that you can see text1.txt in the right pane.

10. Expand the other index files, so that you can see that they contain the files below:

Normal.bkf	text1.txt
Incremental1.bkf	text2.txt
Incremental2.bkf	text3.txt
Differential1.bkf	text4.txt
Differential2.bkf	text4.txt text5.txt

11. To restore the directory completely, you must restore Normal, Incremental1, Incremental2, and Differential2.

12. Check the **Data directory of the Normal.bkf** box.

13. Check the **D: directory of the Incremental1.bkf** box. Note the error. Click **No**. Click **Next**. Click **Finish**. Click **OK** to confirm the backup file. Click **Close** when the restore is complete.

14. In the command prompt window, type **ntbackup** and press **Enter**. Click the link to enter **Advanced** mode. Click the **Restore and Manage Media** tab.

15. Double-click **Incremental1.bkf** and check the **D:** drive. Click **Start Restore**. Click **OK** to confirm. Click **OK** to confirm the file location. Close the Restore Progress window when the restore is complete.

16. Use the same procedure to restore Incremental2.bkf and Differential2.bkf.

17. Close the Backup Utility. Close the command prompt window.

Certification Objectives

Objectives for Microsoft Exam #70-290: Managing and Maintaining a Microsoft Windows Server 2003 Environment:

- Restore backup data.

REVIEW QUESTIONS

1. If a directory was deleted after the Thursday backup, in which order should you restore the directory? The backup schedule: Mon:Diff; Tues:Diff; Wed:Diff; Thurs:Diff; Fri:Normal.

   a. Mon, Tues, Wed, Thurs

   b. Fri, Mon, Tues, Wed, Thurs

   c. Fri, Thurs

   d. Thurs

2. If a directory was deleted after the Thursday backup, in which order should you restore the directory? The backup schedule: Mon:Normal; Tues:Inc; Wed:Normal; Thurs:Inc; Fri:Inc.

   a. Mon, Thurs

   b. Mon, Tues, Wed, Thurs

   c. Thurs

   d. Wed, Thurs

3. If a directory was deleted after the Thursday backup, in which order should you restore the directory? The backup schedule: Mon:Diff; Tues:Diff; Wed:Inc; Thurs:Inc; Fri:Normal.

   a. Fri, Tues, Wed, Thurs

   b. Fri, Wed, Thurs

   c. Fri, Thurs

   d. Wed, Thurs

12

4. True or False? Using the NTBACKUP application, an administrator cannot back up files and folders that he or she has no permission to access.

5. Which of the following can be done in the Advanced Restore options? (Choose all that apply.)

   a. Restore to an alternate location.

   b. Change ownership of restored files to another user.

   c. Remove security settings.

   d. Restore to a CD.

LAB 12.3 CONFIGURING A BACKUP SCHEDULE

Objectives

The goal of this lab is to learn how to use the task scheduler portion of NTBACKUP to set a typical ongoing backup schedule.

Materials Required:

This lab will require the following:

- A Windows Server 2003 system installed and configured according to the instructions at the beginning of this lab manual

Estimated completion time: **15 minutes**

Activity Background

Most servers back up to tape or other removable media. To balance efficiency of storage size/speed of completion with ease of restoration, you would typically mix differential and incremental backups to follow up on a weekly normal backup. In this scenario, we will be backing up to disk but planning as if it was to be implemented on removable media changed daily. An eight-tape schedule would have four tapes for Mon–Thurs and four tapes for a Friday normal backup, one tape per week rotated monthly. Plan to use differential backups the first couple of days following the normal backup when there are fewer changed files. Incremental backups would be used later in the week, when the size and processing time of continuing differential backups becomes impractical. We will also schedule a single monthly backup for archival purposes.

ACTIVITY

Activity

1. If necessary, log on to your domain using the **AdminXX** account (where *XX* is your assigned student number).

2. Click **Start**. Click **Run**. Type **ntbackup**. Click **OK**. Click the link to Advanced Mode.

3. Click the **Schedule Jobs** tab. Double-click **today's date** to start the Backup Wizard. Click **Next**. Click **Next** to back up everything on the computer.

4. In the Type a name for this backup box, type **Weekly Normal**. Click **Next**. The backup type should be set to Normal, by default. Click **Next**. Click the **Verify data after backup** check box. Click **Next**. Click the **Replace the existing backups** option button. Click **Next**.

5. Enter the Job name **Weekly Normal**. Click **Set Schedule**. In the Schedule Task drop-down box, select **Weekly**. Click to deselect **Mon** and select **Fri** (as shown in Figure 12-4). Click **OK**.

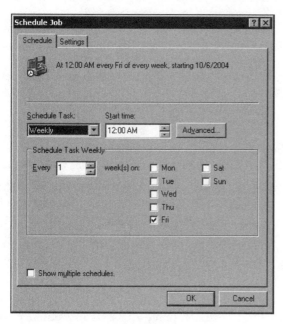

Figure 12-4   Weekly schedule

6. In the Set Account Information window, enter and confirm your AdminXX password. This account will be the user who has the authority to run the task. Click **OK**.

7. Click **Next** in the Backup Wizard. You are asked again for account information; this is the user that will run and own the backup. These users do not need to be the same, but we will continue to use the AdminXX user. Confirm your password and click **OK**. Click **Finish**.

8. Back in the calendar, double-click the first **Monday** after the new schedule begins. Click **Next**. Click **Next** to back up everything on the computer.

9. Name the backup **Daily Differential**. Click **Next**. Select the backup type **Differential**. Click **Next**. Confirm that the Verify data after backup check box is selected and click **Next**. Click the **Replace the existing backups** option button. Click **Next**.

10. Enter the Job name **Daily Differential**. Click **Set Schedule**. Select **Weekly** in the drop-down box. Leave Monday selected. Select **Tuesday**. Click **OK**. Enter and confirm your AdminXX password. Click **OK**. Click **Next**. Enter and confirm your AdminXX password again and click **OK**. Click **Finish**.

11. In the calendar, double-click the first **Wednesday** of the new schedule. Click **Next** to start the wizard. Click **Next**. Name the backup **Daily Incremental**.

NOTE

Ideally, you would be backing up to removable media like tape. This lab is backing up to disk. Therefore, if the Wednesday and Thursday backups are saved to one backup file and we selected Replace the existing backups, then both incremental backups would be useless. The Thursday backup would overwrite the backup of the day before. If you are not backing up to removable media daily, then you should create a separate backup job for each day of the week, or select to append and remove it from your catalog after the weekly normal backup to prepare for next week's schedule.

12. Click **Next**. Select the backup type **Incremental**. Click **Next**. Click **Next**. Click the **Replace the existing backups** option button. Click **Next**.

13. Enter the Job Name **Daily Incremental**. Click **Set Schedule**. Select **Weekly**. Select **Wed** and **Thu**. Click **OK**. Confirm Credentials. Click **OK**. Click **Next**. Confirm Credentials again. Click **OK**. Click **Finish**.

14. The last job to add is a monthly copy to be kept offsite for archival purposes. Double-click the last **Saturday** of this month. Click **Next** to start the wizard. Click **Next**.

15. Name the backup **Monthly Copy**. Click **Next**. Select the backup type **Copy**. Click **Next**. Click **Next**. Click the **Replace the existing backups** option button. Click **Next**.

16. Name the job **Monthly Copy**. Click **Set Schedule**. In the drop-down box, select **Monthly**. Select the second option button and use the drop-down boxes to select the **last Saturday** of the month (as shown in Figure 12-5). Click **OK**. Confirm Credentials. Click **OK**.

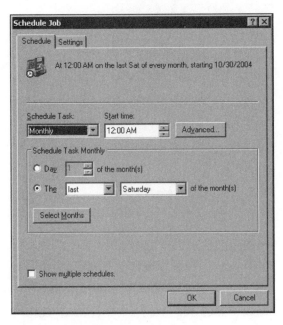

Figure 12-5 Monthly schedule

17. Click **Next**. Confirm Credentials. Click **Finish**.

12

18. In the Calendar (as shown in Figure 12-6), you can click any scheduled event to confirm its properties. Close the Backup Utility.

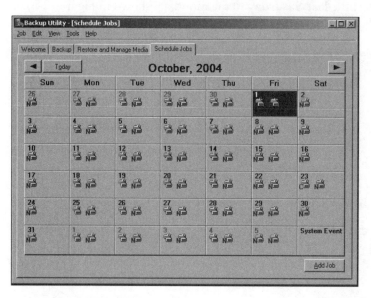

Figure 12-6   Scheduled backups

19. Click **Start**. Click **Control Panel**. Right-click **Scheduled Tasks** and click **Open**.

20. Double-click the **Weekly Normal** task. Notice the long command line in the Run box. (The command can be read easier if you copy and paste into Notepad. The important things to note are that a backup selection file called "Weekly Normal.bks" was created, and where it is located. If a backup fails to run, check that this file still exists.)

21. Disable the backup tasks. On the Task tab, deselect **Enabled (scheduled task runs at specified time)**. Click **OK**. Repeat with each scheduled backup task to disable them all. Close the Scheduled Tasks window.

Certification Objectives

Objectives for Microsoft Exam #70-290: Managing and Maintaining a Microsoft Windows Server 2003 Environment:

- Schedule backup jobs.

REVIEW QUESTIONS

1. What is the extension for a backup selection file?

   a. .dbf

   b. .bkf

   c. .bak

   d. .bks

2. By default, how many hours will a scheduled backup job run before the task scheduler ends the task?

   a. 12

   b. 24

   c. 48

   d. 72

3. Backups cannot be directly saved to which of the following media? (Choose all that apply.)

   a. Hard disk

   b. CD-R

   c. Zip disk

   d. Tape

4. A member server could not schedule a backup of which of these types of data?

   a. Everything on this computer

   b. Selected data files

   c. Active Directory

   d. System State

5. True or False? The same backup job can be scheduled to run several times a day.

LAB 12.4 PREPARING FOR AUTOMATED SYSTEM RECOVERY

Objectives

The goal of this lab is to learn how to prepare for an Automated System Recovery (ASR) using NTBACKUP.

12

Materials Required:

This lab will require the following:

- A Windows Server 2003 system installed and configured according to the instructions at the beginning of this lab manual

- One blank, formatted 1.44 MB floppy disk

- Approximately 1.8 GB free on the D: drive

Estimated completion time: **30 minutes**

Activity Background

In order to be able to repair your server using the ASR feature, you must create an ASR backup after every significant configuration change. Upon completion, you will have a .bkf file, which can be saved to disk or removable media, and a floppy disk that contains information about the backup and disk configuration.

Activity

ACTIVITY

1. If necessary, log on to your domain using the **AdminXX** account (where *XX* is your assigned student number).

2. Click **Start**. Click **Run**. Type **ntbackup**. Click **OK**.

3. Click the link to enter Advanced Mode.

4. On the Welcome tab, click the **Automated System Recovery Wizard** button.

5. Read the Welcome page. Note that the ASR backup does not include your data, which must be backed up separately. Click **Next**.

6. In the Backup media or file name box, type **D:\Backup\ASR backup.bkf**. Click **Next**. Click **Finish**.

7. The backup (as shown in Figure 12-7) may take up to 30 minutes. Insert the floppy disk when prompted (as shown in Figure 12-8) and click **OK**.

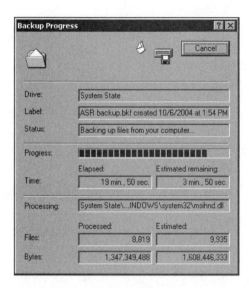

Figure 12-7   ASR Backup Progress

Figure 12-8   A floppy disk is required to restore the ASR backup

8. Once complete, close the status window. Close the Backup Utility.

9. Click **Start**. Right-click **My Computer** and click **Explore**.

10. Double-click the **D:** drive. Click the **Backup** folder. Notice the size of the ASR backup.bkf file. If necessary, click **View** on the menu bar, then click **Details**. Note that the backup is too large to fit on a 700 MB CD-R.

11. Click the **C:** drive. Click the **WINDOWS** folder. Click the **repair** folder. Note the files asr.sif, asrpnp.sif, and setup.log. These are the same files that were copied to your floppy disk. Along with ASR backup.bkf, these are the files you will need to have available to restore your system using ASR.

12. Remove the floppy from your system. Close all windows.

12

Certification Objectives

Objectives for Microsoft Exam #70-290: Managing and Maintaining a Microsoft Windows Server 2003 Environment:

- Implement Automated System Recovery (ASR).

REVIEW QUESTIONS

1. When should you perform an ASR backup?

   a. Weekly

   b. Annually

   c. Anytime configuration is changed

   d. Only when the server fails

2. An ASR set can be restored using which of the following recovery tools?

   a. Recovery Console

   b. Installation CD

   c. Boot disk

   d. Safe Mode

3. Which of the following files are required to restore an ASR set? (Choose all that apply.)

   a. asr.sif

   b. boot.ini

   c. asrpnp.sif

   d. ASR Backup Set.bkf

4. If the floppy disk is lost but you still have access to your server, where could you find the files you need to restore an ASR backup?

   a. C:\Windows

   b. C:\Windows\System32\Drivers\Etc

   c. C:\Windows\repair

   d. C:\Windows\Dev\Floppy0

5. An ASR backup is created with which application?

   a. Backup Utility

   b. Add or Remove Programs

   c. Computer Management

   d. ERD.exe

LAB 12.5 USING THE BOOT LOGGING FEATURE

Objectives

The goal of this lab is to learn how to activate the boot logging startup option.

Materials Required:

This lab will require the following:

- A Windows Server 2003 system installed and configured according to the instructions at the beginning of this lab manual

Estimated completion time: **10 minutes**

Activity Background

12

There are several troubleshooting options that can be enabled during boot. A simple, but effective, tool is the boot logging option. When enabled, it records whether drivers are loaded or not. This is most useful when your server is experiencing unexplained failures of devices or the entire server.

ACTIVITY

Activity

1. If necessary, log on to your domain using the **AdminXX** account (where *XX* is your assigned student number).

2. Click **Start**. Click **Shut Down**.

3. Set the What do you want the computer to do? drop-down box to **Restart**. Type **Boot log test** in the Comment box. Click **OK**.

4. When your server reboots and comes to the Please select the operating system to start screen, press the **F8** key.

5. Use your up and down arrow keys to select **Enable Boot Logging**. Press **Enter**.

6. Select the **Windows Server 2003** operating system. Press **Enter**.

7. Log on to your domain using the **AdminXX** account (where *XX* is your assigned student number).

8. Click **Start**. Click **Run**. Type **c:\windows\ntbtlog.txt**. Press **Enter**.

9. Notepad opens. Examine the boot log.

10. Close all windows.

Certification Objectives

Objectives for Microsoft Exam #70-290: Managing and Maintaining a Microsoft Windows Server 2003 Environment:

■ Monitor server hardware.

REVIEW QUESTIONS

1. What is the variable for the system directory (C:\Windows in this case)?

   a. System

   b. Systemroot

   c. Systemdrive

   d. Path

2. The boot log lists what kind of events? (Choose all that apply.)

   a. Services starting

   b. Volumes loading

   c. Drivers loading

   d. Stop errors

3. True or False? Selecting the Last Known Good startup option will also enable boot logging.

4. What key is used to access the advanced startup options?

   a. F1

   b. F4

   c. F8

   d. Delete

5. True or False? Boot logging cannot be enabled over the network; you must be physically at the computer.

13

ADMINISTERING WEB RESOURCES

Labs included in this chapter:

♦ Lab 13.1 Creating, Deleting, and Displaying Web Site Virtual Directories Using IISVDIR.VBS

♦ Lab 13.2 Creating, Deleting, and Listing FTP Sites Using IISFTP.VBS

♦ Lab 13.3 Creating, Deleting, and Displaying FTP Virtual Directories Using IISFTPDR.VBS

♦ Lab 13.4 Configuring and Testing FTP Site Security Using NTFS Permissions

♦ Lab 13.5 Configuring and Testing FTP Site Security Using IIS Permissions

Microsoft MCSE Exam #70-290 Objectives	
Objective	Lab
Manage Internet Information Services (IIS).	13.1, 13.2, 13.3, 13.4, 13.5
Manage security for IIS.	13.1, 13.2, 13.3, 13.4, 13.5

LAB 13.1 CREATING, DELETING, AND DISPLAYING WEB SITE VIRTUAL DIRECTORIES USING IISVDIR.VBS

Objective

The goal of this lab activity is to use the IISVDIR.VBS command-line utility to create, delete, and display information about virtual directories on a Windows Server 2003 system running IIS.

Materials Required

This lab will require the following:

- Windows Server 2003 installed and configured according to the instructions at the beginning of this lab manual

Estimated completion time: **10 minutes**

Activity Background

The IISVDIR.VBS script allows virtual directories to be managed from the command line, which provides administrators with an alternative to using the Internet Information Services (IIS) Manager console to perform these tasks.

ACTIVITY

Activity

1. Log on to your domain using your **AdminXX** account (where *XX* is your assigned student number).

2. Click **Start** and then click **My Computer**. Double-click drive **D:** to view its contents. Right-click an area of blank space, select **New**, and then click **Folder**. Name the new folder **vdir**. Create an additional folder on drive D: named **vdir2** and then close My Computer.

3. Click **Start**, select **Administrative Tools**, and then click **Internet Information Services (IIS) Manager**.

4. If necessary, click the **plus sign (+)** next to your server to expand it. Click the **plus sign (+)** next to **Web Sites** to expand it.

5. Right-click **Default Web Site**, select **New**, and then click **Virtual Directory**.

6. At the Welcome to the Virtual Directory Creation Wizard screen, click **Next**.

7. At the Virtual Directory Alias screen, type **TEST** in the Alias text box. Click **Next**.

8. At the Web Site Content Directory screen, type **D:\vdir** in the Path text box. Click **Next**.

9. At the Virtual Directory Access Permissions screen, click **Next**.

10. Click **Finish** to complete the wizard. Close the Internet Information Services (IIS) Manager window.

11. Click **Start** and then click **Run**. In the Open text box, type **cmd** and click **OK**.

12. At the command line, type **cd c:\windows\system32** and press **Enter**.

13. Type **cscript iisvdir.vbs /?** and press **Enter**. This will display the help topics associated with the IISVDIR.VBS script. Read through the available settings and options.

14. Type **cscript iisvdir.vbs /query "Default Web Site"** and press **Enter**. This will display a list of any virtual directories currently available, such as the TEST virtual directory created earlier in this lab activity. The output of this command will display the new virtual directory name in the ALIAS column and the path to the directory in the Physical Root column (as shown in Figure 13-1). Additional virtual directories may also be present, depending upon the configuration of your server.

15. At the command line, type **cscript iisvdir.vbs /create "Default Web Site" TEST2 d:\vdir2** and press **Enter**. This will create a new virtual directory in the root of the default Web site named TEST2, using the physical path d:\vdir2 (as shown in Figure 13-2).

16. At the command line, type **cscript iisvdir.vbs /query "Default Web Site"** and press **Enter**. Confirm that the new virtual directory created in Step 15 now exists.

17. At the command line, type **cscript iisvdir.vbs /delete "Default Web Site"/TEST2** and press **Enter**. This will delete the virtual directory created in Step 15.

13

18. Close all open windows and log off, unless you intend to proceed directly to the next lab activity.

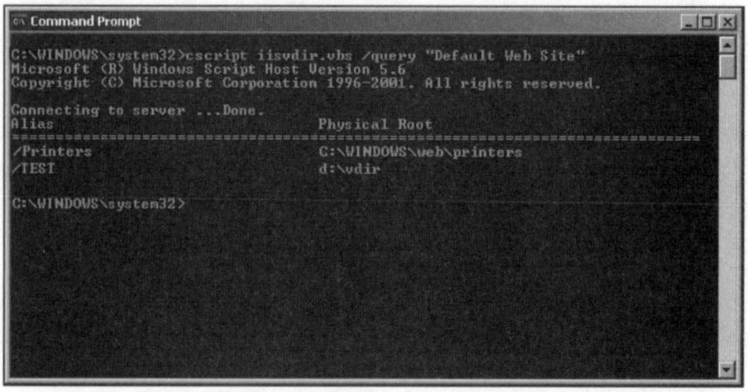

Figure 13-1 Viewing the output of the IISVDIR.VBS/query command

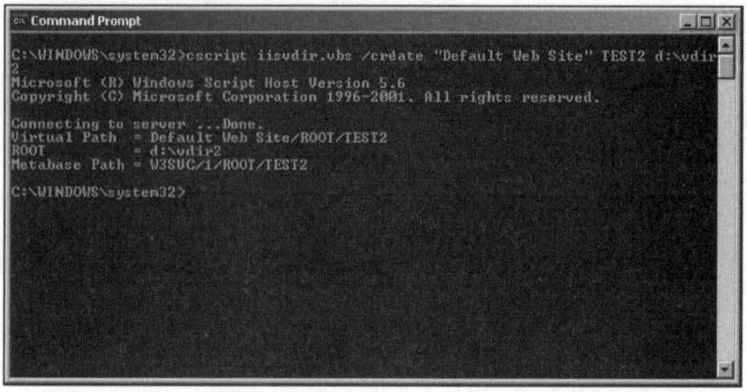

Figure 13-2 Viewing the output of the IISVDIR.VBS/create command

Certification Objectives

Objectives for Microsoft Exam #70-290: Managing and Maintaining a Microsoft Windows Server 2003 Environment:

- Manage Internet Information Services (IIS).

- Manage security for IIS.

REVIEW QUESTIONS

1. Which of the following commands must precede the IISVDIR.VBS command from the command line?

   a. wscript

   b. cscript

   c. script

   d. vbasic

2. True or False? The IISVDIR.VBS command can be used to delete a Web site.

3. Which of the following commands would effectively delete a virtual directory named TEST at the root of a Web site named Corporate when using the IISVDIR.VBS command?

   a. cscript iisvdir.vbs /delete corporate/test

   b. cscript iisvdir.vbs /delete corporate test

   c. cscript iisvdir.vbs /delete corporate –test

   d. cscript iisvdir.vbs /d corporate/test

4. Which of the following switches is used to specify a username with the IISVDIR.VBS command?

   a. /un

   b. /username

   c. /user

   d. /u

5. The _____, _____, and _____ switches are used with the IISVDIR.VBS command to delete, create, or list virtual directories, respectively.

LAB 13.2 CREATING, DELETING, AND LISTING FTP SITES USING IISFTP.VBS

Objective

The goal of this lab activity is to use the IISFTP.VBS command-line utility to create, delete, and list information about FTP virtual servers on a Windows Server 2003 system running IIS.

Materials Required

This lab will require the following:

- Windows Server 2003 installed and configured according to the instructions at the beginning of this lab manual

> Estimated completion time: **15 minutes**

Activity Background

The IISFTP.VBS script allows FTP virtual servers to be managed from the command line. This provides administrators with an alternative to using the Internet Information Services Manager console to perform these tasks. For example, an administrator might use the IIS-FTP.VBS script to manage an FTP virtual server from within a Telnet session.

Activity

1. If necessary, log on to your domain using your **AdminXX** account (where *XX* is your assigned student number).

2. Click **Start** and then click **My Computer**. Double-click drive **D:** to view its contents. Right-click an area of blank space, select **New**, and then click **Folder**. Name the new folder **newftp** and then close My Computer. This folder will be used as the root of a new FTP site that you will create in this lab activity.

3. Click **Start** and then click **Run**. In the Open text box, type **cmd** and click **OK**.

4. At the command line, type **cd c:\windows\system32** and press **Enter**.

5. Type **cscript iisftp.vbs /?** and press **Enter**. This will display the help topics associated with the IISFTP.VBS script. Read through the available settings and options.

6. Type **cscript iisftp.vbs /create d:\newftp FTP2 /b 99 /i 192.168.1.XX** (where *xx* is your assigned student number) and press **Enter**. This will create a new FTP site named FTP2, with a root directory of d:\newftp. The /b switch specifies the port associated with the FTP site (the default port, 21, is already in use on the default FTP site), and the /i switch specifies the IP address on which this FTP site will respond. The output from this command is displayed in Figure 13-3.

7. At the command line, type **cscript iisftp.vbs /query** and press **Enter**. This will list all of the FTP sites currently available on your server (as shown in Figure 13-4).

8. At the command line, type **cscript iisftp.vbs /stop FTP2** and press **Enter**. This will stop the FTP2 site.

9. Type **cscript iisftp.vbs /query** and press **Enter**. Confirm that the status of the FTP2 site is STOPPED.

10. Type **cscript iisftp.vbs /start FTP2** and press **Enter**. This will restart the FTP2 site.

11. At the command line, type **cscript iisftp /delete FTP2** and press **Enter**. This will delete the FTP2 site from your server completely.

12. Close all open windows and log off, unless you intend to proceed directly to the next lab activity.

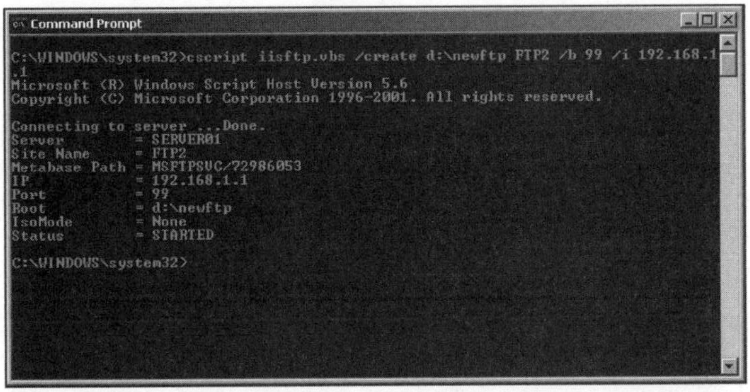

Figure 13-3   Viewing the output of the IISFTP.VBS/create command

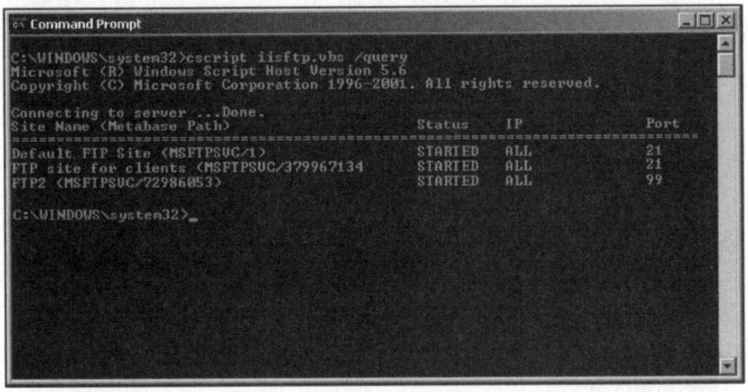

Figure 13-4   Viewing the output of the IISFTP.VBS/query command

Certification Objectives

Objectives for Microsoft Exam #70-290: Managing and Maintaining a Microsoft Windows Server 2003 Environment:

- Manage Internet Information Services (IIS).

- Manage security for IIS.

REVIEW QUESTIONS

1. Which of the following switches will stop an FTP site named FTP99?

   a. cscript iisftp.vbs /stopped ftp99

   b. cscript iisftp.vbs /stop ftp99

   c. cscript iisftp.vbs /pause ftp99

   d. cscript iisftp.vbs /s ftp99

2. Which of the following switches is used in conjunction with the IISFTP.VBS/create command to specify the port on which a new FTP site will listen for requests?

   a. /p

   b. /b

   c. /port

   d. /tcpport

3. Which of the following switches is used in conjunction with the IISFTP.VBS/create command to specify the IP address on which a new FTP site will listen for requests?

   a. /address

   b. /a

   c. /i

   d. /ip

4. True or False? The IISFTP.VBS command can be used to create new FTP sites.

5. Which of the following commands would be used to list all FTP sites on a remote server named Server2?

   a. cscript iisftp.vbs /query /s server2

   b. cscript iisftp.vbs /query /server server2

   c. cscript iisftp.vbs /query server2

   d. cscript /query /s:server2

LAB 13.3 CREATING, DELETING, AND DISPLAYING FTP VIRTUAL DIRECTORIES USING IISFTPDR.VBS

Objective

The goal of this lab activity is to use the IISFTPDR.VBS command-line utility to create, delete, and display information about FTP virtual directories on a Windows Server 2003 system running IIS.

Materials Required

This lab will require the following:

- Windows Server 2003 installed and configured according to the instructions at the beginning of this lab manual

Estimated completion time: **15 minutes**

Activity Background

The IISFTPDR.VBS script allows FTP virtual directories to be managed from the command line, which provides administrators with an alternative to using the Internet Information Services Manager console to perform these tasks. For example, on a server with a large number of virtual directories to be managed or modified, an administrator might enter a series of these commands to a single batch file to automate the process.

13

ACTIVITY

Activity

1. If necessary, log on to your domain using your **AdminXX** account (where *XX* is your assigned student number).

2. Click **Start** and then click **My Computer**. Double-click drive **D:** to view its contents. Right-click an area of blank space, select **New**, and then click **Folder**. Name the new folder **ftp-vdir**. Create an additional folder on drive D: named **ftp-vdir2** and then close My Computer.

3. Click **Start**, select **Administrative Tools**, and then click **Internet Information Services (IIS) Manager**.

4. If necessary, click the **plus sign (+)** next to your server to expand it. Click the **plus sign (+)** next to **FTP Sites** to expand it.

5. Right-click **Default FTP Site**, select **New**, and then click **Virtual Directory**.

6. At the Welcome to the Virtual Directory Creation Wizard screen, click **Next**.

7. At the Virtual Directory Alias screen, type **TEST** in the Alias text box. Click **Next**.

8. At the Web Site Content Directory screen, type **D:\ftp-vdir** in the Path text box. Click **Next**.

9. At the Virtual Directory Access Permissions screen, click **Next**.

10. Click **Finish** to complete the wizard. Close the Internet Information Services (IIS) Manager window.

11. Click **Start**, then **Run**. Type **cmd** in the Open text box, then press **Enter**. At the command prompt, type **cd c:\windows\system32**, then press **Enter**.

12. Type **cscript iisftpdr.vbs /?** and press **Enter**. This will display the help topics associated with the IISFTPDR.VBS script. Read through the available settings and options.

13. Type **cscript iisftpdr.vbs /query "Default FTP Site"** and press **Enter**. This will display a list of any virtual directories currently available, such as the TEST virtual directory created earlier in this lab activity. The output of this command will display the new virtual directory name in the ALIAS column and the path to the directory in the Physical Root column (as shown in Figure 13-5).

14. At the command line, type **cscript iisftpdr.vbs /create "Default FTP Site" TEST2 d:\ftp-vdir2** and press **Enter**. This will create a new virtual directory in the root of the Default FTP Site named TEST2, using the physical path d:\ftp-vdir2 (as shown in Figure 13-6).

15. At the command line, type **cscript iisftpdr.vbs /query "Default FTP Site"** and press **Enter**. Confirm that the new virtual directory created in Step 14 now exists.

16. At the command line, type **cscript iisftpdr.vbs /delete "Default FTP Site"/TEST2** and press **Enter**. This will delete the virtual directory created in Step 14.

17. Close all open windows and log off, unless you intend to proceed directly to the next lab activity.

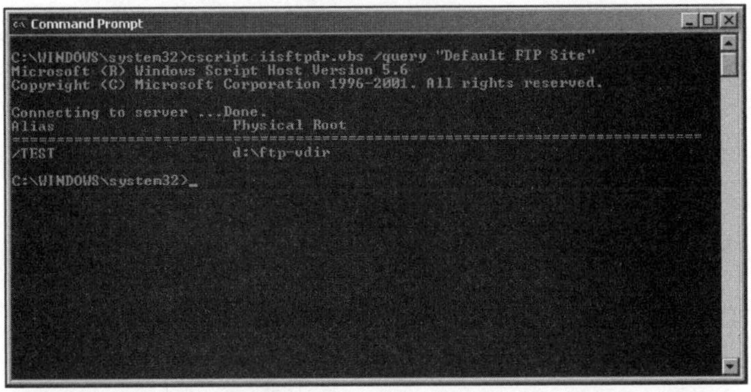

Figure 13-5　Viewing the output of the IISFTPDR.VBS/query command

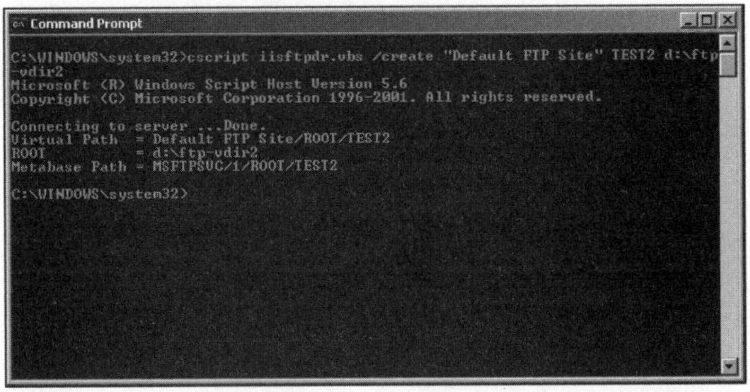

Figure 13-6　Viewing the output of the IISFTPDR.VBS/create command

13

Certification Objectives

Objectives for Microsoft Exam #70-290: Managing and Maintaining a Microsoft Windows Server 2003 Environment:

■ Manage Internet Information Services (IIS).

■ Manage security for IIS.

REVIEW QUESTIONS

1. Which of the following commands would be issued to create a new virtual directory named DOCS with a local path of D:\documents on an FTP site named FTPSERVER on the local machine?

   a. cscript iisftpdr.vbs /create ftpserver docs d:\documents

   b. cscript iisftpdr.vbs /create d:\documents ftpserver docs

   c. cscript ftp iisftpdr.vbs /create d:\documents ftpserver

   d. cscript iisftpdr.vbs /create d:\documents docs ftpserver

2. True or False? The IISFTPDR.VBS/query command will display the current status of the FTP site associated with a listed virtual directory.

3. Which of the following represent switches available with the IISFTPDR.VBS command? (Choose all that apply.)

   a. /s

   b. /u

   c. /p

   d. /query

4. Which of the following switches is used to supply a password with the IISFT-PDR.VBS command?

   a. /p

   b. /password

   c. /setpass

   d. /passwd

5. True or False? The IISFTPDR.VBS command can be used to delete a virtual directory on an FTP site located on a remote system.

LAB 13.4 CONFIGURING AND TESTING FTP SITE SECURITY USING NTFS PERMISSIONS

Objective

The goal of this lab activity is to test the impact of implementing different NTFS permissions on a folder configured as an FTP virtual directory.

Materials Required

This lab will require the following:

- Windows Server 2003 installed and configured according to the instructions at the beginning of this lab manual

---

Estimated completion time: **5 minutes**

Activity Background

When both NTFS and IIS permissions are configured for a folder, the more restrictive of the two permissions is applied to users. In this activity, you will configure NTFS permissions to determine the impact that they have when a user connects to a server and tries to upload a file.

Activity

1. If necessary, log on to your domain using your **AdminXX** account (where *XX* is your assigned student number).

2. Click **Start** and then click **My Computer**. Double-click drive **D:** to view its contents.

3. Right-click the **ftp-vdir** folder and click **Properties**.

4. Click the **Security** tab and then click the **Advanced** button.

5. Uncheck the **Allow inheritable permissions from the parent to propagate to this object and all child objects** check box.

6. When the Security dialog box appears, click **Remove**.

7. Click **OK** to close the Advanced Security Settings for ftp-vdir window. When the Security dialog box appears, click **Yes**.

8. Click the **Add** button. In the Select Users, Computers, or Groups window, type **Everyone** in the Enter the object names to select (examples) text box and click **OK**.

9. In the Permissions for Everyone section, check the **Full Control** check box in the **Allow** column. This grants the Everyone group the full control NTFS permission on the ftp-vdir folder. Click **OK** and then close the My Computer window.

10. Click **Start**, select **Administrative Tools**, and then click **Internet Information Services (IIS) Manager**.

11. If necessary, click the **plus sign (+)** next to your server to expand it. Click the **plus sign (+)** next to FTP Sites to expand it, if necessary.

12. Click the **plus sign (+)** next to Default FTP Site to expand it, if necessary.

13. Right-click the **TEST** virtual directory and click **Properties**.

13

14. On the Virtual Directory tab, select the **Write** check box. This will ensure that the FTP permissions on this virtual directory allow all users both to download (read) and to upload (write) files to this folder using FTP (as shown in Figure 13-7). Click **OK** and then minimize the Internet Information Services (IIS) Manager window.

15. Click **Start** and then click **Run**. In the Open text box, type **cmd** and then click **OK**.

16. At the command line, type **cd c:\WINDOWS\system32** and press **Enter**.

17. Type **ftp localhost** and press **Enter**.

18. At the User prompt, type **AdminXX** (where *XX* is your assigned student number) and press **Enter**.

19. At the Password prompt, type the password for your AdminXX account and press **Enter**.

20. At the ftp> prompt, type **cd TEST** and press **Enter**. This command switches you into the TEST virtual directory.

21. At the ftp> prompt, type **bin** and press **Enter**. This will change the transfer type from ASCII to Binary.

22. At the ftp> prompt, type **put setup.bmp** and press **Enter**. This will upload the setup.bmp file to the TEST virtual directory, since both the configured IIS and NTFS permissions allow users to write to the directory.

23. At the ftp> prompt, type **bye** and press **Enter**. This will exit the FTP utility. Minimize the command prompt window.

24. Click **Start** and then click **My Computer**. Double-click drive **D:** to view its contents. Right-click the **ftp-vdir** folder and click **Properties**.

25. Click the **Security** tab. In the Permissions for Everyone section, deselect all check boxes in the Allow column with the exception of the Read check box, which should remain checked. This limits the Everyone group to read access only on the ftp-vdir folder. Click **OK** and then close My Computer.

26. Maximize the command prompt window. At the command line, type **ftp localhost** and press **Enter**.

27. At the User prompt, type **AdminXX** (where *XX* is your assigned student number) and press **Enter**.

28. At the Password prompt, type the password for your AdminXX account and press **Enter**.

29. At the ftp> prompt, type **cd TEST** and press **Enter**. This command switches you into the TEST virtual directory.

30. At the ftp> prompt, type **bin** and press **Enter**. This will change the transfer type from ASCII to Binary.

31. At the ftp> prompt, type **put setup.bmp** and press **Enter**. Because the configured NTFS permissions for the ftp-vdir folder no longer allow write access, the upload will fail with an Access is denied message (as shown in Figure 13-8). Note that the upload fails even though the configured permissions in IIS still allow both read and write access. This is because when IIS and NTFS permissions conflict, the more restrictive permission applies.

32. At the ftp> prompt, type **bye** and press **Enter**.

33. Close all open windows and log off, unless you intend to proceed directly to the next lab activity.

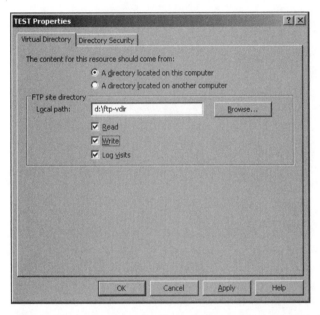

Figure 13-7   Configuring IIS permissions for a virtual directory

Figure 13-8   Attempting to upload a file without the NTFS write permission

Certification Objectives

Objectives for Microsoft Exam #70-290: Managing and Maintaining a Microsoft Windows Server 2003 Environment:

- Manage Internet Information Services (IIS).

- Manage security for IIS.

Review Questions

1. From which tab in the properties of a virtual directory are IIS permissions configured?

   a. Directory Security

   b. Virtual Directory

   c. Security

   d. IIS Security

2. Not having the NTFS _____ permission will deny a user from downloading files from a virtual directory.

3. Not having the NTFS _____ permission will deny a user from uploading files to a virtual directory.

4. Which of the following commands is used to upload files using the command-line FTP utility included with Windows Server 2003?

   a. get

   b. put

   c. upload

   d. upl

5. True or False? Any user with the NTFS full control permission to a virtual directory has the ability to upload or download files, regardless of the IIS permissions configured.

LAB 13.5 CONFIGURING AND TESTING FTP SITE SECURITY USING IIS PERMISSIONS

Objective

The goal of this lab activity is to test the impact of implementing different IIS permissions on a folder configured as an FTP virtual directory.

Materials Required

This lab will require the following:

- Windows Server 2003 installed and configured according to the instructions at the beginning of this lab manual

---

Estimated completion time: **10 minutes**

Activity Background

When both NTFS and IIS permissions are configured for a folder, the more restrictive of the two permissions is applied to users. In this activity, you will configure IIS permissions to determine the impact that they have when a user connects to a server and tries to manage files or navigate between directories.

Activity

1. If necessary, log on to your domain using your **AdminXX** account (where *XX* is your assigned student number).

2. Click **Start** and then click **My Computer**. Double-click drive **D:** to view its contents.

3. Right-click the **ftp-vdir** folder and click **Properties**. Click the **Security** tab.

4. In the Permissions for Everyone section, select the **Full Control** check box in the **Allow** column. This grants the Everyone group the full control NTFS permission on the ftp-vdir folder. Click **OK** and then close the My Computer window.

5. Click **Start**, select **Administrative Tools**, and then click **Internet Information Services (IIS) Manager**.

6. If necessary, click the **plus sign (+)** next to your server to expand it. Click the **plus sign (+)** next to FTP Sites to expand it, if necessary.

7. Click the **plus sign (+)** next to Default FTP Site to expand it, if necessary.

8. Right-click the **TEST** virtual directory and click **Properties**.

9. On the Virtual Directory tab, deselect the **Read** and **Write** check boxes. This will ensure that the FTP permissions on this virtual directory deny users the ability both to download (read) and to upload (write) files to this folder using FTP, even though NTFS permissions on the folder give the Everyone group full control. Click **OK** and then minimize the Internet Information Services (IIS) Manager window.

10. Click **Start** and then click **Run**. In the Open text box, type **cmd** and then click **OK**.

11. At the command line, type **cd c:\WINDOWS\system32** and press **Enter**.

13

12. Type **ftp localhost** and press **Enter**.

13. At the User prompt, type **AdminXX** (where *XX* is your assigned student number) and press **Enter**.

14. At the Password prompt, type the password for your AdminXX account and press **Enter**.

15. At the ftp> prompt, type **cd TEST** and press **Enter**. Notice that an Access is denied message appears (as shown in Figure 13-9). This is because all users have been denied the IIS read permission for the denied.

16. At the ftp> prompt, type **bye** and press **Enter**. This will exit the FTP utility.

17. Close all open windows and log off.

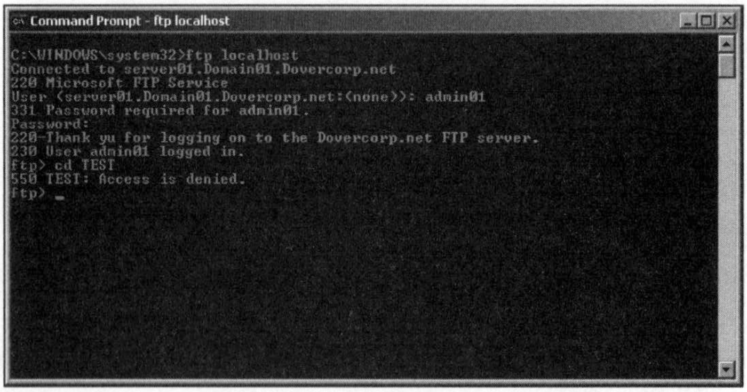

Figure 13-9   Attempting to download a file without the IIS read permission

Certification Objectives

Objectives for Microsoft Exam #70-290: Managing and Maintaining a Microsoft Windows Server 2003 Environment:

- Manage Internet Information Services (IIS).

- Manage security for IIS.

REVIEW QUESTIONS

1. What will happen if a user with the full control NTFS permission to a virtual directory attempts to upload a file, given that users have been granted both the read and write IIS permissions?

   a. The upload will fail.

   b. The upload will succeed.

   c. There is not enough information to answer this question.

2. Which of the following commands is used to change to a different directory when connected to an FTP server, using the FTP client included with Windows Server 2003?

   a. chngdir

   b. cd

   c. chdir

   d. chgdir

3. On which port will an FTP respond to requests by default?

   a. 20

   b. 21

   c. 22

   d. 23

4. True or False? When NTFS and IIS permissions are combined, the most restrictive permission will apply.

5. The _____ command can be used to disconnect from an FTP session.

13

SECURITY BASICS FOR WINDOWS SERVER 2003

Labs included in this chapter:

♦ Lab 14.1 Creating a Security Template

♦ Lab 14.2 Analyzing Security Settings Using SECEDIT and Security Configuration and Analysis

♦ Lab 14.3 Applying Security Template Settings Using SECEDIT

♦ Lab 14.4 Archiving Security Events for Database Analysis

♦ Lab 14.5 Restoring Security Settings to Default Using SECEDIT

Microsoft MCSE Exam #70-290 Objectives	
Objective	Lab
Configure file system permissions.	14.1, 14.3, 14.5
Troubleshoot user authentication issues.	14.1, 14.2, 14.3
Troubleshoot user accounts.	14.2
Monitor and analyze events.	14.4
Manage and implement disaster recovery.	14.5

Lab 14.1 Creating a Security Template

Objectives

The goal of this lab is to learn how to create a custom security template.

Materials Required

This lab will require the following:

■ A Windows Server 2003 system installed and configured according to the instructions at the beginning of this lab manual

Estimated completion time: **20 minutes**

Activity Background

An administrator uses a security template to define, edit, and save baseline security settings to be applied to computers with common security requirements to meet organizational security standards. Templates help ensure that a consistent setting can be applied to multiple machines and be easily maintained. In this lab, you will create a new security template.

ACTIVITY

Activity

1. If necessary, log on to your domain using your **AdminXX** account (where *XX* is your assigned student number).

2. Close any open windows.

3. Click **Start**. Click **Run**. Type **cmd**. Click **OK**.

4. Type **D:**. Press **Enter**.

5. Type **mkdir temp**. Press **Enter**.

6. Close the command prompt window.

7. Click **Start**. Click **Run**. Type **mmc**. Click **OK**.

8. Use the keyboard shortcut **CTRL+M** to open the Add/Remove Snap-in window.

9. Press **ALT+D** to add a new snap-in. Scroll down and click **Security Templates**. Click **Add**. Click **Close**. Click **OK**.

10. Click the **plus sign (+)** next to Security Templates to expand the tree.

11. Click the **plus sign (+)** next to C:\WINDOWS\security\templates to view the templates that currently exist in this directory.

12. Right-click **Security Templates**. Click **New Template Search Path** (as shown in Figure 14-1).

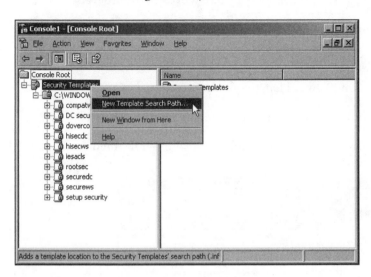

Figure 14-1 Creating a new template search path

13. Click **My Computer**. Click **D:**. Click the **temp** directory. Click **OK**.

14. In the mmc folder, right-click **D:\temp**. Click **New Template**. Enter the template name **Custom DC Security** and the description **New custom security template for domain controllers** (as shown in Figure 14-2). Click **OK**.

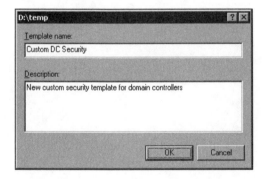

Figure 14-2 Custom Security template

15. If necessary, double-click **D:\temp** to expand it. Double-click **Custom DC Security**. Double-click **Account Policies**. Click **Password Policy**.

14

16. Set the following options, as shown in Figure 14-3:

    Enforce password history – **12 passwords remembered**

    Maximum password age – **31 days**

    Minimum password age – **0 days**

    Minimum password length – **8 characters**

    Password must meet complexity requirements – **Enabled**

    Store password using reversible encryption – **Disabled**

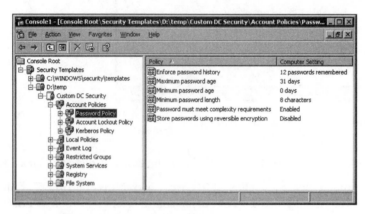

Figure 14-3   New password policy

17. Click **Account Lockout Policy** and set the following options, as shown in Figure 14-4:

Account lockout duration – **30 minutes**

Account lockout threshold – **5 invalid logon attempts**

Reset account lockout counter after – **30 minutes**

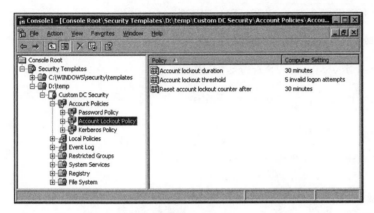

Figure 14-4 New account lockout policy

14

18. Double-click **Local Policies**. Click **Audit Policy**. Set the following options, as shown in Figure 14-5:

Audit account logon events – **Success, Failure**

Audit account management – **Success, Failure**

Audit directory service access – **Failure**

Audit logon events – **Success, Failure**

Audit object access – **No auditing**

Audit policy change – **Success, Failure**

Audit privilege use – **Success, Failure**

Audit process tracking – **No auditing**

Audit system events – **Success, Failure**

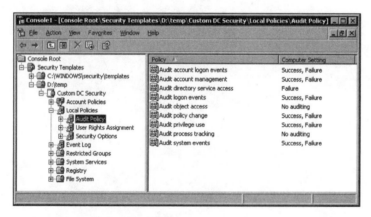

Figure 14-5   New audit policy

19. Click **Security Options**. In this section, there are many options that an administrator may want to be set on a domain controller, but you will only set one at this time. If the following option were enabled, you would open your server to a denial of service attack. Set the following option: Audit: Shut down system immediately if unable to log security audits – **Disabled**.

20. Click **File System**. Note that there are no items configured.

21. Double-click **C:\WINDOWS\security\templates**. Double-click **DC Security**. Right-click **File System**. Click **Copy**.

22. Click the **minus sign (–)** next to C:\WINDOWS\security\templates to collapse the tree.

23. Right-click the **File System** folder beneath the Custom DC Security template and click **Paste**.

24. Note that new File System security entries have been added to the policy.

25. Right-click **File System**. Click **Add File**.

26. In the chooser window, click **Local Disk (D:)**. Click **temp**. Click **OK**.

27. In the Database Security for D:\temp window, click **Users**. Click **Remove**. Click **OK**.

28. In the Add Object window, click **Replace existing permissions on all subfolders and files with inheritable permissions** (as shown in Figure 14–6). Click **OK**.

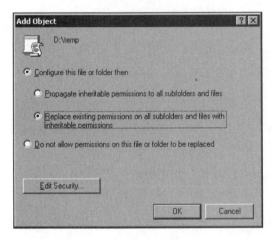

Figure 14-6   Set object security

29. Right-click **Custom DC Security**. Click **Save**.

30. Close the console window. Click **No**.

14

Certification Objectives

Objectives for Microsoft Exam #70–290: Managing and Maintaining a Microsoft Windows Server 2003 Environment:

- Configure file system permissions.

- Troubleshoot user authentication issues.

REVIEW QUESTIONS

1. Which of the following is not a Local Policy that can be set in a security template?

   a. Security Options

   b. Audit Policy

   c. Remote Access Policy

   d. User Rights Assignment

2. Which local security option should be disabled to prevent a potential denial of service attack?

   a. Network Access: Let Everyone permission apply to anonymous users

   b. Interactive Logon: Do not require CTRL+ALT+DEL

   c. Audit: Audit the access of global system objects

   d. Audit: Shut down system immediately if unable to log security audits

3. Which of the following account lockout policy configurations would lock out a user after more than 2 invalid logon attempts in one day?

   a. Account lockout threshold – 2 invalid logon attempts

   Reset account lockout counter after – 1,440 minutes

   b. Account lockout threshold – 3 invalid logon attempts

   Reset account lockout counter after – 1,440 minutes

   c. Account lockout threshold – 2 invalid logon attempts

   Reset account lockout counter after – 24 hours

   d. Account lockout threshold – 3 invalid logon attempts

   Reset account lockout counter after – 24 hours

4. Which of the following audit settings should be configured to audit local logons to this domain controller?

   a. Audit account logon events

   b. Audit account management

   c. Audit logon events

   d. Audit system events

5. Which of the following audit settings should be configured to audit logons to the domain?

   a. Audit account logon events

   b. Audit account management

   c. Audit logon events

   d. Audit system events

LAB 14.2 ANALYZING SECURITY SETTINGS USING SECEDIT AND SECURITY CONFIGURATION AND ANALYSIS

Objectives

The goal of this lab is to learn how to perform a security analysis using SECEDIT.

Materials Required

This lab will require the following:

■ A Windows Server 2003 system installed and configured according to the instructions at the beginning of this lab manual

■ The Custom DC Security template configured as in Lab 14.1

Estimated completion time: **10 minutes**

Activity Background

14

In Chapter 14, you learned how to perform a security analysis using the Security Configuration and Analysis console snap-in. This is easy enough to perform on a single computer, but to perform this analysis periodically on all the servers on your network would require a physical visit to each. SECEDIT is a command-line tool that allows you to script an analysis and run it either interactively or using Task Scheduler. To view the results of the analysis, you still must use the Security Configuration and Analysis console snap-in.

Activity

1. If necessary, log on to your domain using your **AdminXX** account (where *XX* is your assigned student number).

2. Close any open windows.

3. Click **Start**. Click **Run**. Type **cmd**. Click **OK**.

4. Type **D:**, then press **Enter**.

5. Type **cd temp**, then press **Enter**.

6. Type **secedit /analyze /db %computername%.sdb /cfg "Custom DC Security.inf" /log %computername%.log**. Press **Enter**.

7. The %computername% variable will be replaced by the server name. Type **dir**, then press **Enter**. You will see two new files: SERVERXX.sdb and SERVERXX.log.

8. Type **serverxx.log** (where xx is replaced by your student number), then press **Enter**. The log will open in Notepad. Press **CTRL+F** to open the Find dialog box in Notepad. Type **Mismatch** and click **Find Next**. The log will indicate a mismatch whenever a configuration element exists in the template and on the local system, but the associated values differ. Click **Cancel** to close the Find dialog box. Press **F3** a few times to continue to find mismatches in the log file. Close Notepad.

9. Click **Start**. Click **Run**. Type **mmc**. Click **OK**.

10. Press **CTRL+M** to open the Add/Remove Snap-in window. Press **ALT+D** to add a new snap-in. Scroll down and click **Security Configuration and Analysis**. Click **Add**. Click **Close**. Click **OK**.

11. Right-click **Security Configuration and Analysis** and click **Open Database**.

12. In the File name box, type **d:\temp\serverxx.sdb** (where xx is your assigned student number). Click **Open**.

13. Double-click **Account Policies**. Double-click **Password Policy**. Note how your current settings differ from the template.

14. Close all windows.

Certification Objectives

Objectives for Microsoft Exam #70-290: Managing and Maintaining a Microsoft Windows Server 2003 Environment:

- Troubleshoot user authentication issues.

- Troubleshoot user accounts.

REVIEW QUESTIONS

1. What is the primary advantage the secedit/analyze command has over using the graphical Security Configuration and Analysis?

   a. Runs faster

   b. Results in a smaller .sdb file

   c. Can be scripted

   d. Can be used by the guest account

2. In a SECEDIT analysis log, what indicates a difference in configured values between the analyzed computer and the template?

    a. Not defined

    b. Mismatch

    c. Blank, no entry

    d. Failure

3. In a SECEDIT analysis log, what indicates when a value exists in the computer but not in the template?

    a. Not configured

    b. Mismatch

    c. Blank, no entry

    d. Failure

4. If the /log switch is not specified, what is the default location of the scesrv.log file?

    a. %windir%\security\logs

    b. windir\security\logs

    c. C:\Windows\security

    d. The current directory

5. Which command will perform a security analysis?

    a. secedit /analyse

    b. secedit /configure

    c. secedit /analyze

    d. dsa.msc

14

LAB 14.3 APPLYING SECURITY TEMPLATE SETTINGS USING SECEDIT

Objectives

The goal of this lab is to learn how to apply a security template using the command-line tool SECEDIT.

Materials Required

This lab will require the following:

- A Windows Server 2003 system installed and configured according to the instructions at the beginning of this lab manual

- The Custom DC Security template configured as in Lab 14.1

Estimated completion time: **10 minutes**

Activity Background

SECEDIT is also used from the command line to apply security templates or specified areas of a template. As it is a command-line tool, it can be scripted to run on all of your servers, if necessary.

ACTIVITY

Activity

1. If necessary, log on to your domain using your **AdminXX** account (where *XX* is your assigned student number).

2. Close any open windows.

3. Click **Start**. Click **Run**. Type **cmd**. Click **OK**.

4. Type **d:**, then press **Enter**.

5. Type **cd temp**, then press **Enter**.

6. Use SECEDIT to configure your server with the settings in the Custom DC Security template. Type **secedit /configure /db confdb.sdb /cfg "Custom DC Security.inf" /log confdb.log /areas securitypolicy**. Press **Enter**.

7. View the log in Notepad. Type **confdb.log**, then press **Enter**. Notice that there is no mention of file system items. Specifying the securitypolicy area limits the configuration to account policies, audit policies, event log settings, and security options. To include all configuration items in the template, you would not specify any areas. To configure the file system permissions alone, you would run the same command specifying the filestore area (as below).

8. Close **Notepad**.

9. Type **secedit /configure /db confdb.sdb /cfg "Custom DC Security.inf" /log confdb.log /areas filestore**. Press **Enter**.

10. Type **confdb.log**, then press **Enter**. Note that file permissions could not be set for any file that does not exist on the system, and a warning was added to the log. Close **Notepad**.

11. Type **secedit /analyze /db %computername%.sdb /log afterconfig.log**. Press **Enter**.

12. Type **afterconfig.log**, then press **Enter**. Search for any mismatched settings. Close **Notepad**.

13. Manually refresh the computer policy settings. Type **gpupdate**, then press **Enter**.

14. Close all windows.

Certification Objectives

Objectives for Microsoft Exam #70-290: Managing and Maintaining a Microsoft Windows Server 2003 Environment:

- Configure file system permissions.

- Troubleshoot user authentication issues.

REVIEW QUESTIONS

1. Which of the following is not a valid area to be specified in a secedit /configure command?

   a. services

   b. filestore

   c. filesystem

   d. securitypolicy

2. Which area includes settings for the event log?

   a. securitypolicy

   b. user_rights

   c. filestore

   d. regkeys

3. What is the extension of a security template file?

   a. .sdb

   b. .fin

   c. .inf

   d. .log

14

4. What is the extension of a security analysis database?

    a. .inf

    b. .sad

    c. .sbd

    d. .sdb

5. Which command refreshes computer and user group policy settings?

    a. secedit /refreshpolicy

    b. gpupdate

    c. secedit /gpupdate

    d. gpresult

LAB 14.4 ARCHIVING SECURITY EVENTS FOR DATABASE ANALYSIS

Objectives

The goal of this lab is to learn how to save security events, filtered or complete, to a format that can be imported to a database or spreadsheet application for analysis.

Materials Required:

This lab will require the following:

- A Windows Server 2003 system installed and configured according to the instructions at the beginning of this lab manual

Estimated completion time: **15 minutes**

Activity Background

Security events may need to be saved for years as part of a comprehensive security plan. The chapter discussed saving event logs in the .evt event log format. Events can also be saved as comma-delimited or tab-delimited files for import into a spreadsheet, database, or other data analysis tool.

ACTIVITY

Activity

1. If necessary, log on to your domain using your **AdminXX** account (where *XX* is your assigned student number).

2. Close any open windows.

3. Click **Start**. Click **Run**. Type **eventvwr**. Click **OK**.

4. Click **Security**. Right-click **Security** and click **Save Log File As** (as shown in Figure 14-7).

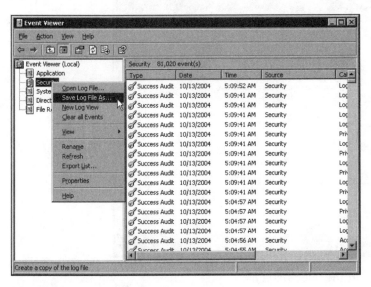

Figure 14-7   Save the complete log file

5. Click the **Save as type** drop-down box and click **CSV (Comma delimited) (*.csv)**.

6. In the File name box, type **d:\temp\full log.csv**. Click **Save**.

7. View the file. Click **Start**. Click **Run**. Type **d:\temp\full log.csv**. Click **OK**.

8. Close Notepad.

9. You can also save particular groups of events to a .csv file. In the Event Viewer window, right-click **Security**. Click **Properties**.

10. Click the **Filter** tab. For Event source, select **Security**. For Category, select **Account Management**. Click **OK**.

14

11. Right-click **Security**. Click **Export List** (as shown in Figure 14-8).

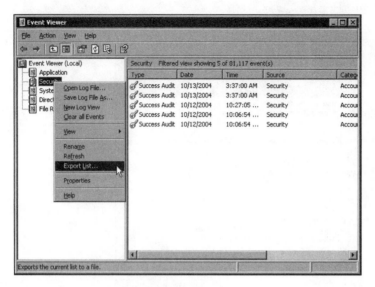

Figure 14-8 Export the filtered log file

12. In the Save as type drop-down box, click **Text (Comma delimited) (*.csv)**. In the File name box, type **d:\temp\filtered log.csv**. Click **Save**.

13. View the file. Click **Start**. Click **Run**. Type **d:\temp\filtered log.csv**. Click **OK**.

14. Close **Notepad**.

15. Close **Event Viewer**. When you restart Event Viewer, it will return to default view settings.

Certification Objectives

Objectives for Microsoft Exam #70-290: Managing and Maintaining a Microsoft Windows Server 2003 Environment:

- Monitor and analyze events.

REVIEW QUESTIONS

1. Which of the following is not a valid format to export a filtered list of events?

   a. Text (Tab delimited)

   b. Text (Space delimited)

   c. Text (Comma delimited)

   d. Unicode Text (Comma delimited)

2. True or False? It is not possible to filter by Event ID.

3. Which of the following event types can be filtered out? (Choose all that apply.)

   a. Success audit

   b. Failure audit

   c. Critical

   d. Error

4. True or False? If an event log has been exported as a .csv file it cannot be imported back into the event log.

5. Which of the following event logs cannot be cleared without generating an event?

   a. Application

   b. Security

   c. System

   d. Directory Service

14

LAB 14.5 RESTORING SECURITY SETTINGS TO DEFAULT USING SECEDIT

Objectives

The goal of this lab is to restore the default security settings for a domain controller.

Materials Required

This lab will require the following:

- A Windows Server 2003 system installed and configured according to the instructions at the beginning of this lab manual

Estimated completion time: **15 minutes**

Activity Background

Setup security.inf includes all of the security settings from when the server was first installed. DC security.inf includes the security settings from when the server was promoted to a domain controller. Restoring the domain controller server security configuration to defaults is accomplished by using SECEDIT to build one combined .sdb file of both templates, and then applying it. Note that this should be done on an as-needed basis for individual servers and that this should not be rolled out using group policy, because Setup security.inf will be different depending on how the server was originally installed. You must use Setup security.inf from the computer you wish to restore to defaults.

ACTIVITY

Activity

1. If necessary, log on to your domain using your **AdminXX** account (where *XX* is your assigned student number).

2. Close any open windows.

3. Click **Start**. Click **Run**. Type **cmd**. Click **OK**. The following commands and the expected results are shown in Figure 14-9.

4. Type **D:**, then press **Enter**.

5. Type **cd temp**, then press **Enter**.

6. Type **secedit /import /db default.sdb /cfg "c:\windows\security\ templates\setup security.inf"**. Press **Enter**.

7. Type **secedit /import /db default.sdb /cfg "c:\windows\security\ templates\DC security.inf"**. Press **Enter**.

8. In this case, you will only restore the settings that were changed in the course of this lab. In your own environment, you may want to omit the /areas switch and fully restore the combined settings. Type **secedit /configure /db default.sdb /areas securitypolicy filestore /log default.log**. Press **Enter**.

9. Type **gpupdate**, then press **Enter**.

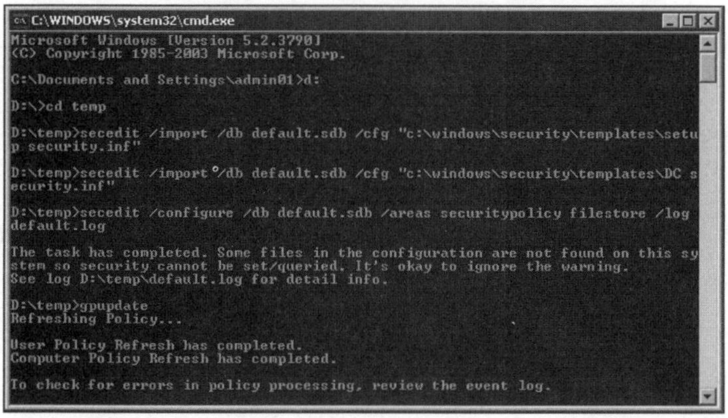

Figure 14-9 Restoring security defaults using SECEDIT.exe

10. Review the log. Type **default.log**, then press **Enter**. Close Notepad.

11. Close the command prompt window.

Certification Objectives

Objectives for Microsoft Exam #70-290: Managing and Maintaining a Microsoft Windows Server 2003 Environment:

- Configure file system permissions.

- Manage and implement disaster recovery.

REVIEW QUESTIONS

1. Which of the following users would not have the rights necessary to restore security settings using SECEDIT unless specifically granted the right?

   a. Members of the Domain Admins group

   b. The local administrator account

   c. Members of the Local Administrators group

   d. Members of the Domain Users group

2. Which of the following template files should only be applied to domain controllers?

   a. setup security.inf

   b. hisecws.inf

   c. hisecdc.inf

   d. rootsec.inf

3. Which of the following template files should only be applied to the computer on which the file originated?

   a. setup security.inf

   b. hisecws.inf

   c. hisecdc.inf

   d. rootsec.inf

4. Which of the following template files should only be applied to workstations and member servers?

   a. setup security.inf

   b. hisecws.inf

   c. hisecdc.inf

   d. rootsec.inf

5. Which of the following commands will merge DC security.inf into a previously configured security database named default.sdb?

   a. type "DC security.inf" >> default.sdb

   b. secedit /merge /db default.sdb /cfg "DC security.inf"

   c. secedit /import /db default.sdb /cfg "DC security.inf"

   d. secedit /import /db default.sdb /cfg DC security.inf